Drug Legalization in Federalist Constitutional Democracies

This book uses the Canadian cannabis legalization experiment, analyzed in the historical context of wider drug criminalization in Canada and placed in an international perspective, to examine important lessons about the differential implementation of federal law in jurisdictions within federalist constitutional democracies. Utilizing a socio-legal, interdisciplinary methodology, the work provides a comprehensive history of Canada's federal drug policy and engages in a critical appraisal of its provincial implementation. It also presents a significant international and comparative component, bringing in analyses of the status of drug legalization in other federalist constitutional democracies. Readers of the book will thus gain a comprehensive knowledge of drug legalization in federalist constitutional democracies. They will also better understand the political and cultural factors that impact upon differential implementation of federal law in individual jurisdictions, including, but not limited to, legacies of racism and stigmatization of drug use. Using the experience of Canada and other countries, future challenges and lessons to be learned for states considering federal drug legalization are analyzed and explained. The book will be a valuable resource for students, academics and policy-makers in the areas of Criminal Law, Constitutional Law, Criminology, Socio-Legal Studies, Indigenous Studies, and Drug and Health Policy Studies.

Daniel Alati is a professor in the Sociology Department, MacEwan University, Canada. His research falls into the categories of comparative criminal justice, comparative national security and anti-terrorism law, and criminal law and procedure.

Drug Legalization in Federalist Constitutional Democracies

The Canadian Cannabis Case Study in Comparative Context

Daniel Alati

LONDON AND NEW YORK

First published 2023
by Routledge
4 Park Square, Milton Park, Abingdon, Oxon OX14 4RN

and by Routledge
605 Third Avenue, New York, NY 10158

Routledge is an imprint of the Taylor & Francis Group, an informa business

© 2023 Daniel Alati

The right of Daniel Alati to be identified as author of this work has been asserted in accordance with sections 77 and 78 of the Copyright, Designs and Patents Act 1988.

All rights reserved. No part of this book may be reprinted or reproduced or utilized in any form or by any electronic, mechanical, or other means, now known or hereafter invented, including photocopying and recording, or in any information storage or retrieval system, without permission in writing from the publishers.

Trademark notice: Product or corporate names may be trademarks or registered trademarks, and are used only for identification and explanation without intent to infringe.

British Library Cataloguing-in-Publication Data
A catalogue record for this book is available from the British Library

Library of Congress Cataloging-in-Publication Data
A catalog record for this book has been requested

ISBN: 978-1-032-06109-2 (hbk)
ISBN: 978-1-032-06112-2 (pbk)
ISBN: 978-1-003-20074-1 (ebk)

DOI: 10.4324/9781003200741

Typeset in Galliard
by Apex CoVantage, LLC

To my partner, Laura, whose endless love and support is a blessing I will always cherish. I love you mucho to the moon and back schmoopie.

Contents

Acknowledgements xi

1 Introduction 1
  1.1 Aims and Objectives 3
  1.2 Methodology 4
  1.3 Chapter Summaries 6

2 Historical Evolution of Canada's Federal Drug Policy 13
  *2.1 The Passage of the Opium Act and the Beginning of
    Prohibition 14*
  *2.2 The LeDain Commission Inquiry and Subsequent Political
    Indifference 17*
  *2.3 "The War on Drugs" and the Passage of the Controlled
    Drugs and Substances Act 19*
  *2.4 The Turn of the Century: A Return to Drug Policy Reform
    Inertia 24*
  *2.5 The Turn of the Century: Legal Challenges Prompt Changes
    to Medical Cannabis Regulation 26*
  *2.6 The Passage of the 2018 Cannabis Act: A Missed
    Opportunity 29*
  *2.7 Voices From the Front Lines: Indigenous Community and
    Cannabis Industry Leaders Echo Academic Concerns 34*
  2.8 Conclusion 42

3 Provincial Implementation of Cannabis Legalization 46
  3.1 Federalism Issues: Cooperation or Unilateralism? 46
  *3.2 Federalism Issues: Further Exclusion of Indigenous
    Participation 50*
  *3.3 Broad Trends and Issues Associated with Provincial
    Implementation 54*

viii *Contents*

3.4 *Provincial Implementation of Cannabis Legalization in Ontario 60*

3.5 *Provincial Implementation of Cannabis Legalization in Alberta 64*

3.6 *Provincial Implementation of Cannabis Legalization in Quebec 65*

3.7 *Provincial Implementation of Cannabis Legalization in British Columbia 67*

3.8 *Provincial Implementation of Cannabis Legalization in Saskatchewan 68*

3.9 *Provincial Implementation of Cannabis Legalization in Manitoba 70*

3.10 *Provincial Implementation of Cannabis Legalization in Canada's Eastern Provinces 71*

3.11 *Conclusion: Is a Course Correction Necessary? 72*

4   Status of Drug Legalization in Other Federalist Constitutional Democracies   77

4.1 *Commonwealth Jurisdictions 77*

    4.1.1 Australia 77

    4.1.2 Jamaica 80

    4.1.3 New Zealand 81

    4.1.4 South Africa 82

    4.1.5 United Kingdom 84

4.2 *European Countries 86*

    4.2.1 Czech Republic 86

    4.2.2 Germany 87

    4.2.3 Italy 89

    4.2.4 Malta 90

    4.2.5 Netherlands 91

    4.2.6 Portugal 93

    4.2.7 Spain 96

    4.2.8 Switzerland 97

4.3 *Latin America 98*

    4.3.1 Argentina 98

    4.3.2 Brazil 100

    4.3.3 Chile 101

    4.3.4 Columbia 102

    4.3.5 Costa Rica 103

    4.3.6 Mexico 104

    4.3.7 Paraguay 106

Contents ix

4.3.8   _Peru 107_
4.3.9   _Uruguay 108_
4.4 _United States 111_
4.4.1   _Alaska 113_
4.4.2   _Arizona 114_
4.4.3   _California 115_
4.4.4   _Colorado 117_
4.4.5   _Connecticut 119_
4.4.6   _Illinois 120_
4.4.7   _Maine 121_
4.4.8   _Massachusetts 122_
4.4.9   _Michigan 124_
4.4.10 _Montana 125_
4.4.11 _Nevada 126_
4.4.12 _New Jersey 127_
4.4.13 _New Mexico 128_
4.4.14 _New York 129_
4.4.15 _Oregon 130_
4.4.16 _Vermont 132_
4.4.17 _Virginia 133_
4.4.18 _Washington State 134_
4.5 _Conclusion 137_

5   Lessons Learned and Future Challenges   154
5.1 _Lessons Learned: Indigenous Exclusion Must Be_
Addressed 155
5.2 _Lessons Learned: Time to Write a New Chapter in Canada's_
Racist Drug History 157
5.3 _Lessons Learned from Abroad: Other Jurisdictions Have_
Done More to Promote Social Equity, Broader Drug Policy
Liberalization, and Harm Reduction Approaches 160
5.4 _Future Challenges: The Government Should Listen to the_
"Voices" of its Industry 168
5.4.1   _Future Challenges: Changes to the Excise Tax and_
Related Issues 168
5.4.2   _Future Challenges: The Inadequacy of Health Canada_
Must Be Addressed 170
5.4.3   _Future Challenges: Marketing and Advertising_
Restrictions Need to Be Relaxed 172
5.4.4   _Future Challenges: The Issue of Market_
Concentration 174

x *Contents*

    *5.4.5 Future Challenges: The Regulation of Consumption
Lounges 175*

    *5.4.6 Future Challenges: The Need for More Transparent
Data 176*

  5.5 Conclusion: Where to Begin? 177

6 Conclusion   181

  *6.1 Recommendations for Future Change to Cannabis (and
Wider Drug) Policy in Canada 182*

  *6.2 Looking Towards the Future: Directions for Future
Research 191*

Index   194

Acknowledgements

I wish to thank my current academic institution, Grant MacEwan University, for their generous support of the research project that led to this publication. Through a Social Sciences and Humanities Research Council of Canada (SSHRC) Internal Grant, funding was provided for two undergraduate student research assistants who were invaluable to the development of this research project. I am indebted to Sara Tanasichuk and Letishia Soungie-Krammer for their tireless effort and hard work.

I also thank my parents, Mary and Gino Alati, for their endless love and support of my personal and academic endeavours throughout my life. They have consistently aided in my personal and professional development, and I would not be the person I am today without them.

To the Indigenous community leaders and cannabis industry members who contributed to the research for this book, I thank you for your time and insights. Your "voices" have shed light on several critical concerns, and this book is more powerful because of their inclusion. I look forward to continuing our relationship with an eye towards future positive changes that will make Canada's cannabis industry (and wider drug policy) more fair, equitable, and efficient.

To Anna Gallagher, my Routledge Editorial Assistant, thank you for your understanding and guidance throughout this process. You are an invaluable asset to your organization.

Last, but certainly not least, I am indebted to my partner, Laura Gill, for her patience and support during a truly extraordinary year. Academic publishing of this magnitude is difficult enough absent a once in a century global pandemic, but your love and kindness made the process a wonderful journey. I love you and thank you. This book would not have been possible were it not for you.

1 Introduction

When the Liberal Party of Canada announced their 2015 election campaign promise to legalize cannabis,[1] it was virtually impossible to foresee what legalization would look like from province to province across the country. Even after the party's subsequent victory in the 2015 federal election, an enormous amount of work would be required to fulfil this promise within the government's self-imposed tight timeline. As a result,

> Cannabis legalization became the most intense national policymaking exercise Canada has undertaken in over a generation. Hundreds of strategic and operational policy decisions needed to be made across hundreds of public and private organizations before recreational cannabis was legalized on October 17, 2018.[2]

Thus, the Canadian cannabis case study provides for a once in a lifetime analysis of how drug legalization in federalist constitutional democracies occurs. The legislative process behind federal cannabis legalization in and of itself requires in-depth analysis and needs to be situated within the wider historical context of drug policy in Canada. By the time the 2018 federal Cannabis Act[3] was passed, several important legal and constitutional questions remained unanswered, especially those pertaining to Indigenous reconciliation, self-governance, and jurisdiction.[4] Similarly, questions were (rightly) raised about the federal legislation's silence on

---

1 Josh Elliott, "Liberals 'Committed' to Legalizing Marijuana: Trudeau" (30 September 2015), online: *CTV News* #x003C;www.ctvnews.ca/politics/election/liberals-committed-to-legalizing-marijuana-trudeau-1.2588260>
2 Jared Wesley & Kyle Murray, "To Market or Demarket? Public-Sector Branding of Cannabis in Canada" (2021) 53:7 Administration & Society 1078 at 1081
3 *Cannabis Act*, SC 2018, c 16
4 For excellent discussion of these issues, see: Konstantia Koutouki & Katherine Lofts, "Cannabis, Reconciliation, and the Rights of Indigenous Peoples: Prospects and Challenges for Cannabis Legalization in Canada" (2019) 56:3 Alberta Law Review 709; Andrew Crosby, "Contesting Cannabis: Indigenous Jurisdiction and Legalization" (2019) 62:4 Canadian Public Administration 634

DOI: 10.4324/9781003200741-1

2   Introduction

social justice, with critics arguing that the legislation did not sufficiently address a long history of racist and classist drug policy in this country that has disproportionately affected minority and marginalized communities.[5] Moreover, "In federations like Canada, creating a fully integrated, nationwide policy framework is a daunting collective action problem. The task is even more challenging when jurisdiction over the policy area is divided, as is the case with cannabis regulation in Canada".[6] As such, analyzing how each province would subsequently go about the business of implementing a scheme for the controlled distribution of cannabis provides important insights into the operation of jurisdictions within federalist constitutional systems. These analyses are usefully placed into the comparative context of jurisdictions around the world that have similarly moved towards cannabis (and wider drug policy) liberalization in recent years.

This book argues that the Canadian cannabis legalization experiment, analyzed in the historical context of wider drug criminalization in Canada, and placed in an international perspective, provides important lessons about the differential implementation of federal law in jurisdictions within federalist constitutional democracies. It utilizes a socio-legal, interdisciplinary, and comparative methodology that the author has previously employed in several publications focused on a different policy sphere (national security).[7] It provides a comprehensive history of federal drug policy in Canada and engages in critical appraisals of Canada's past, present, and future drug policy. It also has a significant international/comparative component, bringing in analyses of the status of drug liberalization in other federalist constitutional democracies. In so doing, it places Canada's recent drug liberalization experiment within the wider context

---

5 For example, see: Jenna Valleriani et al, "A Missed Opportunity? Cannabis Legalization and Reparations in Canada" (2018) 109 Canadian Journal of Public Health 745; Akwasi Owusu-Bempah, "Where Is the Fairness in Canadian Cannabis Legalization? Lessons to Be Learned from the American Experience" (2021) 55:2 Journal of Canadian Studies 395

6 Jared Wesley, "Beyond Prohibition: The Legalization of Cannabis in Canada" (2019) 62:4 Canadian Public Administration 533 at 538–539

7 Daniel Alati, *Domestic Counter-Terrorism in a Global World: Post-9/11 Institutional Structures and Cultures in Canada and the United Kingdom* (New York: Routledge, 2017); Daniel Alati & Graham Hudson, "Secret Evidence in Civil Litigation Against the Government: The Lasting Impact of UN Security Council Resolution 1373 on Due Process in Canada and the UK" in Arianna Vedaschi & Kim Lane Scheppele, eds, *9/11 and the Rise of Global Anti-Terrorism Law: How the UN Security Council Rules the World* (Cambridge: Cambridge University Press, 2021); Daniel Alati, "Countering Radicalization to Violent Extremism: A Comparative Study of Canada, the UK and Southeast Asia" (2020) 14:2 International Journal of Law and Political Sciences 88; Graham Hudson & Daniel Alati, "Behind Closed Doors: The Judicial Administration of Secret Trials in Canada" (2018) 44:1 Queen's Law Journal 1; Feng Lin & Daniel Alati, "From 'Occupy Central' to Democracy: Is a Referendum for Hong Kong Feasible and Desirable?" (2016) 10:2 Asian Journal of Comparative Law 259; Daniel Alati, "Current National Security and Human Rights Issues in the UK, Canada and Hong Kong" (2015) 22 ILSA Journal of International and Comparative Law 91; Daniel Alati, "Cowardly Traitor or Heroic Whistleblower? The Impact of Edward Snowden's Disclosures on Canada and the United Kingdom's Security Establishments" (2015) 3:1 Lincoln Memorial Law Review 91

Introduction 3

of moves towards drug liberalization in relevant jurisdictions all around the world. This comparative component helps place Canada's efforts in context, allowing for lessons learned to be discussed both in terms of Canada's domestic policy itself, as well as for discussions about how the comparative experience of other jurisdictions may usefully bring to light areas for future improvement. These analyses and discussions are particularly important at this time, given that statutory review of the Cannabis Act was mandated to begin within three years of its operation.[8]

1.1 Aims and Objectives

The overall aim of this book is to place Canadian cannabis (and wider drug) policy in a historical and comparative context. As such, several objectives flow from this, including: 1) providing for a comprehensive analysis of the historical evolution of Canada's federal drug policy, in order to better understand more recent developments including the legalization of cannabis; 2) engaging in critical analyses of the legislative process behind, and eventual passage of, the federal Cannabis Act, including a specific focus on Indigenous exclusion and lack of participation in the process and a critical appraisal of whether Canada's long racist and classist drug policy history was sufficiently addressed both throughout the process and in the subsequent legislation; 3) comprehensively surveying provincial implementation of the federal legislation, with an eye towards identifying any notable similarities and differences amongst provinces and analyzing the complex interplay of jurisdictional issues that existed during this implementation; 4) elucidating whether a cooperative federalism operated in the provincial implementation of federal legislation and, if so, to what extent; 5) comprehensively surveying drug policy liberalization in jurisdictions around the world, with an eye towards placing Canada's past, present, and future wider drug policy in comparative context; and 6) illustrating lessons to be learned from the early years of Canada's cannabis legalization, with an eye towards future improvement of both the country's legal cannabis regime as well as its wider drug policy. To this end, the book aims to make a crucial contribution to a field of literature that is topical, ever-growing, and focused on a policy environment that is fast-moving. Cannabis legalization is in its infancy and will soon be subjected to a (hopefully substantive) statutory review. As such, it is hoped that the various analyses within this book will serve the future purpose of indicating key and necessary areas of reform.

---

8 Cannabis Act, *supra* note 3, s 151.1 (1). The end of this three-year timeline occurred in October 2021. The Cannabis Act mandates that a review be laid before both the House and Senate within 18 months of this date. As of late February 2022, Health Canada had indicated that the review had not yet begun. See Solomon Israel, "Canada's Cannabis Legalization Review Running Late, as Industry Hopes for Reforms" (25 February 2022), online: *MJBiz Daily* <https://mjbizdaily.com/canadas-cannabis-legalization-review-running-late-as-industry-hopes-for-reforms/>

4   *Introduction*

1.2 Methodology

The methodology utilized in this book was largely developed through the author's first book publication,[9] and was subsequently used and refined in several other publications.[10] This methodology is socio-legal and interdisciplinary, blending core aspects of traditional legal research methods (documentary analyses) and sociological research methods (qualitative material). Traditional legal research methods are utilized all throughout the book, largely through documentary analyses that look at sources, including, but not limited to, case law, legislation, legislative summaries, reports from commissions of inquiry, Hansard debates, relevant reports of both House and Senate committees, official government responses and press releases, and secondary source materials (including academic articles, industry publications, non-governmental organization publications, and news media articles). This material is particularly useful when it comes to understanding and analyzing the historical evolution of any given policy, but in a fast-evolving policy area like cannabis legalization, there are often analytical gaps that need to be filled in. As noted by Wesley, "In a quickly moving policy area like cannabis reform, scholars must be in close contact with practitioners in the public, private, and non-profit sectors in order to stay abreast of new developments and advancements in the field".[11] As such, qualitative interviews with cannabis industry leaders were utilized to fill in gaps and add context to the traditional documentary analyses. They were particularly useful for analyses of the provincial implementation of cannabis legalization, as a significant lack of available provincial data makes analysis difficult. As noted by Armstrong, "Provincial cannabis agencies have the most information about recreational sales, especially where they operate all the stores; but despite public ownership, public mandates, and public attention, most provide minimal public disclosure".[12] The provincial secrecy surrounding legal cannabis implementation data stands in stark contrast to the proactive disclosure practised by several U.S. states,[13] and, as such, qualitative interviews were necessary for a full picture of the challenges associated with implementation to be painted. Moreover, cannabis industry leaders were extremely useful in providing appraisals of aspects of the federal legislation that have had an impact on their work within the industry. Similarly, Indigenous communities were largely excluded from the public consultation on the Cannabis

---

9   Daniel Alati, *Domestic Counter-Terrorism in a Global World: Post-9/11 Institutional Structures and Cultures in Canada and the United Kingdom* (New York: Routledge, 2017)

10 See note 7

11 Wesley, *supra* note 6, at 546

12 Michael Armstrong, "Legal Cannabis Market Shares During Canada's First Year of Recreational Legalization" (2021) 88 International Journal of Drug Policy, DOI: <>https://doi.org/10.1016/j.drugpo.2020.103028> at 2

13 Michael Armstrong, "Canada's Provinces and Territories Should Disclose Cannabis Data to Support Research" (2021) 193:10 CMAJ 341

Act[14] and from various other stages of the legislative process. Qualitative interviews with leaders of Indigenous communities thus shed light on Indigenous perspectives on the impacts of cannabis legalization that were not otherwise available in publicly available materials.

Unlike some sociological research that seeks to engage qualitative participants with an eye towards arriving at some kind of "representative" or "generalizable" set of opinions, this research did not seek to do so. From its outset, the qualitative component of the research was meant to be supplementary, providing key information that otherwise could not have been accessed through publicly available material. Issues of time and limited resources also precluded a wider, more generalizable qualitative component. While this may be considered for future research projects in this area, it was simply not possible at this early stage in this research. Prospective interview participants were identified through a comprehensive scan of the available documentary material. In some cases, "snowball" sampling was used when interview participants suggested colleagues that may also be interested in participation. Participants were drawn from jurisdictions across the country, representing various relevant communities and industry segments. Indigenous community leaders were authoritative, representing their own individual communities and also sharing experience from having held higher-level governance positions. Cannabis industry expert participants were similarly representative of the higher-level executive branch of the industry. Most were CEOs of their companies or worked in executive-level positions within large cannabis firms. Confidentiality dictates that any further information about these participants cannot be shared, including any potential information that may identify them or put their anonymity at stake. As such, all participants have been assigned a random letter identifier to be used for purposes of citation throughout this book. Semi-structured interviews were conducted based on relevant topics identified through the documentary analyses. These interviews were largely conducted virtually due to the COVID-19 pandemic. Participation was voluntary, and participants were informed of their rights to decline to answer specific questions and withdraw from the interview at any time. None of the research participants saw the need to exercise either of these rights. The qualitative research component conformed to the standards set by the author's institutional Research Ethics Board.

Furthermore, this book utilized a comparative research methodology that is backstopped by a well-established theoretical framework and literature. This book's methodology situates itself within the literature on comparative criminal justice and cultural comparativism.[15] In a nutshell, the cultural comparativist

---

14 Health Canada, *Proposed Approach to The Regulation of Cannabis* (Ottawa: Health Canada, 2017); Health Canada, *Proposed Approach to The Regulation of Cannabis: Summary of Comments Received During the Public Consultation* (Ottawa: Health Canada, 2018): In the former document, the word "Indigenous" is found a grand total of two times in 75 pages. In the latter, it is found 3 times in 40 pages

15 For the seminal text on this research methodology, see: David Nelken, *Comparative Criminal Justice: Making Sense of Difference* (Los Angeles: Sage Publications, 2010)

6 *Introduction*

seeks to go beyond rule-comparison by considering the social, political, and cultural dynamics that shape laws differently in different jurisdictions.[16] Since the field of comparative legal studies lacks a discipline-wide consensus about the goals and methods of comparison,[17] researchers are often faced with a choice between formal (and very literal) analyses of different legal rules or broader analyses that encompass the "historical, social, economic, political, cultural and psychological context which has made that rule or proposition what it is".[18] This book decisively chooses the latter, as is evidenced by its extensive focus on the historical evolution of Canada's drug policy in Chapter 2. Furthermore, it has been argued that "purely doctrinal comparative legal studies that focus on the black letter of the law in different jurisdictions can miss out on key differences in the legal and political cultures and structures of states".[19] For example, any nuanced and informed analysis of the Cannabis Act's actual contents requires a broader understanding of crucial legal and political cultures and structures in Canada. It is for this very reason that Canada's system of federalism is extensively discussed in Chapter 3.[20] Lastly, comparative analyses inevitably require a researcher to make choices, particularly in relation to the jurisdictions to be surveyed. In this project, many of these choices were dictated by space, access, and suitable grounds for comparison. As is noted in Chapter 4, space precluded a discussion of every single federalist constitutional democracy that has either criminalized or liberalized cannabis (and wider drug) use at some time in its history. Moreover, jurisdictions from Asian, African and Middle Eastern regions were not discussed largely because of a lack of available (English language in particular) academic and documentary material. Jurisdictions in these regions also lack some necessary sufficient bases for comparative analyses, namely a federalist constitutional democracy and a legal system similar to the common-law system practised in Canada.

1.3 Chapter Summaries

Chapter 2 provides a thorough and comprehensive account of Canada's federal drug policy history dating back to the passage of the country's first consequential drug legislation, the Opium Act.[21] It subsequently analyzes several key periods of time and historical developments within this history, including: 1) the years

---

16 For further examples of research works that fall within this methodology, see: Pierre Legrand, "Comparative Legal Studies and the Matter of Authenticity" (2006) 1 Journal of Comparative Legal Studies 365; Liora Lazarus, *Contrasting Prisoner's Rights: A Comparative Examination of Germany and England* (Oxford: Oxford University Press, 2004)

17 David Nelken, *Comparative Criminal Justice and Globalization* (Farnham, UK: Ashgate, 2011) at 91

18 Pierre Legrand, "How to Compare Now" (1996) 16 Journal of Legal Studies 232 at 234

19 Alati, *supra* note 9, at 12

20 Chapter 3.1

21 *Opium Act*, RSC 1908, c 50

Introduction 7

following the passage of the Opium Act and the beginning of prohibition;[22] 2) the LeDain Commission inquiry and subsequent political indifference;[23] 3) the "War on Drugs" and the passage of the Controlled Drugs and Substances Act (CDSA);[24] 4) a return to drug policy reform inertia at the turn of the century;[25] 5) changes to medical cannabis regulation prompted by legal challenges at the turn of the century;[26] and 6) the passage of the 2018 Cannabis Act.[27] Through these analyses, it becomes clear that the historical evolution of Canada's federal drug policy has largely been driven by racist, classist, and colonial motivations that have allowed for punitive measures resulting in the exclusion of, and disproportionate impact on, Canada's Indigenous, minority, and marginalized communities.[28] Using this history, cannabis legalization is placed in historical context, and it is argued that the Cannabis Act represents a *missed opportunity* to the extent that it did not address this history through consultation, consideration, and inclusion of the communities historically most affected by cannabis prohibition. Documentary analyses illustrate a severe lack of consultation with Indigenous communities, as well as a complete absence of any social justice measures in the Cannabis Act that could and should have provided redress for the minority and marginalized groups historically most affected by cannabis prohibition. Qualitative interviews with Indigenous community and cannabis industry leaders express sentiments that further reiterate these arguments, adding further context from those who have been on the front lines of cannabis legalization in this country.[29]

Chapter 3 focuses on the period following the passage of the federal Cannabis Act to discuss the unique and intense policy environment that existed during a tight timeline for its implementation in provinces across the country. It has been argued that

> In federations like Canada, creating a fully integrated, nationwide policy framework is a daunting collective action problem. The task is even more challenging when jurisdiction over the policy area is divided, as is the case with cannabis regulation in Canada.[30]

---

22 Chapter 2.1
23 Chapter 2.2
24 Chapter 2.3
25 Chapter 2.4
26 Chapter 2.5
27 Chapter 2.6
28 For more on this subject, see: Neil Boyd, "The Origins of Canadian Narcotics Legislation: The Process of Criminalization in Historical Context" (1984) 8:1 Dalhousie Law Journal 102; Robert Solomon & Melvyn Green, "The First Century: The History of Non-Medical Opiate Use and Control Policies in Canada, 1870–1970" in Patricia Blackwell & Judith Erickson, eds, *Illicit Drugs in Canada: A Risky Business* (Scarborough: Nelson Canada, 1988) 88; Andrew Hathaway, "The Legal History and Cultural Experience of Cannabis" (2009) 5:4 Visions Journal 12
29 Chapter 2.7
30 Wesley, *supra* note 6, at 538–539

8 *Introduction*

As such, the chapter necessarily begins with analyses of the implementation of legal cannabis in Canada that call into question the existence of a "cooperative federalism"[31] in the country and instead suggest that the federal government exercised strong coercive force over the policy choices that were supposedly within the jurisdiction of the provinces.[32] Furthermore, Indigenous exclusion is once again discussed to the extent that it is a historical issue with Canadian federalism that has further manifested itself through legal cannabis implementation in the provinces, recreating an unfortunate historical pattern of exclusion and settler colonialism that had previously occurred with other substances such as alcohol and tobacco.[33] Here once again, qualitative interviews with Indigenous community leaders are used to add context from those who have been affected by the provincial implementation of legal cannabis. The chapter then discusses general trends and issues related to implementation that were common across all provinces throughout the country,[34] including: 1) supply issues that plagued the rollout of legalization in its first year; 2) strict marketing and advertising rules laid out by the federal government that impacted the ability of companies in provinces across the country to compete; 3) a lack of available and transparent data from the provinces, which has made it difficult to assess legal cannabis implementation; and 4) the trickle-down effect of the Cannabis Act's complete lack of social justice and social equity provisions, resulting in a glaring lack of diversity in each province's cannabis industry and concerns that the "legacy market" are being denied access to the legal cannabis economy.[35] It is argued that the commonality of these issues in provinces across Canada is further evidence of the federal government's strong coercive force over the policy choices of provinces.[36] The chapter concludes with province-specific analyses of the differences, peculiarities, challenges, and successes of each province's legal cannabis implementation,[37]

31 For an extensive and thoughtful discussion of cooperative federalism in Canada, see: Peter Bowal et al, "Regulating Cannabis: A Comparative Exploration of Canadian Legalization" (2020) 57:4 American Business Law Journal 677
32 Chapter 3.1
33 Chapter 3.2
34 Chapter 3.3
35 "Legacy market" is a term used throughout the book to refer to a large segment of Canada's pre-legalization cannabis industry, broadly encompassing those who operated therapeutic dispensaries to provide cannabis to patients while the substance was still illegal, openly challenging cannabis prohibition in the process
36 For excellent discussions of the federal government's role in "policy coercion" related to cannabis legalization, see: Andrew Train & Dave Snow, "Cannabis Policy Diffusion in Ontario and New Brunswick: Coercion, Learning, and Replication" (2019) 62:4 Canadian Public Administration 549; Maude Benoit & Gabriel Levesque, "What Can Cannabis Legalisation Teach Us About Canadian Federalism?" (2019), online: *Fifty Shades of Federalism* <http://50shadesoffederalism.com/policies/what-can-cannabis-legalisation-teach-us-about-canadian-federalism/>
37 Chapters 3.4–3.10 provide analyses of legal cannabis implementation in Ontario, Alberta, Quebec, British Columbia, Saskatchewan, Manitoba and Canada's Eastern Provinces (New Brunswick, Nova Scotia, Newfoundland and Labrador, and Prince Edward Island)

Introduction 9

suggesting that more research and data will be needed to assess the success of implementation in the years to come.

Chapter 4 provides a comprehensive account of cannabis (and wider drug) policy liberalization in jurisdictions around the world. Forty jurisdictions are analyzed, representing a significant scan of jurisdictions within the Commonwealth,[38] Europe,[39] Latin America,[40] and several states within the United States.[41] These analyses reveal several jurisdictions with globally significant markets, population size, and political significance that have moved towards recreational cannabis legalization, including, but not limited to, Mexico,[42] Uruguay,[43] Malta,[44] South Africa,[45] Germany,[46] Portugal,[47] Switzerland,[48] and several U.S. states. Moreover, and importantly, the jurisdictional scan reveals various trends associated with wider drug policy liberalization that may be relevant to future drug policy reform in Canada, including: 1) several jurisdictions have moved towards broader drug policy liberalization through the decriminalization, defelonization, or legalization of illicit substances other than cannabis; 2) several jurisdictions (especially in the United States) have included social justice (pardons) and/or social equity (prioritization of equity applicants, financial assistance, etc.) provisions in their cannabis legalization regulatory schemes; and 3) several jurisdictions have implemented public health-oriented drug policies and programs, including syringe exchanges, sanctioned drug consumption sites, etc.[49] It is thus suggested that there are lessons to be learned for Canada based on the comparative experiences of the jurisdictions surveyed.

Chapter 5 begins by noting that the Cannabis Act is scheduled to undergo a statutory review to assess the impacts of cannabis legalization in its early years. It thus argues that any review or legislative reform of cannabis legalization that occurs in the future should take note of various lessons learned stemming from the analyses in this book, namely: 1) the need to address a long and unfortunate history of Indigenous exclusion that continued through the passage and implementation of the Cannabis Act;[50] 2) the need to address Canada's long and unfortunate history of racist and classist drug policy, specifically through the use of social justice mechanisms such as automatic record expungement for past

38 Chapter 4.1
39 Chapter 4.2
40 Chapter 4.3
41 Chapter 4.4
42 Chapter 4.3.6
43 Chapter 4.3.9
44 Chapter 4.2.4
45 Chapter 4.1.4
46 Chapter 4.2.2
47 Chapter 4.2.6
48 Chapter 4.2.8
49 Chapter 4.5
50 Chapter 5.1

10 *Introduction*

possession-related cannabis offences;[51] and 3) the need to learn lessons from other jurisdictions that have better implemented social equity provisions alongside cannabis legalization, engaged in wider drug policy reform by decriminalizing substances other than cannabis, and more generally moved towards harm reduction measures with an eye towards re-orienting their approach to drug addiction from a criminal justice issue to a public health issue.[52] The chapter concludes by identifying issues that, whilst not readily apparent at the time of the passage of the Cannabis Act, are nonetheless future challenges that have manifested during its implementation and must be addressed, including: 1) necessary changes to the excise tax;[53] 2) the inadequacy of Health Canada as a regulator;[54] 3) necessary changes to marketing and advertising restrictions;[55] 4) the growing issue of market concentration;[56] 5) the regulation of consumption lounges;[57] and 6) the need for more transparent data.[58] The chapter concludes by lamenting the delayed beginning of the statutory review of the Cannabis Act, particularly given the long list of legislative reform issues that need to be addressed to provide for a more equitable and effective system of legalized cannabis in the future.

Chapter 6 concludes the text by succinctly and concisely re-iterating recommendations for future change based on the analyses throughout this text. It does so alongside select qualitative material from the Indigenous community and cannabis industry leaders who participated in the research for this book. In doing so, it connects the "voices" from the front lines of cannabis legalization with the broader documentary analyses throughout the text to highlight future steps for legislative reform. It also provides for a brief discussion of key areas of analysis that might be necessary as cannabis (and wider drug) policy moves forward into its next phase in the years to come.

Alati, Daniel, "Countering Radicalization to Violent Extremism: A Comparative Study of Canada, the UK and Southeast Asia" (2020) 14:2 International Journal of Law and Political Sciences 88

Alati, Daniel, "Cowardly Traitor or Heroic Whistleblower? The Impact of Edward Snowden's Disclosures on Canada and the United Kingdom's Security Establishments" (2015) 3:1 Lincoln Memorial Law Review 91

Alati, Daniel, "Current National Security and Human Rights Issues in the UK, Canada and Hong Kong" (2015) 22 ILSA Journal of International and Comparative Law 91

Alati, Daniel, *Domestic Counter-Terrorism in a Global World: Post-9/11 Institutional Structures and Cultures in Canada and the United Kingdom* (New York: Routledge, 2017)

51 Chapter 5.2
52 Chapter 5.3
53 Chapter 5.4.1
54 Chapter 5.4.2
55 Chapter 5.4.3
56 Chapter 5.4.4
57 Chapter 5.4.5
58 Chapter 5.4.6

Alati, Daniel & Hudson, Graham, "Secret Evidence in Civil Litigation Against the Government: The Lasting Impact of UN Security Council Resolution 1373 on Due Process in Canada and the UK" in Arianna Vedaschi & Kim Lane Scheppele, eds, *9/11 and the Rise of Global Anti-Terrorism Law: How the UN Security Council Rules the World* (Cambridge: Cambridge University Press, 2021)

Armstrong, Michael, "Canada's Provinces and Territories Should Disclose Cannabis Data to Support Research" (2021) 193:10 CMAJ 341

Armstrong, Michael, "Legal Cannabis Market Shares During Canada's First Year of Recreational Legalization" (2021) 88 International Journal of Drug Policy, DOI: <https://doi.org/10.1016/j.drugpo.2020.103028> at 2

Benoit, Maude & Levesque, Gabriel, "What Can Cannabis Legalisation Teach Us About Canadian Federalism?" (2019), online: *Fifty Shades of Federalism* <http://50shadesoffederalism.com/policies/what-can-cannabis-legalisation-teach-us-about-canadian-federalism/>

Bowal, Peter, Kisska-Schulze, Kathryn, Haigh, Richard & Ng, Adrienne, "Regulating Cannabis: A Comparative Exploration of Canadian Legalization" (2020) 57:4 American Business Law Journal 677

Boyd, Neil, "The Origins of Canadian Narcotics Legislation: The Process of Criminalization in Historical Context" (1984) 8:1 Dalhousie Law Journal 102

Cannabis Act, SC 2018, c 16

Crosby, Andrew, "Contesting Cannabis: Indigenous Jurisdiction and Legalization" (2019) 62:4 Canadian Public Administration 634

Elliott, Josh, "Liberals 'Committed' to Legalizing Marijuana: Trudeau" (30 September 2015), online: *CTV News* <www.ctvnews.ca/politics/election/liberals-committed-to-legalizing-marijuana-trudeau-1.2588260>

Hathaway, Andrew, "The Legal History and Cultural Experience of Cannabis" (2009) 5:4 Visions Journal 12

Health Canada, *Proposed Approach to the Regulation of Cannabis* (Ottawa: Health Canada, 2017)

Health Canada, *Proposed Approach to the Regulation of Cannabis: Summary of Comments Received During the Public Consultation* (Ottawa: Health Canada, 2018)

Hudson, Graham & Alati, Daniel, "Behind Closed Doors: The Judicial Administration of Secret Trials in Canada" (2018) 44:1 Queen's Law Journal 1

Israel, Solomon, "Canada's Cannabis Legalization Review Running Late, as Industry Hopes for Reforms" (25 February 2022), online: *MJBiz Daily* <https://mjbizdaily.com/canadas-cannabis-legalization-review-running-late-as-industry-hopes-for-reforms/>

Koutouki, Konstantia & Lofts, Katherine, "Cannabis, Reconciliation, and the Rights of Indigenous Peoples: Prospects and Challenges for Cannabis Legalization in Canada" (2019) 56:3 Alberta Law Review 709

Lazarus, Liora, *Contrasting Prisoner's Rights: A Comparative Examination of Germany and England* (Oxford: Oxford University, 2004)

Legrand, Pierre, "Comparative Legal Studies and the Matter of Authenticity" (2006) 1 Journal of Comparative Legal Studies 365

Legrand, Pierre, "How to Compare Now" (1996) 16 Journal of Legal Studies 232

Lin, Feng & Alati, Daniel, "From 'Occupy Central' to Democracy: Is a Referendum for Hong Kong Feasible and Desirable?" (2016) 10:2 Asian Journal of Comparative Law 259

12 *Introduction*

Nelken, David, *Comparative Criminal Justice and Globalization* (Farnham, UK: Ashgate, 2011)

Nelken, David, *Comparative Criminal Justice: Making Sense of Difference* (Los Angeles: Sage Publications, 2010)

Opium Act, RSC 1908, c 50

Owusu-Bempah, Akwasi, "Where Is the Fairness in Canadian Cannabis Legalization? Lessons to Be Learned from the American Experience" (2021) 55:2 Journal of Canadian Studies 395

Solomon, Robert & Green, Melvyn, "The First Century: The History of Non-Medical Opiate Use and Control Policies in Canada, 1870–1970" in Patricia Blackwell & Judith Erickson, eds, *Illicit Drugs in Canada: A Risky Business* (Scarborough: Nelson Canada, 1988) 88

Train, Andrew & Snow, Dave, "Cannabis Policy Diffusion in Ontario and New Brunswick: Coercion, Learning, and Replication" (2019) 62:4 Canadian Public Administration 549

Valleriani, Jenna, Lavalley, Jennifer & McNeil, Ryan, "A Missed Opportunity? Cannabis Legalization and Reparations in Canada" (2018) 109 Canadian Journal of Public Health 745

Wesley, Jared, "Beyond Prohibition: The Legalization of Cannabis in Canada" (2019) 62:4 Canadian Public Administration 533

Wesley, Jared & Murray, Kyle, "To Market or Demarket? Public-Sector Branding of Cannabis in Canada" (2021) 53:7 Administration & Society 1078

2 Historical Evolution of Canada's Federal Drug Policy

Legislative changes are a product of the historical evolution of policy, especially in common-law jurisdictions operating under a federalist constitutional order. It is thus necessary to analyze Canada's long history of drug prohibition to best understand its more recent direction towards drug liberalization. This chapter provides a comprehensive account of the historical evolution of Canada's federal drug policy. In doing so, it focuses on several key periods of time and substantial historical developments, namely: 1) the passage of the Opium Act and the beginning of prohibition;[1] 2) the LeDain Commission Inquiry and subsequent political indifference;[2] 3) the "War on Drugs" and the passage of the Controlled Drugs and Substances Act (CDSA);[3] 4) a return to drug policy inertia at the turn of the century;[4] 5) changes to medical cannabis regulation prompted by legal challenges at the turn of the century;[5] and 6) the legislative process behind, and eventual passage of, the 2018 Cannabis Act.[6] The chapter concludes with "voices from the front lines", a select sample of qualitative material collected through interviews with Indigenous community and cannabis industry leaders.[7] The analyses that follow below tell a story of drug policy in Canada that has mainly been instigated by racist and classist forces, born less out of real concerns with increased drug use and more out of hysteria, moral panic, and mythology. They suggest that more recent developments towards drug liberalization in Canada, though momentous, nonetheless recreate a pattern whereby the communities – Indigenous, minority, and marginalized – historically most affected by drug criminalization have been excluded from meaningful engagement and inclusion.

1 Chapter 2.1
2 Chapter 2.2
3 Chapter 2.3
4 Chapter 2.4
5 Chapter 2.5
6 Chapter 2.6
7 Chapter 2.7

DOI: 10.4324/9781003200741-2

14 History of Canada's Federal Drug Policy

2.1 The Passage of the Opium Act and the Beginning of Prohibition

The impetus behind drug prohibition in Canada began well before the eventual passage of the Opium Act[8] in 1908. Before this time, the use of opiates in Canada was unregulated, with some scholars suggesting that the use of alcohol and tobacco was considered a greater threat to public health and morals.[9] The passage of the Opium Act has been described by numerous scholars as less of a response to a real drug consumption problem and more of a reflection of the anti-immigrant and anti-Asian sentiment of the time. As noted by Boyd,

> Canada's decision to make opiate use illegal was not substantially the product of an ethic of consumer protection. The legislation is better understood as reflecting a fear of socio-economic and socio-cultural assimilation, a fear that was exacerbated by the Chinese who were successfully making their way in the young nation of Canada.[10]

The passage of the Opium Act took place after a major labour demonstration in 1907, prompting the Deputy Minister of Labour, William Lyon Mackenzie King, to visit British Columbia. King was reportedly shocked by the existence of the opium trade in British Columbia, namely that opium smoking was becoming more prevalent among white people and that Chinese opium merchants were making vast profits in the opium trade. As a result, "elimination of the opium 'menace' was to become the primary focus of King's early political career".[11] The 1908 Opium Act was lenient in comparison to the legislation that would come in the years to follow, as it did not prohibit simple possession nor use of the drug. Much more harsh legislation was passed in the form of the 1911 Opium and Narcotic Drug Act,[12] which significantly increased the severity of penalties (including imprisonment) and expanded enforcement powers.[13] While there are various academic explanations and accounts of the two decades that would follow the passage of this legislation, the consistent theme of these accounts (and indeed much of Canada's drug prohibition history overall) is that "since its inception,

---

8 *Opium Act*, RSC 1908, c 50

9 Giselle Dias, "Canada's Drug Laws: Prohibition Is Not the Answer" in J. Thomas et al, eds, *Perspectives of Canadian Drug Policy* (Ontario: The John Howard Society of Canada, 2003) 9–24 at 10

10 Neil Boyd, "The Origins of Canadian Narcotics Legislation: The Process of Criminalization in Historical Context" (1984) 8:1 Dalhousie Law Journal 102 at 117

11 Dias, *supra* note 9, at 11

12 RSC 1911, c 17

13 Robert Solomon & Melvyn Green, "The First Century: The History of Non-Medical Opiate Use and Control Policies in Canada, 1870–1970" in Patricia Blackwell & Judith Erickson, eds, *Illicit Drugs in Canada: A Risky Business* (Scarborough: Nelson Canada, 1988) 88–104 at 92–93

drug prohibition has been used to demonize non-white and poor consumers of illegal drugs".[14]

There is extensive evidence of this theme all throughout the literature on Canada's early drug prohibition history. As noted by Carstairs,

> Although the middle and upper classes also used drugs, especially alcohol, to excess, by the 1920s, the drugs prohibited under the Opium and Narcotic Drug Act seem to have been used primarily by working-class people. The middle and upper-class people who did use opiates and cocaine often were able to obtain supplies through doctors. They had little contact with the illicit market and rarely faced criminal sanctions for their drug use. This was not true for working-class users.[15]

The passage of these early prohibitionist drug laws did very little to quell the swelling of Anti-Asian views. Racist and anti-immigrant sentiment allowed the rapid proliferation of prosecutorial powers with little to no debate, as is evidenced by the fact that marijuana was added to the list of prohibited substances in 1923 with the Health Minister's simple assertion, "There is a new drug in the schedule".[16] The writings of Emily Murphy, well documented in the academic literature on early prohibition, provide a particularly illuminating historical record of the sentiment of the time. Murphy, a police magistrate and judge of the Edmonton juvenile court, was commissioned by Maclean's magazine to write a series of 1920 articles on the problem of drug abuse, which ultimately formed the basis of her book, *The Black Candle*. Murphy's writings, which were filled with racist and unflattering descriptions of Chinese drug addicts, "brought the Vancouver drug panic to a larger Canadian audience".[17] There is a clear distinction between the description and treatment of white drug addicts and Chinese drug users and, as such, "White drug use and Chinese drug use thereby were delineated as two quite separate problems".[18] The sensationalist rhetoric hardly provided for an impartial account of the actual effects of various drugs, suggesting instead that all drugs provided for the same problems: "moral degeneration, crime, physical and mental deterioration and disease".[19]

It is against this backdrop that several substantial legislative provisions (and enforcement mechanisms) related to drug prohibition were developed and

---

14 Scott Bernstein et al, "The Regulation Project: Tools for Engaging the Public in the Legal Regulation of Drugs" (2020) 86 International Journal of Drug Policy 1 at 2

15 Catherine Carstairs, "Deporting 'Ah Sin' to Save the White Race: Moral Panic, Racialization, and the Extension of Canadian Drug Laws in the 1920's" (1999) 16:1 University of Toronto Press 65 at 82

16 Boyd, *supra* note 10, at 12: Boyd notes that the addition garnered no discussion in the House of Commons

17 Carstairs, *supra* note 15, at 76

18 *Ibid*

19 Boyd, *supra* note 10, at 129

16 History of Canada's Federal Drug Policy

consolidated during the 1920s. The blame of Chinese-Canadians for the drug use of white youth prompted the increase of maximum sentences for trafficking and possession from one year to seven in 1921 and allowed for new legal precedents to be set for the search of people and places without a warrant with limited rights to appeal.[20] At the same time, the rhetoric around drug use left little to no space for discussion of treatment, as "neither the government or social services organizations were willing to spend money on the treatment and rehabilitation of the socially disadvantaged dope fiend".[21] By the end of the decade, rhetoric and language surrounding the "nefarious trafficker" and their role in the drug problem had become so entrenched in the national consciousness that the availability of "whipping" as a punishment available to judges for trafficking offences was almost an afterthought in the debates on the 1929 consolidation of the Opium and Narcotic Drug Act.[22] In this type of societal climate, very little space was reserved for the consideration of whether such powers and prohibitions were even necessary. Few people had even heard of marijuana when it was outlawed in 1923, and it was more than a decade before the first arrests for cannabis possession were even reported.[23] Nonetheless, by the time the 1920s had concluded, there was a substantial volume of prohibitionist drug policy on Canada's statute books. The Opium and Narcotic Drug Act would indeed stand the test of time. As noted by Riley, "The Opium and Narcotic Drug Act of 1929 was Canada's main instrument of drug policy for the next forty years".[24]

It was not until several decades later that drug prohibition would again become part of the national conversation. Even though illegal drug use was declining during the 1950s, the media published sensationalist accounts of drug-addicted youth in Canada.[25] By the 1960s, the use of marijuana among educated, white youth of higher means and social status began to raise concern.[26] This was despite the fact that the 1961 Narcotic Control Act was in place, legislation that has been argued to be "one of the most punitive drug laws enacted by a Western nation at that time".[27] Available penalties of up to seven years imprisonment for illicit drug possession seemed to have had only a slight deterrent effect on cannabis use rates, which climbed sharply during the decade despite a large amount of enforcement resources being allocated to combat the problem.[28] During this time, "the demonization of illicit drug users continued, and punitive laws, prison time, and

---

20 Carstairs, *supra* note 15, at 66–68
21 *Ibid* at 81
22 *Ibid* at 80
23 Andrew Hathaway, "The Legal History and Cultural Experience of Cannabis" (2009) 5:4 Visions Journal 12
24 Diane Riley, *Drugs and Drug Policy in Canada: A Brief Review & Commentary* (Ottawa: Senate of Canada, 1998) at 4
25 Solomon and Green, *supra* note 13, at 102
26 Hathaway, *supra* note 23, at 12
27 Susan Boyd & Donald MacPherson, "Community Engagement – The Harms of Drug Prohibition: Ongoing Resistance in Vancouver's Eastside" (2018) 200 BC Studies 87 at 90
28 Riley, *supra* note 24, at 4

History of Canada's Federal Drug Policy   17

abstinence from criminalized drugs remained the primary goals of drug policy in Canada".[29] The law itself began to pose a problem, as a "criminal conviction was a serious consequence for otherwise conforming, law-abiding young Canadians".[30] At the same time, the "dope fiend" mythology that had been utilized so successfully to justify prohibition for decades was losing much of its rhetorical weight. As noted by Dias,

> When a substantial proportion of the population is engaging in drug use it is difficult to maintain myths that are not supported by experience. Most of the people arrested on drug charges during the "cannabis controversy: did not fit the "drug fiend" stereotype, and the law was criticized for making criminals out of white middle class youth.[31]

The 1960s were characterized by a "narrowing of the social distance between drug users and the mainstream of society", and the "law was widely assailed for making criminals of middle class youth".[32] In glaring contrast to the racist and classist motivations behind the strict prohibition of drugs in the 1920s, sympathetic views towards middle-class drug use (and a very real issue with court backlog) created "pressures for the liberalization of Canada's drug laws".[33] As a result, in 1969, the Commission of Inquiry into the Non-Medical Use of Drugs (most commonly referred to as the LeDain Commission) was formed to "address growing concern about drug use and appropriate responses".[34]

2.2 The LeDain Commission Inquiry and Subsequent Political Indifference

As noted by Hathaway, the LeDain Commission Inquiry was not lacking in scope or diligence, engaging in extensive research, consulting experts, and holding public hearings across the country over a three-year period.[35] As noted in its fourth and *Final Report*,[36] the Commission held public hearings in 27 cities, including Ottawa and every provincial capital, and received a total of 639 submissions from

---

29 Boyd & MacPherson, *supra* note 27, at 90
30 Hathaway, *supra* note 23, at 12
31 Dias, *supra* note 9, at 11
32 Patricia G. Erickson, "Recent Trends in Canadian Drug Policy: The Decline and Resurgence of Prohibitionism" (1992) 121:3 Political Pharmacology: Thinking About Drugs 239 at 247
33 Walter Cavalieri & Diane Riley, "Harm Reduction in Canada: The Many Faces of Regression" in Richard Pates & Diane Riley, eds, *Harm Reduction in Substance Use and High-Risk Behaviour: International Policy and Practice* (London: Wiley-Blackwell, 2012) 382–394 at 382
34 Riley, *supra* note 24, at 4
35 Hathaway, *supra* note 23, at 12
36 Commission of Inquiry into the Non-Medical Use of Drugs, *Final Report of the Commission of Inquiry into the Non-Medical Use of Drugs* (Ottawa: Information Canada, 1973)

18   *History of Canada's Federal Drug Policy*

organizations and individuals.[37] The end result of the Commission's work was a set of several recommendations across multiple reports in support of drug law liberalization. In its *Interim Report*,[38] the Commission

> essentially concluded that cannabis, compared to other prohibited drugs like heroin or cocaine, was a relatively innocuous substance, and that especially personal use should not be subject to criminal or other punitive consequences, which it considered more harmful than the direct risks of the drug.[39]

As noted by Riley, "The majority of the commissioners recommended a graduate withdrawal from criminal sanctions against users, along with the development of less coercive and costly alternatives to replace the punitive application of criminal law".[40] Around the same time, several similar inquiries into cannabis policy in other countries (including the 1968 Wootton Report in Britain, the 1972 Shafer Commission in the United States, and the 1971/1972 Dutch Commissions) produced recommendations that were consistent with those made by the LeDain Commission.[41] At home in Canada, while there was public and media support for the LeDain Commission's proposals to make cannabis control more lenient, "there was no tangible political action – the door was simply opened to a decade of indecision".[42] This has prompted some to observe that "The LeDain Commission served the role of most Royal Commissions: it delayed action on a controversial issue long enough for the public demand for action to subside. Interest in the reform of drug policy gradually declined".[43]

The years that followed the LeDain Commission, a massive and thoughtful undertaking that put forth a fundamentally re-oriented view of the approach Canada could and should take towards drug control, have understandably been characterized by scholars as a period of political indifference. According to Erickson,

> Other proposals for legal changes were made but never implemented. For example, a major reform that attracted substantial political attention in 1968, 1970, 1974 and 1980 but was not approved, was a proposal to move

37   *Ibid* at 6
38   Commission of Inquiry into the Non-Medical Use of Drugs, *Interim Report of the Commission of Inquiry into the Non-Medical Use of Drugs* (Ottawa: Information Canada, 1970)
39   Benedikt Fischer, Cayley Russell & Neil Boyd, "A Century of Cannabis Control in Canada" in Tom Decorte, Simon Lenton & Chris Wilkins, eds, *Legalizing Cannabis: Experiences, Lessons and Scenarios* (England: Routledge, 2020) 89–115 at 89
40   Riley, *supra* note 24, at 4
41   Benedikt Fischer et al, "Cannabis Law Reform in Canada: Is the 'Saga of Promise, Hesitation and Retreat' Coming to an End?" (2003) 45:3 Canadian Journal of Criminology and Criminal Justice 265
42   *Ibid* at 271
43   Riley, *supra* note 24, at 4

cannabis from the Narcotic Control Act to the less restrictive Food and Drug Act.[44]

It should be noted that amendments made to the Criminal Code in the early 1970s did allow for absolute and conditional discharges as sentencing options in drug possession cases.[45] The closest thing to meaningful reform came in 1974 when Bill S-19 was tabled in the Senate. That legislation – which proposed to limit cannabis penalties to a $100 fine with no option for imprisonment, as well as to eliminate criminal records through an automatic discharge mechanism – later died on the order paper in the House of Commons.[46] There are many explanations for the indifference exhibited during this period. Erickson suggests that greater efficiency of the courts in processing drug offenders "helped reduce pressure for meaningful law reform".[47] It has also been suggested that "The post-LeDain Commission years saw numerous political declarations of intent (e.g. in the platforms of federal parties, but usually only when in opposition)".[48] It is unclear why the political will for reform was absent, despite the fact that "In the space of a decade (1970s) cannabis possession convictions grew from less than 1,000 per year to more than 40,000".[49] Many politicians (likely in an effort to download the responsibility for drug enforcement to the courts) "increasingly suggested that the courts could provide for practical decriminalization of cannabis-use offences if they saw fit, by giving discharges or probation".[50] This reasoning largely ignored the fact that discharged offenders would still obtain a criminal record and, as such, "the mass production of 'cannabis criminals' continued throughout the 1970s".[51]

2.3 "The War on Drugs" and the Passage of the Controlled Drugs and Substances Act

Despite the lack of political action, the work of the LeDain Commission ushered in a new kind of dialogue about drug use in Canada, namely that of "harm reduction". As noted by Cavalieri and Riley, the work of the Commission represented "an important step in the development of a policy of harm reduction in Canada".[52] It is also important to note that publicly funded treatment services grew following the recommendations of the Commission.[53] By the mid-1980s,

44 Erickson, *supra* note 32, at 246
45 Riley, *supra* note 24, at 4
46 Fischer et al, *supra* note 41, at 271
47 Erickson, *supra* note 32, at 246
48 Fischer, Russell & Boyd, *supra* note 39, at 90
49 Riley, *supra* note 24, at 5
50 Fischer et al, *supra* note 41, at 271–272
51 *Ibid* at 272
52 Cavalieri & Riley, *supra* note 33, at 382
53 Boyd & MacPherson, *supra* note 27, at 90

20 History of Canada's Federal Drug Policy

there was a growing societal acknowledgement of "the serious limitations of law enforcement and education in reducing the demand for drugs".[54] At the same time, it appears as though the use of illicit drugs was declining, with marijuana arrest activity and sentence severity diminishing in Canada.[55] As a result, "the urgency of earlier drug policy debates was replaced by public and political indifference".[56] The indifferent views of the public and politicians would change sharply, however, towards the latter half of the decade. The catalyst for this change was the 1986 declaration by United States President Ronald Reagan of a new "War on Drugs". Within two days of President Reagan's declaration,

> Prime Minister Brian Mulroney departed from his prepared text to announce that "Drug abuse has become an epidemic and undermines our economic as well as our social fabric" . . . drugs thus returned to the social and political agenda.[57]

It is indeed notable how quickly events subsequently transpired, after more than a decade of political indifference towards drug law reform. The U.S. war on drugs ushered in a "new era of drug prohibition and law enforcement"[58] in Canada. In 1987, Prime Minister Mulroney's government announced "Canada's Drug Strategy" and created a Federal Drug Secretariat that engaged in wide-ranging consultations with community groups and agencies, tasked with the "objectives of reducing the harm to individuals, families and communities from the abuse of drugs".[59]

Canada's Drug Strategy was expressed using the language of "harm reduction" and a "balanced approach to supply and demand reduction", prompting "some renewed hope for cannabis law reform".[60] The decade that followed surely caused this hope to dissipate. As noted by Erickson, "Proposals to increase the surveillance and detection of drug users or sellers and to restrict their liberty became more common. Workplace drug testing and zero tolerance were undoubtedly influenced by the American example".[61] The American media played a key role during this period in propagating and facilitating an existential threat mythology that had not been seen in Canada since the early 1900s. This was particularly true of cocaine, especially in the form of crack, which the U.S. media "portrayed as the drug that finally fulfilled all of the expectations of the 'demon drug' mythology".[62] The drug panic around cocaine and crack was "imported from

---

54 Cavalieri & Riley, *supra* note 33, at 383
55 Erickson, *supra* note 32, at 244
56 *Ibid* at 248
57 *Ibid*
58 Dias, *supra* note 9, at 12
59 Erickson, *supra* note 32, at 248
60 Fischer et al, *supra* note 41, at 272
61 Erickson, *supra* note 32, at 249
62 *Ibid* at 254

History of Canada's Federal Drug Policy 21

the United States as part of a larger cultural infiltration, with its highly negative evaluations of illicit drug use and users".[63] The racist and classist elements of this drug panic were clearly evident at the time and, with the benefit of hindsight, have been rightly criticized as such. As noted by Dias, "The war on drugs opens the back door to re-instituting a form of slavery. The powerful people in society use the war on drugs to justify incarcerating minorities".[64] There is no shortage of academics who suggest that the U.S. war on drugs was used "as a proxy to promote hidden agendas related to race and social control".[65] It is against this backdrop that the work of Canada's Drug Strategy in the late 1980s and early 1990s must be considered. When it was first established, the strategy was given $210 million dollars in funding to be applied in equal parts to enforcement, treatment and prevention, and was "clearly influenced by the latest American War on Drugs".[66] The strategy was initially funded for a five year period and extended for another five years in April 1992 before "sunsetting" in 1997. During this period of time, the budget related to the health aspects of drug use reduction was significantly slashed.[67] In a move symbolic of the lack of focus on, and funding for, health aspects of drug use reduction, "The Policy and Research Unit of the Canadian Centre on Substance Abuse, which had begun to research and document alternatives to drug prohibition, was closed in 1996 as part of the demise of the Drug Strategy".[68]

The result of this 10-year span – one that began with great promise for a drug policy based on "harm reduction" – was the passage and implementation of the *Controlled Drugs and Substances Act*[69] in 1996. The new legislation, first introduced as Bill C-85 by the Conservative government in 1982 and then as Bill C-7 by the incoming Liberal government, retained a number of core aspects of its punitive predecessor, the Narcotic Control Act: 1) it retained cannabis on Schedule 1, continuing the punitive criminalization of simple possession; 2) an original draft of the law doubled the maximum penalties for first offences of simple possession to a $2,000 fine and/or 12 months imprisonment; and 3) it retained the seven-year maximum for cases decided by way of indictment.[70] The legislation was technically a "health bill", introduced into the House of Commons by the Minister of Health, but commentators have noted that "its content came primarily from the Department of Justice and

---

63 *Ibid*
64 Dias, *supra* note 9, at 17
65 Barbara Macrae, "Drug Policy in Canada: War If Necessary but Not Necessarily War" in J. Thomas et al, eds, *Perspectives of Canadian Drug Policy* (Ontario: The John Howard Society of Canada, 2003) 43–74 at 44
66 Riley, *supra* note 24, at 5
67 *Ibid*: Riley notes that the health budget for drugs was cut to 40% of its former amount during this time
68 *Ibid*
69 SC 1996, c 19
70 Fischer et al, *supra* note 41, at 272–273

22   *History of Canada's Federal Drug Policy*

the Office of the Solicitor General. The bill was drafted by a senior member of the Department of Justice".[71] The legislation attracted considerable criticism during its debate:

> Parliamentary and Senate committee hearings on Bill C-7 generated widespread opposition to the draft law, from a wide spectrum of witnesses – lawyers, addiction researchers, medical and public health experts, even the Canadian Police Association critiqued the bill for its broad punitive approach to drug use . . . an opposition group of MPs within the Liberal caucus advocated more liberal cannabis provisions in the final version of the new drug law.[72]

Some positive developments resulted from submissions made during the legislation's readings and hearings, including a "lessening of penalties for possession of cannabis for personal use so that simple possession would become a summary offence. Nonetheless, such possession was to remain a criminal offence".[73] The legislation also received scrutiny in the Senate Standing Committee on Justice and Constitutional Affairs in late 1995, with the Law Union of Ontario, the Addiction Research Foundation, and the Canadian Foundation for Drug Policy calling for an independent review of the bill.[74] This never occurred, and the current form of the CDSA would subsequently come into effect in 1996.

The Controlled Drugs and Substances Act has since been criticized comprehensively for its punitive orientation, even though it was "touted by some government officials as a *de facto* cannabis decriminalization and a step that had reconciled cannabis-use control with the values of the Canadian public".[75] As noted by Riley, the CDSA

> is soundly prohibitionist and rather than retreating from the drug war rhetoric of the past it extends the net of prohibition further still. The problems related to criminalizing drug users, the social and economic costs of this approach, and its failure to reduce drug availability have still not been addressed. As a result, the costs, both financial and human, of illicit drug use remain unnecessarily high while the costs of criminalizing illicit drug use continue to rise, steadily, predictably and avoidably.[76]

---

71 Riley, *supra* note 24, at 16
72 Fischer et al, *supra* note 41, at 273
73 Riley, *supra* note 24, at 16
74 *Ibid*
75 Fischer et al, *supra* note 41, at 273
76 Riley, *supra* note 24, at 5

History of Canada's Federal Drug Policy 23

Taking into account the work done by the LeDain Commission nearly two decades earlier, the CDSA is truly representative of a marked departure from the values and principles that the Commission espoused. As Erickson notes,

> A wealth of drug research dating back to the Le Dain Commission (1969–1973) was ignored. . . . Canada was one of the first countries to subject the scope and nature of modern criminal drug prohibition to intense scrutiny and consider major reforms of its laws. Yet, the new drug law ensconced the severe maximum penalties and extensive police powers found in the previous *Narcotics Control Act* and added resources to aid even more efficient arrest and prosecution of illicit drug users and sellers.[77]

Relatedly, and ironically, the CDSA simultaneously claimed a need for compliance with international treaties but failed to consider "alternatives to conviction or punishment that are set out in those treaties".[78] For many, the Controlled Drugs and Substances Act was seen as a missed opportunity, particularly because of the wealth of evidence in support of harm reduction that was put forth in the years following the passage of the Narcotic Control Act. As noted by Erickson,

> Much evidence was presented about the costs of allowing the criminal justice response to dominate over more harm reducing alternatives for addicted users. Except for a vague clause about rehabilitation and treatment in appropriate circumstances, little changed from the previous law.[79]

These costs were made immediately evident in the aftermath of the passage of the CDSA. Arrests for drug offences reached new highs during this time, with estimates of simple cannabis possession accounting for around 50% of the 60,000 drug offences per year.[80] Moreover, the early evidence documented in larger cities suggested the weight of these costs was not allocated equally as a result of "selective enforcement involved in drug arrests, targeting the homeless, minorities and other more vulnerable segments of what is a much more homogeneous drug using population".[81]

---

77 Patricia G. Erickson, "A Persistent Paradox: Drug Law and Policy in Canada" (1999) 4:2 Canadian Journal of Criminology 275 at 275
78 Riley, *supra* note 24, at 16–17: Riley also notes that there was room within the related UN Conventions for the removal of criminal penalties for possession of certain drugs for personal use, noting that several countries including Australia, Italy, Spain and Germany had done this without compromising their position with respect to the treaties
79 Erickson, *supra* note 77, at 278
80 Fischer et al, *supra* note 41, at 274
81 Erickson, *supra* note 77, at 278: Erickson's concern about the selective enforcement involved in drug arrests has certainly stood the test of time. The over-representation of these groups in the Canadian criminal justice system for drug-related crimes is discussed extensively in Chapter 2.7

24 History of Canada's Federal Drug Policy

2.4 The Turn of the Century: A Return to Drug Policy Reform Inertia

According to Erickson and Hyshka, "The first decade of the new millennium was marked by further failures to decriminalize cannabis possession and an ongoing inertia in drug policy reform".[82] A closer look at the turn of the century in Canada's drug policy history reveals that, despite significant legal developments and increasing drug use and criminalization problem, very little tangible legislative reform occurred. In the year 2001, 91,920 incidents related to the CDSA were reported by the police, a 3% increase from the year before and a "continuation of an upward trend in drug offences that began in 1994".[83] Of these offences, cannabis offences were primarily responsible for the overall increase, accounting for about three-quarters of all drug-related incidents (with 70% of the cannabis-related incidents being for possession).[84] During this time, a number of key research and policy groups were publicly advocating for cannabis law reform, including the Canadian Centre on Substance Abuse, the Canadian Association of Chiefs of Police, and the Centre for Addiction and Mental Health.[85] Two substantial parliamentary committees would study the issue in the early 2000s – the Senate Special Committee on Illegal Drugs and the House of Commons Special Committee on the Non-Medical Use of Drugs. In September 2002, the Senate Special committee "recommended the legalization of cannabis, arguing that a public health approach should be taken towards drug use".[86] In doing so, the Committee wrote, "We know our proposals are provocative, they will meet with resistance. However, we are also convinced that Canadian society has the maturity and openness to welcome an informed debate".[87] The Special Senate Committee recommendations included a licensing system for the legal production and sale of cannabis products, treating cannabis use and supply like alcohol. The Committee called for "even more fundamental changes to the system of cannabis control than the LeDain Commission had suggested some thirty years earlier".[88]

The House of Commons Special Committee was far more restrained in the recommendations it put forth. Nonetheless, in December 2002, the House of

---

82 Patricia E. Erickson & Elaine Hyshka, "Four Decades of Cannabis Criminals in Canada 1970–2010" (2010) 2:4 Amsterdam Law Forum 1 at 1

83 Josee Savoie, "Crime Statistics in Canada, 2001" (2001) 22:6 Juristat 1–22 <>https://www150.statcan.gc.ca/n1/en/pub/85-002-x/85-002-x2002006-eng.pdf?st=dr2u M6zM> accessed 28 December 2021

84 *Ibid*

85 Fischer et al, *supra* note 41, at 275

86 Canada, Parliament, Library of Parliament, *Legislative Summary: Bill C-45: An Act Respecting Cannabis and to Amend the Controlled Drugs and Substances Act, the Criminal Code and Other Acts,* Pub. No. 42-1-C45-E (Ottawa: Parliamentary Information and Research Service, 2018) at 4

87 Canada, Parliament, Special Senate Committee on Illegal Drugs, *Cannabis: Our Position for a Canadian Public Policy* (September 2002) (Chair: Pierre Claude Nolin)

88 Fischer et al, *supra* note 41, at 278

History of Canada's Federal Drug Policy   25

Commons Special Committee "recommended that the use of cannabis remain illegal, but that the Minister of Health establish a comprehensive strategy for decriminalizing the possession and cultivation of not more than thirty grams of cannabis for personal use".[89] The work of this Committee had been shaped by the introduction of a private member's bill (C-344) that "proposed making possession and trafficking in small amounts of cannabis a 'ticketable' rather than a criminal offence".[90] The House Committee's recommendations have been characterized as a

> middle-of-the-road attempt, on the one hand, to eliminate the criminal status, consequences and costs of cannabis-use control under current law . . . but, on the other hand, not to sanction cannabis use by completely dismantling the mechanisms of legal control and punishment.[91]

In response to these two committee reports, the Federal Government introduced Bill C-38 in May 2003, which proposed "legislative reforms that would decriminalize possession of small amounts of cannabis, while imposing tough penalties on cannabis grow operators".[92] More specifically, the legislation would decriminalize the possession of less than 15 grams of cannabis and less than 1 gram of hashish by making it a non-criminal offence subject to a fine between $100 and $400 under the Contraventions Act.[93] In doing so, it is argued that "The government's ultimate goal was to increase enforcement against cannabis users with the logic being that police officers would be less hesitant to charge cannabis offenders with a non-criminal offence".[94] Bill C-38 would nonetheless never make it into Canadian law, dying on the order paper with the prorogation of Parliament in 2003. A new version of the legislation, Bill C-10, which included amendments that would allow for the cultivation of up to three plants for personal use, would also later die on the order paper following the May 2004 dissolution of Parliament.[95]

While considerable public support for cannabis decriminalization existed during this period of time, "the period of attempted reforms ended with the election of a new more socially conservative government in 2006".[96] The incoming Conservative government, led by Prime Minister Stephen Harper, "made it categorically clear that they were not going to resume or continue these unfinished efforts, in that they considered cannabis a harmful drug".[97] Under Harper's leadership, a

---

89 Library of Parliament, *supra* note 86, at 4
90 *Ibid*
91 Fischer et al, *supra* note 41, at 278–279
92 Library of Parliament, *supra* note 86, at 4
93 Erickson & Hyshka, *supra* note 82, at 3
94 *Ibid* at 4
95 *Ibid*
96 Erickson & Hyshka, *supra* note 82, at 5
97 Fischer, Russell & Boyd, *supra* note 39, at 92

26 *History of Canada's Federal Drug Policy*

new $64 million dollar National Anti-Drug Strategy was launched that officially "put an end to the prior government's plan to decriminalize possession of small quantities of marijuana and removed drug issues from the Ministry of Health, leaving them solely under the jurisdiction of the Ministry of Justice".[98] The new national strategy "removed the government's commitment to harm reduction, emphasized law enforcement over treatment and prevention, and promised to introduce mandatory minimum sentencing for cannabis and other drug-related offenses under the CDSA".[99] During this period of time, the rate for cannabis offences almost doubled, despite the overall crime rate in Canada continuously declining, and, by 2013, about three-quarters of drug offences were cannabis-related, with the large majority (around 80%) for personal possession.[100] As was the case during the 1990s, the movement towards "harm reduction" in drug policy also significantly suffered during this period of time. As noted by Cavalieri and Riley,

> Harm reduction's regression in Canada is part of a larger context of the federal government's demonization of drugs and the people who use them. This is a well-funded propaganda campaign, which appeals to fear, prejudice and greed. As a result, we are experiencing a value shift which is deeply upsetting and does not augur well for harm reduction, the well-being of people who use illicit drugs or for any marginalized people.[101]

2.5 The Turn of the Century: Legal Challenges Prompt Changes to Medical Cannabis Regulation

During the same period described above, while recreational drug policy reform remained stagnant, a series of significant and high-profile cases pertaining to medical cannabis were being adjudicated by Canada's highest courts. In 1999, Health Canada initiated a federal medicinal cannabis program in response to the Ontario Court of Justice's decision in the *Wakeford*[102] case. This made Canada the first country after the international prohibition of cannabis to initiate such a program.[103] In *Wakeford*, the Court recognized the legal right of a person living with HIV/AIDS (and facing cannabis possession and cultivation charges) to access cannabis without fear of arrest, instructing "Health Canada to create a process allowing for legal

---

98 Cavalieri & Riley, *supra* note 33, at 388
99 Akwasi Owusu-Bempah & Alex Luscombe, "Race, Cannabis and the Canadian War on Drugs: An Examination of Cannabis Arrest Data by Race in Five Cities" (2020) 91 International Journal of Drug Policy 1 at 2
100 Fischer, Russell & Boyd, *supra* note 39, at 92
101 Cavalieri & Riley, *supra* note 33, at 400
102 *Wakeford v. Can.*, 1999 96 O.T.C. 108 (SC)
103 Jürgen Rehm et al, "Medical Marijuana. What Can We Learn from Experiences in Canada, Germany and Thailand?" (2019) 74 International Journal of Drug Policy 47 at 48

access to this medicine".[104] Health Canada responded by pointing to legislation that existed under the CDSA (Section 56) allowing qualified applicants a federal exemption from the law. One year later, this section was again before the courts. In *Parker*,[105] the Ontario Court of Appeal struck down the aforementioned Section 56 program "as unconstitutional when it was revealed that the process was not subject to regulatory oversight and instead granted total discretion to approve or reject potential applicants to the Health Minister".[106] As a result, Health Canada created a governing body to oversee the implementation of the *Marijuana Medical Access Regulations* (MMAR) that replaced the Section 56 exemption process in 2001.[107] Two years later, in *Hitzig*,[108] the Ontario Supreme Court once again found the federal program unconstitutional for creating the "illusion of access", giving the government until July 9 of the same year to establish a legal supplier for medical users under the MMAR.[109] Shortly before that deadline, "Canada became the second nation in the world to put in place a system for access to medical cannabis through a centralized, government administered program".[110] While these cases were all primarily focused on medical cannabis use, "they illustrated the closely connected nature of the medical and recreational cannabis control debate and have had important implications for general cannabis law reform".[111] It has indeed been suggested that the evolution of the medical cannabis access program "paved the way and pre-shaped key features of foundations towards the general legalization of non-medical cannabis use and supply to come".[112]

While it is unquestionably true that the cases described above resulted "in an unprecedented degree of judicial activism",[113] the first decade of medical cannabis access in Canada was nonetheless fraught with numerous practical difficulties. As noted by Rehm, the MMAR were very bureaucratic and restrictive, focusing on a limited number of severe conditions and, as such, "only several hundred participants were enrolled in the program in the first decade of the 21st century, but many more used cannabis to self-medicate illegally".[114] Some estimates suggest that fewer than 5% of the more than 500,000 estimated users of therapeutic cannabis in Canada registered under the MMAR.[115] Numerous studies suggest

---

104 Phillippe Lucas, "Regulating Compassion: An Overview of Canada's Federal Medical Cannabis Policy and Practice" (2008) 5 Harm Reduction Journal 5 at 7
105 *R. v. Parker*, 2000 49 O.R. (3d) 481
106 Lucas, *supra* note 104, at 7
107 *Ibid*
108 *Hitzig v. Can.*, 2003 177 O.A.C. 321 (CA)
109 Lucas, *supra* note 104, at 8
110 *Ibid*
111 Fischer et al, *supra* note 41, at 275–276
112 Fischer, Russell & Boyd, *supra* note 39, at 93
113 Fischer et al, *supra* note 41, at 275
114 Rehm et al, *supra* note 103, at 48
115 Rielle Capler et al, "Are Dispensaries Indispensable? Patient Experiences of Access to Cannabis from Medical Cannabis Dispensaries in Canada" (2017) 47 International Journal of Drug Policy 1 at 2

28 History of Canada's Federal Drug Policy

that similarly large proportions of Canadians turned to the illicit market in the face of overly restrictive barriers to legal access. As such, evaluations of the first decade of medical cannabis access have been unsurprisingly critical: "There is a growing body of evidence that Health Canada's program is not meeting the needs of Canada's medical cannabis patient community, and that it may actually be acting as an impediment to safe and timely access".[116] It has also been suggested that the existence of the medical system was conveniently used by politicians to avoid making decisions regarding decriminalization or legalization of recreational cannabis use. As argued by Rehm,

> In 2013 and 2014, the Canadian government was facing an election in the following year, with the majority of Canadians stating a preference for the legalization of cannabis. With the opposing parties either opting for decriminalization or legalization and with cannabis policy being one of the major topics in the election, the ruling Conservative Party opted to support more lenient regulations for MMJ use.[117]

Analyses of the last decade of medical cannabis regulation point to a welcome, continued evolution of a system that barely resembles that which was established at the turn of the century. The above noted political pressure prompted a fundamental reframing of the medical system in 2013 when the system was relaunched as the Marihuana for Medical Purposes Regulations (MMPR). As noted by Fisher, Russell and Boyd,

> Among several significant changes from the MMAR, Health Canada, as the federal government agency responsible until then, removed itself as the authorizer from the actual approval process for legitimate medical cannabis use. This process and role were now shifted to eligible healthcare professionals including, primarily, but not limited to, physicians.[118]

While there was some controversy amongst physicians about potentially questionable sources of endorsements for medical cannabis use, as well as the expanding range of conditions that were being accepted for treatment, it is clear that the last decade has seen a significant increase in the number of Canadians accessing medical cannabis legally: "In 2001, 100 Canadians were granted legal access to medicinal cannabis, in 2013 there were 37, 800 medical exemptions, and that number rose to over 329, 038 medical client exemptions in 2020".[119] Moreover, it is fair to argue that much of the licensed producer infrastructure that currently

---

116 Lucas, *supra* note 104, at 16
117 Rehm et al, *supra* note 103, at 48
118 Fischer, Russell & Boyd, *supra* note 39, at 94
119 Chelsea Cox, "Implications of the 2018 Canadian Cannabis Act: Should Regulation Differ from Medicinal and non-Medicinal Cannabis Use?" (2021) 125 Health Policy 12 at 13

History of Canada's Federal Drug Policy 29

exists and fuels the non-medical market was developed extensively as a result of the evolution of the medical system. Licensed producers were born out of another new provision of the MMPR, which in essence marked "the formal beginning and establishment of a legitimate, government-regulated – and quickly expanded – commercial cannabis industry in Canada, ironically introduced by the 'anti-cannabis' (but pro-business) Conservative government".[120] Based on the analyses above, it would thus be fair to conclude that the medical cannabis system in Canada, itself the product of unprecedented judicial activism in the early part of the century, has played a key role in establishing the necessary infrastructure for a recreational cannabis system that had remained criminal and plagued by policy reform inertia prior to the enactment of the 2018 Cannabis Act.[121]

2.6 The Passage of the 2018 Cannabis Act: A Missed Opportunity

Unsurprisingly, given the massive size and scale of the cannabis legalization undertaking, the story of the 2018 Cannabis Act[122] starts many years before its eventual passage, dating back to a 2015 Liberal government election promise to legalize and regulate cannabis "right away".[123] After winning a majority in the 2015 election, Justin Trudeau and his Liberal government faced numerous policy questions and challenges if they were to make good on their promise: 1) they were operating on a self-imposed, tight timeline to deliver a legalization framework within a couple of years of election; 2) they needed to provide a federal framework that would address and respect the role of provinces and municipalities in a way that would reconcile often conflicting powers between different levels of government in a federalist constitutional system; and 3) they were limited in some potential policy choices that had already been pre-decided or shaped by the realities of the existing federal medical cannabis provisions.[124] Significantly,

---

120 Fischer, Russell & Boyd, *supra* note 39, at 95
121 Although focus will now turn to the recreational legalization of Cannabis ushered in by the 2018 Cannabis Act, it is nonetheless important to note that Canada remains the only Federal jurisdiction where two distinct streams for medical and non-medical cannabis access are in place. Ironically, it has been suggested that the recreational legalization of cannabis may result in a variety of impacts on medical cannabis users, including: 1) problems with access, with some studies suggesting that 1 in 4 medical cannabis users have found accessing cannabis more difficult since non-medical legalization; 2) problems with product potency, with the Cannabis Act potency limits potentially falling short of what is required to meet the medical needs of medical cannabis consumers; and 3) insurance, tax and human rights ramifications. For a thorough and thoughtful analysis of these issues, see Cox, *supra* note 119
122 SC 2018, c 16
123 Josh Elliot, "Liberals 'Committed' to Legalizing Marijuana: Trudeau" (September 2015), online: *CTV News* #x003C;www.ctvnews.ca/politics/election/liberals-committed-to-legalizing-marijuana-trudeau-1.2588260>
124 Fischer, Russell & Boyd, *supra* note 39, at 97

30 *History of Canada's Federal Drug Policy*

Trudeau's government had also made Indigenous reconciliation a key aspect of his party's successful election platform,[125] and, as such, there was an expectation that Indigenous communities would be extensively included and consulted during a project of such great national significance. Consequently, on June 30, 2016, the government established a Task Force on Cannabis Legalization and Regulation to "provide it with guidance on the design of the new legislative and regulatory system".[126] The Task Force "engaged with provincial, territorial and municipal governments, experts, parents, advocates, Indigenous governments and representative organizations, employers and industry".[127] The Task Force solicited nearly 30,000 submissions from individuals and organizations as part of an online public consultation.[128] The Task Force's final report, released on November 30, 2016, contained a number of recommendations, including: 1) setting a national minimum age of purchase of 18; 2) suggesting comprehensive restrictions on advertising, promotion, and packaging of cannabis; 3) encouraging economic analysis to ensure tax and price that balances health protection with the goal of reducing the illicit market; 4) stating that distribution and retail sales of cannabis be regulated by the provinces; 5) allowing for personal cultivation of cannabis with a limit of four plants per residence; 6) implementing a limit of 30 grams of cannabis for personal possession; 7) maintaining a separate medical access framework; 8) providing for a systematic review and evaluation of legalization; and 9) engaging with Indigenous governments and representative organizations to explore opportunities for their participation in the cannabis market.[129] It is important to note that absent from the myriad recommendations found in the report is any mention of engaging communities that have been traditionally over-policed and over-represented in the criminal justice system due to cannabis criminalization, nor is there any significant discussion of pardons or redress for past criminal records.

On these latter points (Indigenous consultation and historical redress for over-represented groups), the work of the Task Force and, subsequently, the government, in implementing its recommendations, has been widely criticized. As noted by Crosby, "The campaign promise to legalize cannabis was void of any mention of engagement with Indigenous peoples or addressing the disproportionate

---

125 Susana Mas, "Trudeau Lays Out Plan for New Relationship with Indigenous People" (December 2015), online: *CBC News* #x003C;www.cbc.ca/news/politics/justin-trudeau-afn-indigenous-aboriginal-people-1.3354747>

126 Library of Parliament, *supra* note 86, at 4

127 Canada, Task Force on Cannabis Legalization and Regulation, *A Framework for the Legalization and Regulation of Cannabis in Canada: The Final Report of the Task Force on Cannabis Legalization and Regulation* (Ottawa: Health Canada, 2016) at 2. The insufficiency of consultation with Indigenous communities (both by the Task Force and the government) in the years leading to the Cannabis Act is subject to comprehensive criticism and is discussed further below

128 *Ibid* at 2

129 *Ibid* at 2–7

History of Canada's Federal Drug Policy 31

negative impacts of decades of prohibition and criminalization".[130] Questions were also raised about the composition of the Task Force itself: "Internal Justice Canada files, although heavily redacted, indicate that no Indigenous person was seriously considered to sit as a Task Force member".[131] Moreover, although the Task Force explicitly mentions its analyses of other jurisdictions[132] as part of its study, it has been noted that its report, and the government's subsequent legislation,

> does not seek to provide redress to racialized communities disproportionately affected by drug prohibition in the same way that American legalization does. Many American states, for example, are taking active measures to include racialized populations in the legal cannabis industry and to direct some tax revenue from legal sales back to the communities most harmed by prohibition.[133]

It thus becomes clear that from an early stage of the process that would eventually lead to cannabis legalization in Canada, meaningful engagement with the communities most historically affected by cannabis criminalization was conspicuously absent.

The legislative process behind Bill C-45[134] tells a similar story of exclusion and insufficient consultation. The legislation was introduced into the House of Commons on April 13, 2017 and referred to the House of Commons Standing Committee on Health, whose report was concurred in by the House of Commons on November 21, 2017.[135] On that same day, the Government of Canada launched a public consultation on cannabis regulations.[136] Both the consultation document[137] and the summary of comments received during the public consultation make little to no mention of Indigenous perspectives and opinions on the legislation.[138] Exacerbating this feeling of exclusion and lack of consultation is

---

130 Andrew Crosby, "Contesting Cannabis: Indigenous Jurisdiction and Legalization" (2019) 62:4 Canadian Public Administration 634 at 635
131 *Ibid*
132 Task Force, *supra* note 127, at 2: "The Task Force looked internationally (e.g., Colorado, Washington State, Uruguay) to learn from jurisdictions that have legalized cannabis for non-medical purposes"
133 Owusu-Bempah & Luscombe, *supra* note 99, at 1
134 Bill C-45, *An Act Respecting Cannabis and to Amend the Controlled Drugs and Substances Act, the Criminal Code and Other Acts*, 1st Sess, 42nd Parl, 2015 (as passed by the House of Commons 21 June 2018)
135 *Library of Parliament, supra* note 86, at 1
136 *Ibid* at 30
137 Health Canada, *Proposed Approach to the Regulation of Cannabis* (Ottawa: Health Canada, 2017)
138 Health Canada, *Proposed Approach to the Regulation of Cannabis: Summary of Comments Received During the Public Consultation* (Ottawa: Health Canada, 2018): In the former, the word "Indigenous" is found a grand total of two times in 75 pages. In the latter, it is found 3 times in 40 pages

32   History of Canada's Federal Drug Policy

the fact that Bill C-45 was otherwise subjected to rigorous debate in relation to several other aspects of its content, including: 1) whether cannabis should be legally available to persons under the age of 25; 2) diverse submissions on the restrictions of cannabis promotion and advertising; 3) whether the legislation sufficiently accomplished the government's goal of preventing youth use; 4) ample arguments against the co-availability of alcohol and cannabis; 5) whether home growing provisions for cannabis could be effectively enforced and regulated; and 6) whether the issue of cannabis-impaired driving was sufficiently considered.[139] Notably, the Standing Senate Committee on Aboriginal Peoples began studying the legislation in February 2018, with its final report (released in May 2018) stating,

> There was an alarming lack of consultation, particularly given this Government's stated intentions of developing a new relationship with Indigenous people. . . . Had sufficient consultation occurred, the problems identified by the Committee would likely have been solved, and the solutions incorporated into Bill C-45.[140]

The Committee recommended delaying Bill C-45 for up to one year, particularly with an eye towards negotiations on the implementation of appropriate excise tax collection and sharing agreements.[141] The government issued a response on September 28, 2018, effectively refusing to delay the legislation.[142] Relatedly and crucially, "Indigenous peoples were excluded from the meetings leading to the negotiation and signing of the Coordinated Cannabis Taxation Agreements and thus excluded from benefitting from the excise tax formula".[143]

Despite the concerns noted above, Bill C-45 received its final reading and approval by the Senate on June 7, 2018, having undergone "a total of about 40 – mostly minor – amendments over the revised draft bill version it had received from the government".[144] It received Royal Assent on June 21, 2018 and came into force on October 18, 2018 and, in doing so, it effectively: 1) permitted some cannabis-related activities that had previously been prohibited (possessing 30 grams or less of dried cannabis in public and cultivating up to four plants per residence); 2) prohibited some cannabis-related activities (sale of cannabis to

---

139 Fischer, Russell & Boyd, *supra* note 39, at 100

140 Canada, Parliament, Senate, Standing Senate Committee on Aboriginal Peoples, *The Subject Matter of Bill C-45: An Act Respecting Cannabis and To Amend the Controlled Drugs and Substances Act, the Criminal Code and Other Acts* (May 2018) (Chair: Lillian Eva Dyck) at 8

141 *Ibid* at 16

142 Canada, Parliament, *Government Response to the Eleventh Report of the Standing Senate Committee on Aboriginal Peoples Entitled "the Subject Matter of Bill C-45: An Act Respecting Cannabis and to Amend the Controlled Drugs and Substances Act, the Criminal Code and Other Acts"* (Ottawa: Clerk of the Senate and Clerk of the Parliaments, 2018)

143 Crosby, *supra* note 130, at 636

144 Fischer, Russell & Boyd, *supra* note 39, at 100

minors); 3) listed prohibited activities in relation to cannabis for which a ticket can be issued (rather than prosecution for an indictable or summary offence); 4) provided a framework for permitted and prohibited promotion and advertising; and 5) established a statutory basis on which the designated minister can issue licenses and permits for authorized cannabis-related activities.[145] It has been rightly noted that

> While the Cannabis Act removes cannabis from the Controlled Drugs and Substances Act, it also proposes approximately 45 new criminal offences, including harsher penalties for the possession of illicitly sourced cannabis. . . . So, too, does it authorize up to 14 years in prison for selling cannabis to minors, a grossly disproportionate potential sentence when compared to infractions involving any other legal drug in Canada.[146]

Moreover, the passage of Bill C-46 (the Impaired Driving Act) on June 20, 2018 allows for the possibility that "cannabis-impaired driving could be punished with a prison sentence of up to ten years".[147] The point to be made here is that although cannabis legalization has arrived in Canada, penalties for certain cannabis-related activities remain (or, in some cases, are more punitive), with understandable concern that the historical over-policing and over-representation of certain groups will continue.[148] This concern is exacerbated by the fact that the Cannabis Act was "entirely void of any complementary social justice measures . . . leaving intact laws that have disproportionately and prejudicially impacted Indigenous people and people of colour".[149] Moreover, while the government subsequently passed legislation in 2019 to deal with the issue of pardons,[150] the system implemented has proven ineffective: as of October 2021, only 484 pardons had been issued.[151] As such, both past and future concerns about the disproportionate impact of cannabis criminalization on minority communities remain. Put simply, "Renewed

---

145 Library of Parliament, *supra* note 86, at 1–2
146 Jenna Valleriani et al, "A Missed Opportunity? Cannabis Legalization and Reparations in Canada" (2018) 109 Canadian Journal of Public Health 745 at 746
147 Fischer, Russell & Boyd et al, *supra* note 39, at 99
148 Crosby, *supra* note 130, at 642: "Cannabis legalization has created even more laws to regulate cannabis than in the prohibition era, which are likely to reproduce racial disparities in the post-legal landscape. . . . The punitive nature of the cannabis legalization regime has the potential to disproportionately impact Indigenous and racialized peoples, as has historically been the case surrounding prohibition"
149 Valleriani et al, *supra* note 146, at 745
150 Bill C-93, *An Act to Provide No-Cost, Expedited Record Suspensions for Simple Possession of Cannabis*, 1st Sess, 42nd Parl, 2015 (as passed by the House of Commons 21 June 2019)
151 Peter Zimonjic, "Only 484 Marijuana Pardons Have Been Granted Since Program Started in 2019" (31 October 2021), online: *CBC News* #x003C;www.cbc.ca/news/politics/pot-pardons-still-low-484-1.6230666>: Critics argue that the process is cumbersome and inaccessible, particularly for the most marginalized Canadians who (ironically) are most in need of pardons. It is suggested that full record expungements would be far more effective

34   *History of Canada's Federal Drug Policy*

attention to and intensified regulation of cannabis-impaired driving, trafficking to under-age users, and under-age possession may just as easily maintain (or perhaps worsen) the racial disparities we have documented".[152]

To quote the Task Force on Cannabis Legalization and Regulation, "The current paradigm of cannabis prohibition has been with us for almost 100 years. We cannot, and should not, expect to turn this around overnight. While moving away from cannabis prohibition is long overdue, we may not anticipate every nuance of future policy".[153] This chapter has extensively detailed this nearly 100-year history of cannabis and wider drug policy evolution. The legalization of cannabis brought forth in 2018 was undoubtedly a momentous step forward in this history of Canadian drug policy. Such a massive undertaking was inevitably always going to face a severe learning curve, especially when the timeline committed to by the Liberal government was so tight. As such, it is a very welcome development that a review of the Cannabis Act is mandated by the legislation.[154] Various suggestions for improvement of the federal legislation, as well as the provincial implementation of this legislation, will be discussed in great depth in subsequent chapters of this book. With that said, the analyses above lead to an evaluation of the Cannabis Act (and the legislative process behind it) as a *missed opportunity*. More specifically, it is a missed opportunity on two significant fronts. First, the legalization project in this country should have been one of nation-building and reconciliation aimed at healing relationships with Indigenous communities but was instead a reiteration of a long history of exclusion and a lack of effective consultation. Second, cannabis legalization provided an opportunity to address a long history of racist and classist drug policy in this country but was instead a glaring omission of any substantial measures aimed at providing social justice and reparation. This is especially disappointing given how intuitively these social justice components would have aligned with the country's apparent changed societal attitudes towards the criminalization of cannabis and the prohibition of drug use more generally.

2.7 Voices From the Front Lines: Indigenous Community and Cannabis Industry Leaders Echo Academic Concerns

As noted in Chapter 1, the socio-legal methodology of this book includes a qualitative research component that seeks to supplement or "fill in the gaps" of

---

152 Owusu-Bempah & Luscombe, *supra* note 99, at 7: The authors note that a similar trend occurred in Colorado, Alaska and Washington State following the legalization of recreational cannabis in those jurisdictions

153 Task Force, *supra* note 127, at 1

154 David George-Cosh, "Cannabis Canada Weekly: Government Review Aims to Shape Next Chapter of Legalization" (October 2021), online: *BNN Bloomberg* <https://ampvideo.bnn-bloomberg.ca/cannabis-canada-weekly-government-review-aims-to-shape-next-chapter-of-legalization-1.1667028>

History of Canada's Federal Drug Policy 35

documentary analyses of the publicly available source material. Subsequent chapters of this book similarly use this qualitative material to add necessary context to issues related to provincial implementation of cannabis legalization, as well as highlight additional concerns with the federal legislation that are not discussed here. For space reasons, the qualitative material in this section focuses specifically on the two *missed opportunities* noted above – insufficient consultation of Indigenous communities in the development of federal cannabis legislation and an insufficient commitment in the federal legislation to provide social justice and redress for the communities and people most historically and disproportionately affected by criminalization. The academic literature suggests that there is a "need for Canada to go further in its efforts to legalize by incorporating measures that would do more to address the damages disproportionately suffered by Black and Indigenous people during Canada's war on cannabis".[155] It further notes that "decriminalizing cannabis possession by youth is an important component of equity in cannabis law reform, considering evidence showing that Indigenous and Black people in Canada have been over-represented among those arrested and charged for cannabis".[156] The opinions of the Indigenous community and cannabis industry leaders on the front lines of a post-legalization world discussed below echo these sentiments. Similarly, "concern over the lack of adequate consultation by the government, the application of provincial regulations on reserves and traditional territories, and the exclusion of First Nations from the law's excise tax revenue sharing framework"[157] is also expressed by several of the Indigenous community leaders below. Academic criticism pertaining to this issue has been forceful: "Despite stated commitments to reconciliation and a nation-to-nation relationship, Indigenous peoples were sidelined in the development of a cannabis policy framework, subordinated to federal and provincial governmental authority, and excluded from jurisdictional considerations and economic benefits".[158] The following small sample of the overall qualitative material collected shows that these forceful academic criticisms were indeed indicative of the feelings and opinions of those arguably most affected by cannabis legalization.

Those on the front lines of cannabis legalization have certainly echoed an academic concern regarding the Cannabis Act's notable and disappointing lack

---

155 Akwasi Owusu-Bempah, "Where Is the Fairness in Canadian Cannabis Legalization? Lessons to Be Learned from the American Experience" (2021) 55:2 Journal of Canadian Studies 395–418 at 396

156 Rebecca J. Haines-Saah & Benedikt Fischer, "Youth Cannabis Use and Legalization in Canada – Reconsidering the Fears, Myths and Facts Three Years in" (2021) 30:3 Journal of the Canadian Academy of Child and Adolescent Psychiatry 191 at 195

157 Konstantia Koutouki & Katherine Lofts, "Cannabis, Reconciliation, and the Rights of Indigenous Peoples: Prospects and Challenges for Cannabis Legalization in Canada" (2019) 56:3 Alberta Law Review 709 at 710

158 Crosby, *supra* note 130, at 645

36 History of Canada's Federal Drug Policy

of social justice measures. According to one cannabis industry leader, the federal government

> made it seem as though supporting individuals who have been wrongly affected by this, and those within marginalized communities, would have definitely been front and centre, but it was quickly pushed to the wayside, . . . The legislation could have been tweaked to allow for a more equitable landscape for people to participate.[159]

The impact of this lack of tangible social justice component in the Cannabis Act goes far beyond its very real philosophical ramifications. It is manifesting itself in a shocking lack of diversity in Canada's legal cannabis industry. A recent study by the Centre on Drug Policy evaluation found that "Black and Indigenous people, and women, are vastly underrepresented in leadership positions in the Canadian cannabis industry when compared to their representation in the general population".[160] The study found that 84% of cannabis industry leaders were white, with only 2% Indigenous and only 1% Black.[161] Not surprisingly, the study attributes this severe lack of diversity to a "notable absence of government regulation and adoption of programs that would structurally address the underrepresentation of racialized groups that were disproportionately targeted and punished under prohibition", noting that "business and financial support for members of these groups has been instituted in California, Massachusetts and Illinois".[162] Exacerbating this severe lack of diversity is the fact that "Those who have been historically in the drug war have been among the first to pivot into the legal cannabis industry. This includes many former high-profile police, RCMP officers, and Conservative MPs, who now hold executive roles in many legal cannabis companies in Canada".[163] This paradoxical hypocrisy was not lost on another study participant, who forcefully stated:

> There are many government people that have migrated and found very lucrative cannabis executive positions. . . . The corruption that has occurred with the actual access to licensing it's a real punch in the face to us as Indigenous

---

159 Participant A, 21 July 2021

160 Nazlee Maghsoudi et al, "How Diverse Is Canada's Legal Cannabis Industry? Examining Race and Gender of Its Executives and Directors" (October 2020), online: *Centre on Drug Policy Evaluation* <>https://cdpe.org/publication/how-diverse-is-canadas-legal-cannabis-industry-examining-race-and-gender-of-its-executives-and-directors/> at 1

161 *Ibid*

162 *Ibid*. For more on these initiatives, see: Bryon Adinoff & Amanda Reiman, "Implementing Social Justice in the Transition from Illicit to Legal Cannabis" (2019) 45:6 The American Journal of Drug and Alcohol Abuse 673. They are also extensively discussed in Chapter 4's comparative analyses

163 Valleriani et al, *supra* note 146, at 746

History of Canada's Federal Drug Policy 37

people saying well you were throwing our people in jail for this stuff and now you're sitting there in one of these plush positions.[164]

A cannabis industry leader confirmed that they, too, had seen a complete lack of Indigenous inclusion in their work on cannabis licensing.[165]

This paradox extends beyond Indigenous and minority groups and also applies with respect to another marginalized societal group that has been openly fighting the criminalization of cannabis for decades – the "legacy market", i.e. members of the public who ran therapeutic and compassionate cannabis dispensaries well before legalization and, ironically, continued to supply most medical cannabis consumers throughout most of the 2000s as the medical cannabis system proved ineffective.[166] The legacy market now largely finds itself on the outside looking in, as is noted by one study participant:

> There's a lot of hostility from people that have been it in [legacy market] for years. You know, we've been through the Charter challenges, we've been arrested for having our dispensaries open before it was legal, and here come the suits and the big companies and they're going to take all the money and all the jobs.[167]

The hostility is understandable: a system of cannabis legalization, supposedly based on the philosophy that societal attitudes towards cannabis criminalization have fundamentally changed, should include social justice mechanisms that help to include those who have most disproportionately borne the weight of past criminalization. In fact, it appears that quite the opposite has happened, with those marginalized and over-represented groups facing great barriers to succeeding in the market. Said one participant:

> Legislation is not set up in a way that will help [smaller] businesses prosper. . . . What I feel bad about is the smaller guys that have been a part of this industry and a part of the movement to legalize and change perception of the plant and remove that stigma and now they're in a space like this is killing

---

164 Participant J, 3 June 2021: The participant went on to further state: "There should be formal scrutiny on that and furthermore I'd say there's a reason to investigate that. If there are people that hold positions and you have current policies of non-competition, you know, some of these people weren't out of government very long but yet they're competing for licensing. I don't know something doesn't seem right about that"

165 Participant R, 2 June 2021: "Yeah I haven't worked with many and that right there might speak to something because we've worked with I don't know it must be close to a hundred people that are opening stores and I can't think of any that are Indigenous"

166 See Lucas, *supra* note 104 for a full discussion of the role of therapeutic dispensaries in supplying the medical cannabis market in Canada

167 Participant R, *supra* note 165

38   *History of Canada's Federal Drug Policy*

us from a bureaucracy perspective and an administrative perspective and an inability to generate dollars.[168]

For those in Indigenous communities, the barriers to access are very much indicative of a larger issue with Canadian federalism and a long-standing disagreement about Indigenous rights to self-governance. This was noted by another study participant:

> The Federal government issues licenses for the cultivation of cannabis and leaves the licensing of retail in the hands of the provinces and that's a problem because not all communities including mine allow for the jurisdiction of the province in certain activities especially cannabis, tobacco and alcohol. . . . In essence, the Federal government delegating that to the provinces has created a void and apprehension or disagreements between the community and the province.[169]

The issue of jurisdiction was a common concern raised by other participants:

> In my opinion, all of that discussion went out the door, went out the window as soon as the Federal government amended their laws and the Criminal Code and then downloaded to the province. . . . You've got the Federal and Provincial governments simply dividing the taxes between themselves at some rate they've come to agree on and then at the time First Nations become an afterthought.[170]

According to another participant:

> When the Canadian cannabis consumer crosses that jurisdictional line called a First Nation, the Federal Government is just letting this thing stew and work itself out. It's almost like knowing someone has cancer and you're not doing a damned thing about it.[171]

Other jurisdictional issues noted by participants were more practical than philosophical but constituted perceived and real barriers nonetheless, including

---

168 Participant K, 22 July 2021

169 Participant T, 26 May 2021: On this point, the participant further added: "We have said from the beginning to the Federal Government that we do not want a very similar situation where they pay billions of dollars in excise tax to the Federal government but pay nothing to the community. . . . This is a disadvantage to an Indigenous economy where they have to pay more in fees overall because of the Federal government's lack of recognition or lack of ability of lack of willingness to work with the communities"

170 Participant F, 26 May 2021

171 Participant J, *supra* note 164

language[172] and banking.[173] Thus, the message being sent on tax and jurisdictional issues to the Federal government is clear: "Let's harmonize with the existing laws and let's create interface and let's work with leveling out the playing field on an economic level to address this".[174] Put more forcefully and succinctly by another participant: "The Federal government needs to amend their legislation at a minimum to say they can enter into agreements with the First Nations governments to recognize our jurisdiction".[175]

Participants representing both Indigenous and industry communities roundly agreed that the current barriers to access and success in the legal market are having a directly contradictory effect on one of the Government's prime legalization objectives – eliminating the black market. One participant expresses serious concerns for the safety of his community as a result:

> There's gonna be so much entrenchment of the black market still in the grey market which is why I'm saying let the red market work now within the mainstream and let's work to actually build the legislative amendments and start to readjust the current economic landscape. . . . I fear that if the government waits too long we will have problems in our community and the government will be 100% responsible for the impacts. I hope it's not a lost life.[176]

Similarly, another participant stated: "For any First Nations that'll want to quote unquote legally have a dispensary the only thing that the province is saying is that 'you have to play by our rules'. Well clearly these guys are not playing by your rules. They don't care about your rules".[177] For industry participants, it is the Federal government's tax structure that is providing barriers to success:

> The Government is taking their cut off it on their stamp. . . . I think that's kind of really hurt the objective of tackling the black market because the

---

172 Participant T, *supra* note 169: "If we were to allow for a Cannabis store regulated by Quebec in our community, it would be all in French, employees would have to speak French because it's a crown entity. . . . So that's not gonna work. My community would blow a limb if there was a French sign sitting here let alone having somebody have to speak French to be able to work there. So there's so many things that are just not going to work in my community"

173 *Ibid*: "How the heck can you stir a legitimate economy in a First Nations community when you can't get a product tested bstandards of a licensed tester and you can't open a bank account so they're only driving more of that into the grey market". Another participant, speaking from an industry perspective, also alluded to banking difficulties: "You know, trying to set up a bank account for cannabis at least back in 2019 was nearly impossible. There's only one bank in the entire country that was willing to do banking with us. . . . So there's lots of nuances where the policy or the rules were set out with the actual practical reality that the industry just wasn't ready for it" (Participant S, 30 June 2021)

174 Participant J, *supra* note 164

175 Participant T, *supra* note 169

176 Participant J, *supra* note 164

177 Participant F, *supra* note 170

40 *History of Canada's Federal Drug Policy*

> margin which we're charging, they've got to take their cut first and we kinda take our cut it makes it difficult for us companies to make money at this and it makes the black market better positioned in terms of how they're selling their product.[178]

Another industry participant echoed this sentiment:

> Both federal and provincial bodies constantly say they're in the business of eliminating the illicit market and making cannabis more accessible, making it more affordable. Fantastic. If that's the case, then why are you taking a forty-five percent margin on a product just for literally storing the cannabis. . . . Their objectives don't align with what they're actually doing in the market.[179]

The concerns and frustrations exhibited above are largely in relation to outcomes (i.e. the way the system has operated post-legalization) that are the result of deficiencies in the content and implementation of the federal Cannabis Act. It is worth stating that some of these outcomes could have been avoided had there been better consultation on the front end of the development of the legislation. The academic literature cited above noted an extreme lack of consultation with Indigenous communities, as did the Senate Standing Committee on Aboriginal Peoples when it considered Bill C-45. Study participants explicitly echoed this frustration, and their comments make it clear that there are high levels of cynicism when it comes to possibilities for meaningful reform in the future.[180] One participant lamented an extremely short timeline for participation in consultation:

> Why are we given such short notice to participate, you know we can't participate in that I mean how meaningful is the participation with such a

---

178 Participant S, *supra* note 173: Questions were also raised about whether tax proceeds were being effectively redirected to social initiatives and combatting of the black market: "You've got a Crown corporation taking a good chunk of margin before we can get to the product. . . . You would hope anyways then that the proceeds from that are going into or being redistributed through programs and initiatives that are in line with you know wider societal change and ideals towards the system. And obviously tackling the illicit market which is you know not paying tax and causing more harm than good"

179 Participant K, *supra* note 168: The participant further added: "Yes, there's a greater calling and a greater good that is occurring here, but look I'm trying to run a business to deliver a product that has all sorts of benefits to the end consumer. But in order to be able to do that, and in order to be able to do all those things that the federal government wants us to do like eliminate the illicit market, provide convenience and quality, keep it out of the hands of kids . . . the business needs to thrive and be profitable. Otherwise, nobody will be able to operate in this world and that's what they're getting to. They're literally bankrupting one licensed producer at a time"

180 While the comments that follow reference concerns of Indigenous participants, the "legacy" industry also felt excluded from consultation. For example, see Participant R, *supra* note 165: "Why aren't we talking to the people that have been doing this twenty or thirty or forty years? Some of these people from the legacy market felt a little bit excluded from the process".

short notice. I think that's just laughable. Anywhere else, that would never happen, just simply wouldn't happen, and so you know this leads to the cynicism by First Nations leaders.[181]

Another participant connected the lack of consultation with the tight timeline set by the government to pass legislation:

> There's no secret that this was done very quickly right? I mean, it was an election promise made by the Liberals that they would legalize cannabis and you know they set out to do that very quickly. There was no outreach to any Indigenous communities, especially not mine for sure, about what a framework would look like for legalization.[182]

The same sentiment was echoed by this participant:

> That rapid rate of the legislative process was the first initial challenge and the fact that it, you know, seemed like what the Federal Government was doing is saying well we're not going to do deep engagement with Indigenous communities now because if we do this there will not be legislation by the end of this term . . . let's ram the legislation through and let's apologize to the Indigenous people later.[183]

As a result, there is understandable scepticism of any future consultation or reform: "Well isn't it a little bit damned late to do that after you've already amended all of that legislation, are they actually gonna go back, there's no politician that's going to walk back onto the playing field to correct the score after they've won the game, it's never happened, and it won't happen".[184] Another participant expressed some hope for legislative reform, but nonetheless lamented how long it would be until the issue was back under consideration: "But the problem with that Daniel is everything's been passed already and we're now left with a bad situation where we can't even get legislative amendments in for the next four or five years to recognize First Nations supply chain models. So yeah I'm going to give the Liberals a failing grade on that".[185] Based on the analyses above, the Federal Government may very well need the full 18-month period of statutory review to address the missed opportunities outlined by the Indigenous community and cannabis industry leaders in this section.

181 Participant F, *supra* note 170
182 Participant T, *supra* note 169
183 Participant J, *supra* note 164
184 Participant F, *supra* note 170
185 Participant J, *supra* note 164

42 *History of Canada's Federal Drug Policy*

2.8 Conclusion

This chapter has thoroughly and extensively placed Canada's cannabis legalization within the wider historical context of drug prohibition in the country. In doing so, it has told a story of drug policy in Canada that has mainly been instigated by racist and classist forces, born less out of real concerns with increased drug use and more out of hysteria, moral panic and mythology. More recent developments towards drug liberalization in Canada, though momentous, nonetheless recreate a pattern whereby the communities – Indigenous, minority, and marginalized – historically most affected by drug criminalization have nonetheless been excluded from meaningful engagement and inclusion. This is not simply a matter of academic concern and focus. Indigenous community and cannabis industry leaders have loudly echoed the concerns raised in the academic literature. As such, Canada's move to legalize cannabis has been characterized as a missed opportunity, specifically because it was born out of a process that unfortunately recreates past trends in the country's drug policy history. As the government moves forward (particularly with the statutory review of the Cannabis Act), it would do well to consider ways in which historical legacies of racism, colonialism, exclusion, and insufficient consultation can be meaningfully addressed. Several of the jurisdictions surveyed in Chapter 4's comparative analysis have implemented social justice and social equity mechanisms alongside cannabis legalization, including automatic criminal record expungements, incentives for (and prioritization of) minority license applicants, and re-investment of cannabis tax revenues into the communities historically most affected by drug criminalization. Many jurisdictions have also begun liberalizing *wider* drug policy through the removal of criminal sanctions for personal use and possession of drugs *beyond* cannabis. There is thus ample comparative experience to help guide the future of cannabis (and wider drug) policy reform in the future. Any future reform must necessarily be far more inclusive (particularly with regards to Indigenous consultation) in order to avoid repeating past mistakes and missing future opportunities.

Adinoff, Bryon & Reiman, Amanda, "Implementing Social Justice in the Transition from Illicit to Legal Cannabis" (2019) 45:6 The American Journal of Drug and Alcohol Abuse 673

Bernstein, Scott E., Amirkhani, Emily, Werb, Dan & MacPherson, Donald, "The Regulation Project: Tools for Engaging the Public in the Legal Regulation of Drugs" (2020) 86 International Journal of Drug Policy 1

Bill C-45, *An Act Respecting Cannabis and to Amend the Controlled Drugs and Substances Act, the Criminal Code and Other Acts,* 1st Sess, 42nd Parl, 2015 (as passed by the House of Commons 21 June 2018)

Bill C-93, *An Act to Provide No-Cost, Expedited Record Suspensions for Simple Possession of Cannabis,* 1st Sess, 42nd Parl, 2015 (as passed by the House of Commons 21 June 2019)

Boyd, Neil, "The Origins of Canadian Narcotics Legislation: The Process of Criminalization in Historical Context" (1984) 8:1 Dalhousie Law Journal 102

Boyd, Susan & MacPherson, Donald, "Community Engagement – The Harms of Drug Prohibition: Ongoing Resistance in Vancouver's Eastside" (2018) 200 BC Studies 87

Canada, Parliament, *Government Response to the Eleventh Report of the Standing Senate Committee on Aboriginal Peoples Entitled "The Subject Matter of Bill C-45: An Act Respecting Cannabis and to Amend the Controlled Drugs and Substances Act, the Criminal Code and Other Acts"* (Ottawa: Clerk of the Senate and Clerk of the Parliaments, 2018)

Canada, Parliament, Library of Parliament, *Legislative Summary: Bill C-45: An Act Respecting Cannabis and to Amend the Controlled Drugs and Substances Act, the Criminal Code and Other Acts,* Pub. No. 42–1-C45-E (Ottawa: Parliamentary Information and Research Service, 2018)

Canada, Parliament, Senate, Standing Senate Committee on Aboriginal Peoples, *The Subject Matter of Bill C-45: An Act Respecting Cannabis and to Amend the Controlled Drugs and Substances Act, the Criminal Code and Other Acts* (May 2018) (Chair: Lillian Eva Dyck)

Canada, Parliament, Special Senate Committee on Illegal Drugs, *Cannabis: Our Position for a Canadian Public Policy* (September 2002) (Chair: Pierre Claude Nolin)

Canada, Task Force on Cannabis Legalization and Regulation, *A Framework for the Legalization and Regulation of Cannabis in Canada: The Final Report of the Task Force on Cannabis Legalization and Regulation* (Ottawa: Health Canada, 2016)

Cannabis Act, SC 2018, c 16

Capler, Rielle, Walsh, Zach, Crosby, Kim, Belle-Isle, Lynne, Holtzman, Susan, Lucas, Phillippe & Callaway, Robert, "Are Dispensaries Indispensable? Patient Experiences of Access to Cannabis from Medical Cannabis Dispensaries in Canada" (2017) 47 International Journal of Drug Policy 1

Carstairs, Catherine, "Deporting 'Ah Sin' to Save the White Race: Moral Panic, Racialization, and the Extension of Canadian Drug Laws in the 1920's" (1999) 16:1 University of Toronto Press 65

Cavalieri, Walter & Riley, Diane, "Harm Reduction in Canada: The Many Faces of Regression" in Pates, Richard & Riley, Diane, eds, *Harm Reduction in Substance Use and High-Risk Behaviour: International Policy and Practice* (London: Wiley-Blackwell, 2012) 382–394

Commission of Inquiry into the Non-Medical Use of Drugs, *Interim Report of the Commission of Inquiry into the Non-Medical Use of Drugs* (Ottawa: Information Canada, 1970)

Commission of Inquiry into the Non-Medical Use of Drugs, *Final Report of the Commission of Inquiry into the Non-Medical Use of Drugs.* (Ottawa: Information Canada, 1973)

Controlled Drugs and Substances Act, SC 1996, c 19

Cox, Chelsea, "Implications of the 2018 Canadian Cannabis Act: Should Regulation Differ from Medicinal and non-Medicinal Cannabis Use?" (2021) 125 Health Policy 12

Crosby, Andrew, "Contesting Cannabis: Indigenous Jurisdiction and Legalization" (2019) 62:4 Canadian Public Administration 634

Dias, Giselle, "Canada's Drug Laws: Prohibition Is Not the Answer" in J. Thomas et al, eds, *Perspectives of Canadian Drug Policy* (Ontario: The John Howard Society of Canada, 2003) 9–24

44 History of Canada's Federal Drug Policy

Elliot, Josh, "Liberals 'Committed' to Legalizing Marijuana: Trudeau" (September 2015), online: *CTV News* <www.ctvnews.ca/politics/election/liberals-committed-to-legalizing-marijuana-trudeau-1.2588260>

Erickson, Patricia E. & Hyshka, Elaine, "Four Decades of Cannabis Criminals in Canada 1970–2010" (2010) 2:4 Amsterdam Law Forum 1

Erickson, Patricia G., "A Persistent Paradox: Drug Law and Policy in Canada" (1999) 4:2 Canadian Journal of Criminology 275

Erickson, Patricia G., "Recent Trends in Canadian Drug Policy: The Decline and Resurgence of Prohibitionism" (1992) 121:3 Political Pharmacology: Thinking About Drugs 239

Fischer, Benedikt, Russell, Cayley & Boyd, Neil, "A Century of Cannabis Control in Canada" in Decorte, Tom, Lenton, Simon & Wilkins, Chris, eds, *Legalizing Cannabis: Experiences, Lessons and Scenarios* (England: Routledge, 2020)

Fischer, Benedikt, Ala-Leppilampi, Kari, Single, Eric & Robins, Amanda, "Cannabis Law Reform in Canada: Is the 'Saga of Promise, Hesitation and Retreat' Coming to an End?" (2003) 45:3 Canadian Journal of Criminology and Criminal Justice 265

George-Cosh, David, "Cannabis Canada Weekly: Government Review Aims to Shape Next Chapter of Legalization" (October 2021), online: *BNN Bloomberg* <https://ampvideo.bnnbloomberg.ca/cannabis-canada-weekly-government-review-aims-to-shape-next-chapter-of-legalization-1.1667028>

Haines-Saah, Rebecca, J. & Fischer, Benedikt, "Youth Cannabis Use and Legalization in Canada – Reconsidering the Fears, Myths and Facts Three Years in" (2021) 30:3 Journal of the Canadian Academy of Child and Adolescent Psychiatry 191

Hathaway, Andrew, "The Legal History and Cultural Experience of Cannabis" (2009) 5:4 Visions Journal 12

Health Canada, *Proposed Approach to the Regulation of Cannabis* (Ottawa: Health Canada, 2017)

Health Canada, *Proposed Approach to the Regulation of Cannabis: Summary of Comments Received During the Public Consultation* (Ottawa: Health Canada, 2018)

Hitzig v. Can., (*2003*) 177 O.A.C. 321 (CA)

Koutouki, Konstantia & Lofts, Katherine, "Cannabis, Reconciliation, and the Rights of Indigenous Peoples: Prospects and Challenges for Cannabis Legalization in Canada" (2019) 56:3 Alberta Law Review 709

Lucas, Phillippe, "Regulating Compassion: An Overview of Canada's Federal Medical Cannabis Policy and Practice" (2008) 5 Harm Reduction Journal 5

Macrae, Barbara, "Drug Policy in Canada: War If Necessary but Not Necessarily War" in J. Thomas et al, eds, *Perspectives of Canadian Drug Policy* (Ontario: The John Howard Society of Canada, 2003) 43–74

Maghsoudi, Nazlee, Rammohan, Indhu, Bowra, Andrea, Sniderman, Ruby, Tanguay, Justine, Bouck, Zachary, Scheim, Ayden, Werb, Dan & Owusu-Bempah, Akwasi, "How Diverse Is Canada's Legal Cannabis Industry? Examining Race and Gender of Its Executives and Directors" (October 2020), online: *Centre on Drug Policy Evaluation* <https://cdpe.org/publication/how-diverse-is-canadas-legal-cannabis-industry-examining-race-and-gender-of-its-executives-and-directors/>

Mas, Susana, "Trudeau Lays Out Plan for New Relationship with Indigenous People" (December 2015), online: *CBC News* <www.cbc.ca/news/politics/justin-trudeau-afn-indigenous-aboriginal-people-1.3354747>

Opium Act, RSC 1908, c 50

Owusu-Bempah, Akwasi, "Where Is the Fairness in Canadian Cannabis Legalization? Lessons to Be Learned from the American Experience" (2021) 55:2 Journal of Canadian Studies 395–418

Owusu-Bempah, Akwasi & Luscombe, Alex, "Race, Cannabis and the Canadian War on Drugs: An Examination of Cannabis Arrest Data by Race in Five Cities" (2020) 91 International Journal of Drug Policy

R. v. Parker (2000), 49 O.R. (3d) 481

Rehm, Jürgen, Elton-Marshall, Tara, Sornpaisarn, Bundit & Manthey, Jakob, "Medical Marijuana. What Can We Learn from Experiences in Canada, Germany and Thailand?" (2019) 74 International Journal of Drug Policy 47

Riley, Diane, *Drugs and Drug Policy in Canada: A Brief Review & Commentary* (Ottawa: Senate of Canada, 1998)

Savoie, Josee, "Crime Statistics in Canada, 2001" (2001) 22:6 Juristat 1–22 <https://www150.statcan.gc.ca/n1/en/pub/85-002-x/85-002-x2002006-eng.pdf?st=dr2uM6zM> accessed 28 December 2021

Solomon, Robert & Green, Melvyn, "The First Century: The History of Non-Medical Opiate Use and Control Policies in Canada, 1870–1970" in Blackwell, Patricia & Erickson, Judith, eds, *Illicit Drugs in Canada: A Risky Business* (Scarborough: Nelson Canada, 1988) 88–104

The Opium and Narcotic Drug Act, RSC 1911, c 17

Valleriani, Jenna, Lavalley, Jennifer & McNeil, Ryan, "A Missed Opportunity? Cannabis Legalization and Reparations in Canada" (2018) 109 Canadian Journal of Public Health 745

Wakeford v. Can. (1999), 96 O.T.C. 108 (SC)

Zimonjic, Peter, "Only 484 Marijuana Pardons Have Been Granted Since Program Started in 2019" (31 October 2021), online: *CBC News* <www.cbc.ca/news/politics/pot-pardons-still-low-484-1.6230666>

3 Provincial Implementation of Cannabis Legalization

Chapter 2 described several issues with the legislative process behind, and eventual passage of, the Cannabis Act. In the aftermath of that legislation, a tight timeline for implementation created perhaps the most intense policy environment this country has seen in decades. This chapter begins by discussing how legal cannabis implementation has created a unique policy experiment through which claims of the existence of a Canadian "cooperative federalism" can be assessed.[1] It then moves on to describe how an ongoing, historical issue with Canadian federalism – Indigenous exclusion – further manifested itself in the provincial implementation of legal cannabis.[2] The next section of this chapter notes general trends and issues related to provincial implementation that were common across all provinces throughout the country, largely because of the federal government's role in dictating policy implementation.[3] Focus then turns to province-specific analyses of the differences, peculiarities, challenges and successes of each specific province's legal cannabis implementation.[4] The chapter concludes by noting a need for more research and data in order to properly assess the provincial implementation of legal cannabis, particularly with an eye towards noting a key future issue to be monitored: the growing problem of market concentration.[5]

3.1 Federalism Issues: Cooperation or Unilateralism?

As noted by Bowal et al,

> Similar to the division for other federations, Canada's legislative power is divided between national and subnational units. These powers are largely set out in Canada's Constitution Act, 1867 (CA, 1867). Section 91 grants the national Parliament exclusive powers over certain subject matters, while

1 Chapter 3.1
2 Chapter 3.2
3 Chapter 3.3
4 Chapters 3.4–3.10
5 Chapter 3.11

DOI: 10.4324/9781003200741-3

Section 92 grants sovereign legislative powers to the provinces in other areas.[6]

More specifically, Section 91[7] has historically been interpreted as establishing the federal government's jurisdiction over criminal law matters, while Section 92,[8] with its focus on property and civil rights in the provinces, has been broadly interpreted to encompass many areas of business (including taxation and models of retail) and the administration of justice. As a result, "In federations like Canada, creating a fully integrated, nationwide policy framework is a daunting collective action problem. The task is even more challenging when jurisdiction over the policy area is divided, as is the case with cannabis regulation in Canada".[9] Many scholars have commented on the unique policy experiment that cannabis legalization in Canada has created. Some have argued that it "is especially revealing of the intertwined competing dynamics in the policy-making process at play in Canadian federalism".[10] Others have noted that

> Cannabis legalization became the most intense national policymaking exercise Canada has undertaken in over a generation. Hundreds of strategic and operational policy decisions needed to be made across hundreds of public and private organizations before recreational cannabis was legalized on October 17, 2018.[11]

In this intense policy environment, the federal government (through the Ministers of Health and Justice) oversees the licensing of commercial producers and processors, establishes rules for packaging and branding, oversees the medical cannabis system, sets maximum and minimum ages for possession, establishes sanctions for trafficking and drug-impaired driving, and decides on issues like pardons and amnesty for past convictions.[12] Since commerce, public health, and most of law enforcement fall under provincial jurisdiction, the provinces were theoretically afforded the freedom to choose the distribution, wholesale, and retail models that they deemed most appropriate, but some have argued that

---

6　Peter Bowal et al, "Regulating Cannabis: A Comparative Exploration of Canadian Legalization" (2020) 57:4 American Business Law Journal 677 at 681

7　*Constitution Act, 1867* (UK), 30 & 31 Vict, c 3, reprinted in RSC 1985, App II, No 5, s 91

8　*Ibid* s 92

9　Jared Wesley, "Beyond Prohibition: The Legalization of Cannabis in Canada" (2019) 62:4 Canadian Public Administration 533 at 538–539

10　Maude Benoit & Gabriel Levesque, "What Can Cannabis Legalisation Teach Us About Canadian Federalism?" (2019), online: *Fifty Shades of Federalism* <http://50shadesoffederalism. com/policies/what-can-cannabis-legalisation-teach-us-about-canadian-federalism/>

11　Jared Wesley & Kyle Murray, "To Market or Demarket? Public-Sector Branding of Cannabis in Canada" (2021) 53:7 Administration & Society 1078 at 1081

12　Wesley, *supra* note 9, at 539

48   *Provincial Implementation*

this "entanglement of responsibilities" nonetheless "did not lead to a negotiated project of legalization".[13]

In other areas of great national importance requiring cooperation between the federal government and the provinces, the "Supreme Court of Canada has promoted cooperative federalism in constitutional law, allowing federal and provincial governments to exercise overlapping jurisdiction in certain regulatory areas".[14] Cooperative federalism has been argued to be a modern economic necessity, with the dominant tide of Canadian federalism shifting "from differences and antagonisms to a cooperative tide. . . . As a constitutional principle, cooperative federalism requires collaboration across all government levels to legally manage a formerly illegal drug".[15] That said, the style of leadership adopted by Ottawa during the legalization process has been characterized as an "inflexible unilateralism", particularly in light of the fact that multiple requests from the provinces to delay the legalization date were denied.[16] This has prompted some to observe that, "While cannabis legalization was framed as a collaborative endeavour, the federal government leaned heavily on its jurisdiction over criminal law to force provincial governments into policy specifics".[17] The fact that the federal government planned to implement online sales of cannabis (a provincial jurisdiction) if provinces were uncooperative has further lead to the argument that "Legalization of cannabis, therefore, does not illustrate a joint policy-making process in which the two orders of government are involved, but an imposed decision by the federal government onto its provincial counterparts".[18] Subsequently,

> Canada simultaneously created 13 distinct emerging economies within a mature economic framework. Each of those 13 distinct economic models approached opening their markets somewhat differently, but all of them did so at the same time. As a result, firms seeking to participate in the market had to develop entrepreneurial strategies which evolved in concert with that process, and those with national ambitions needed to develop multiple, parallel strategies.[19]

Provinces generally did not focus on maximizing provincial revenues, instead choosing tight restrictions from the onset of legalization. Train and Snow argue that, "The federal government's coercive policy goals and settings diminished

---

13 Benoit & Levesque, *supra* note 10

14 Bowal et al, *supra* note 6, at 681

15 *Ibid* at 682

16 Benoit & Levesque, *supra* note 10

17 Andrew Train & Dave Snow, "Cannabis Policy Diffusion in Ontario and New Brunswick: Coercion, Learning, and Replication" (2019) 62:4 Canadian Public Administration 549 at 567

18 Benoit & Levesque, *supra* note 10

19 Alice De Koning & John McArdle, "Implementing Regulation in an Emerging Industry: A Multiple-Province Perspective" (2021) 55:2 Journal of Canadian Studies 362 at 364

the incentives for provinces to legislate for a competitive advantage".[20] As such, "The framework for the sale and consumption of cannabis reveals a total absence of coherence between the multiple orders of government involved",[21] leaving entrepreneurs in any given province facing "significant ambiguity around licensing and regulation processes for retail operations, supply chain constraints and production delays that have impacted their business models . . . and inconsistent regulatory frameworks across provinces which have impacted their ability to scale operations".[22]

These issues were unsurprisingly also identified by cannabis industry leaders who have since been navigating the provincial implementation of cannabis legalization. They are worth discussing here as they are microcosms of a Canadian federalist system that produced differential provincial regulatory schemes across the country. One cannabis industry leader argues that

> The legalization from a federal level failed and will continue to fail in the expediting of creating a solely legal market because it put too much onus on the provinces and municipalities to do some more of the heavy lifting. Although the federal government gave us a general framework, the amount of powers that it gave and certain powers that it gave to provincial governments actually are gonna be the cause for inhibiting legalization to be a success.[23]

Another cannabis industry leader makes a similar point, giving a specific example of a logistical issue:

> The government federally legalized cannabis but the way that cannabis was gonna be sold was on the provincial level and that created all sorts of complications especially with the way that cannabis is tracked and how the taxation and the revenue is reported back to the government. Logistically and operationally this creates a lot of complexities for licensed producers. With excise, like you need a separate excise stamp if you wanna send product to Manitoba or Saskatchewan or Ontario. . . . From the start the government should have just made the stamp uniform across the whole country.[24]

---

20 Train & Snow, *supra* note 17, at 568
21 Benoit & Levesque, *supra* note 10
22 De Koning & McArdle, *supra* note 19, at 364
23 Participant A, 21 July 2021. Another study participant echoed this sentiment: "If you're going to be dictating legislation that will help create a new billion-dollar industry and fuel taxation revenue and jobs and innovation, it's in your best interest to foster and allow that to grow. But instead, the mix of the federal and provincial aspect has totally destroyed the ability for any of these companies to flourish both on the licensed producer side and on the retailer side" (Participant K, 22 July 2021)
24 Participant K, 22 July 2021

50 *Provincial Implementation*

Others point to similar practical issues that involve the interplay between federal and provincial regulators. For instance, as one cannabis industry leader noted:

> I find that with the Cannabis Act, which is being enforced by Health Canada, the bodies aren't talking to one another. Like there's this finger pointing game that's going on. . . . If I have some kind of marketing inducement issue Health Canada might send me a letter but I can't get any prescriptive information from my local or provincial regulators.[25]

It has been argued that the regulatory frameworks developed in the provinces "prevented normal business practices and entrepreneurs in the industry responded with work-around strategies".[26] One industry participant lent support to the idea that entrepreneurs have had to come up with innovative solutions while hoping that amendments to federal and provincial legislation might be on the horizon.[27] Nonetheless, in this first stage of provincial legal cannabis implementation, there have been a wide variety of issues faced by industry members, ranging from broad (applicable in provinces all across the country) to specific (issues specific to the regulatory framework of any given province) that remain to be addressed and discussed.[28]

3.2 Federalism Issues: Further Exclusion of Indigenous Participation

No discussion of the issues related to Canadian federalism in the context of provincial legal cannabis implementation would be complete without a discussion of the exclusion of Indigenous participation. As noted in Chapter 2,[29] the legislative process behind, and passage of, the Cannabis Act was characterized as a missed opportunity because of an extreme lack of consultation with, and inclusion of, Indigenous communities. This lack of consultation and inclusion has further manifested itself in the subsequent implementation of cannabis legalization in provinces across the country. As noted by Ben-Ishai:

> The regulation of cannabis on reserve is tied up in larger questions about Indigenous sovereignty. . . . The regulatory framework becomes even more

25 Participant S, 30 June 2021
26 De Koning & McArdle, *supra* note 19, at 367
27 Participant S, *supra* note 25: "The thing that really strikes me is the resilience of people that are really driving the industry. So like in the spaces where there are those regulatory gaps or challenges or miscommunication amongst government bureaucracy, I've really been impressed by the entrepreneurial spirit to drive that system forward. Like it really seems like an area of policy that is the opposite of the traditional conception of trickle down from the top of the government. . . . It's people working on it on the ground day to day that are really encountering these challenges and coming up with innovative solutions for moving forward in a way that is not just financially prosperous but is also just kind of logical and intuitive and overall in line with the overarching goals of legalization"
28 Broad issues with provincial implementation are discussed below in Chapter 3.3. Province-specific issues are discussed in Chapters 3.4–3.10
29 See Chapter 2.6

Provincial Implementation 51

complicated for First Nations who want to take advantage of the opportunities presented by cannabis or have been operating dispensaries for decades. Numerous communities have taken the position that the federal and provincial regulations do not apply to their lands. Others have passed their own laws that meet or exceed the requirements off-reserve. These laws have led to questions about how these communities would enforce their regulations, and about their validity where they conflict with federal legislation.[30]

The exclusion of Indigenous communities from discussions on tax sharing agreements[31] has created a serious implementation issue whereby Indigenous communities (who largely don't recognize the jurisdiction of provinces on their lands) are excluded from participation in the legal system and are effectively exposed to risks from both organized crime and potential criminalization. In Ontario alone, provincial police have estimated that there are 79 unlicensed cannabis distributors operating on 23 First Nations, with some raids of dispensaries having been reported.[32] Many of the same federalism issues pertaining to Indigenous participation in the cannabis industry have historical parallels with the regulation of substances like alcohol and tobacco. As noted by Wesley:

> All provinces handed authority over distribution of cannabis to their well-established liquor control boards, and many based their cannabis retail models on their approaches to selling alcohol. . . . First Nations governments play a subordinate role in these systems. This approach serves to replicate and perpetuate settler colonial systems of authority, to the exclusion of Indigenous self-determination.[33]

Unsurprisingly, Indigenous community leaders advanced several concerns with the implementation of cannabis legalization in the qualitative interviews conducted for this book. According to one participant, the problem began first with the Federal Government:

> The Federal Government passes a law, downloads it into Criminal Code to the provincial government. As soon as it gets downloaded like that, you try to create a law for a First Nation and then you immediately run into Section 88 of the Indian Act. Section 88 of the Indian Act is the general law of application. And that says where there is no treaty, or Federal law, provincial laws will apply. If you never get a chance to build your own law, you're never

---

30 Stephanie Ben-Ishai, "Bankruptcy for Cannabis Companies: Canada's Newest Export?" (2020) 27:2 University of Miami International and Comparative Law Review 226 at 243–244

31 Andrew Crosby, "Contesting Cannabis: Indigenous Jurisdiction and Legalization" (2019) 62:4 Canadian Public Administration 634 at 636

32 Ben-Ishai, *supra* note 30, at 245

33 Wesley, *supra* note 9, at 541

52 *Provincial Implementation*

able to generate commerce where in fact you could actually participate in, financially, solving your own problems.[34]

This is an aspect of Canadian federalism that should have been envisioned as problematic by the federal government but, as one participant notes, has not been addressed:

> The problem is that the federal government can only through legislation enter into agreements with the provinces and not first nations communities or territories which is problematic. We've highlighted that to them and they've said that they would continue to examine options or collaboration but it hasn't happened.[35]

Participants made it clear that they wanted to participate within the "mainstream" framework, but that current federal and provincial agreements constrain any meaningful access:

> We wanna merge into the mainstream to take our place but we don't wanna play in the mainstream framework with the current rules around taxation because we can't even begin to compete or we cannot combat the black market. So competing in the industry, we need to find that baseline and combating the black market we need the resources to do that. So the excise tax is a really important piece and I think if the provinces wanna deal with the black market they're gonna have to work with red market platforms that can work within the mainstream but it's really gonna be about harmonization.[36]

Participants are concerned that the implementation of cannabis regulations closely resembles the regulation of other substances.[37] Another participant also identified a key jurisdictional issue that effectively forced his community to develop its

---

34 Participant F, 26 May 2021

35 Participant T, 26 May 2021: On this issue, the participant further added: "We didn't want the provinces exercising jurisdiction in relation to anything here in an economic development sense. . . . Protect the consumer, protect the community, but also protect our jurisdiction in this industry from the province and the federal government"

36 Participant J, 3 June 2021. On this issue, the participant further added: "We don't want the province to carve into our place of this industry. They can work with us on safety and oversight, but let's negotiate and collaborate at a jurisdictional level on the issue of shared benefit and resource and let's push the black market out of the way"

37 Participant F, *supra* note 34: "The province of Ontario didn't know how to create a distribution system and so they started on this licensing where essentially they never talked to producers. What they did is essentially throw together the stiffest regulations that they could possibly put together from tobacco, from gasoline, from alcohol. They crossbred all those things to make them all the more difficult things, and they made it so difficult for retailers to actually get into the field, they were spending so much money unnecessarily on the process itself that uh, and getting two dollars a gram out of it, they weren't making a whole pile of money"

own cannabis regulations.[38] It becomes clear that, absent any change in federal and provincial government policy, Indigenous communities are going to continue operating in the face of what they (rightly) believe to be systemic discrimination.[39]

As noted by Wesley, "It is difficult to see how governments can continue to exclude Indigenous communities and municipalities from these high-level discussions".[40] The cynical (but also realistic) response might be that eventually, they will be forced to do so if they are truly committed to eliminating the illicit market. Concerns around the prevalence of illicit markets and organized crime activity in Indigenous communities were shared by all study participants. As noted by one community leader,

> It's the layering effect I call it. It's one ill-conceived issue after another and complete denials by the government that they're going to allow us to participate in any part of this economy. And what happens at that point: the economy just goes underground.[41]

Another participant pointed to a grey market in their community being facilitated by a lack of access to product safety testing:

> The way it was developed and implemented created more of a grey market in First Nations communities around cannabis. So it just created more problems. We can't validate safeness because every licensed tester in Canada will not accept a product from an unlicensed facility.[42]

---

38 Participant T, *supra* note 35: "My community is in Ontario and Quebec. If we were a community that worked in collaboration with the provinces around cannabis we theoretically would have two regimes that would be set up. . . . The provinces have different age limits, they have different approaches on what's allowable and what's not. . . . They are practically saying that one community has two sets of delivery methods and that's not acceptable. So that's a reason why we developed our own interim cannabis regulations"

39 Participant J, *supra* note 36: "We as an Indigenous people have the ability and we have the right to be part of Canada's cannabis industry. . . . But you can't make us do that without the proper resources, you can't force us to collect tax for you, we're gonna keep that in the community. . . . Every day that goes by and every day that we lose economic opportunity because the business model doesn't line up with the current content of the legal landscape, it's not only that we don't have access but that's systemic discrimination"

40 Wesley, *supra* note 9, at 545

41 Participant F, *supra* note 34, The participant further added: "The banks cannot legally accept the currency. What do you do with this huge influx of cash that's coming at you at the rate of 35 thousand dollars a week? That pillow is only so big you know you can only stash it so many places. . . . And what comes of that is gonna be guns and drugs then there's potential for human trafficking"

42 Participant T, *supra* note 35. Another participant also lamented the lack of access to product safety testing: "We don't want to poison our own people, and we certainly don't want to poison anybody else, you know, we're doing it for exactly the same reasons as you're doing it but you won't listen, they won't listen, the provincial government won't listen to the First Nation input" (Participant F, *supra* note 34)

54   *Provincial Implementation*

The continued existence of illicit markets in Indigenous communities led one participant to express concern about the likelihood of violence absent some action from the federal and provincial governments: "It's like the government has these pitbulls holding our people against the wall and they're not doing a darn thing about it. They know the black market is in our communities. What are they waiting for? For somebody to get shot?".[43] It is disappointingly clear that Indigenous communities have been excluded from the provincial implementation of cannabis, just as they were excluded from consultations in the legislative process behind the Cannabis Act. This is an issue that should have been foreseen by the federal and provincial governments. Absent further action from the federal government, it can only be hoped that "regulations across the country are likely to evolve as one component of the system (i.e. another province) observes and adopts successful practices from another".[44] It would thus be prudent for provinces to look at the example of Saskatchewan, a province that one industry participant pointed to as a leader in terms of incentivizing Indigenous participation and inclusion.[45]

3.3 Broad Trends and Issues Associated with Provincial Implementation

Given the strong role of the federal government in dictating provincial policy implementation, it is unsurprising that there are general (or broad) issues that have affected legal cannabis implementation in every province. This section focuses on these issues and country-wide trends before moving to analyses of province-specific issues.[46] The first general trend to be noted is the issue of adequate supply, particularly in reference to the first year of legalization implementation. For context, the total monthly sales (online and-in store combined) grew year-on-year from $59 million in December 2018 to $148 million and $297 million in December 2019 and 2020, respectively.[47] This is a quantum leap in a short space of time, but it also speaks to supply issues that largely plagued the first year of legalization implementation in provinces across the country. As noted by Armstrong,

> For the country overall, sales were held back by shortages of dry products and licensed stores. The dry shortage directly impacted sales by making fewer

---

43 Participant J, *supra* note 36

44 De Koning & McArdle, *supra* note 19, at 367

45 Participant R, 2 June 2021: "In Saskatchewan, when they were doing their licensing process, you specifically got extra points for having Indigenous owners or partners and the applicants went out of their way to incorporate them and create a joint venture and work with them and they were all very proud of that fact"

46 Chapters 3.4–3.10

47 Michael Armstrong, "Relationships Between Increases in Canadian Cannabis Stores, Sales and Prevalence" (2021) 228 Drug and Alcohol Dependence, DOI: <>https://doi.org/10.1016/j.drugalcdep.2021.109071> at 1

Provincial Implementation 55

products available and indirectly by causing provinces to delay retail expansion. These results support complaints that product shortages initially were widespread and refute federal government claims of adequate supplies.[48]

Indeed, the "sluggish rollout of retail stores across Canada" has been often attributed to national supply shortages that all provinces seemed to deal with in the first year of legalization.[49] The small number of licensed producers initially authorized by Health Canada led to demand significantly exceeding supply, and, as a result, it is likely that many consumers continued to take advantage of a black market price that was far below what was being offered legally.[50] It is also argued that

> A second phase of market bottleneck emerged as provincial wholesalers were not adequately prepared to accept and distribute high volumes of bulk cannabis products. This was due to several factors. First, provincial wholesalers needed time to develop internal processes and procedures, hire and train staff, establish relationships and negotiate contracts with both producers and retail operators, and integrate systems for receiving, shelving, inventory control and management, and shipping products.[51]

These factors were all part of an inevitable learning curve likely foreseen by the provinces when they requested (unsuccessfully, as noted above) additional time from the federal government before proceeding with legalization.

A second Canada-wide trend is directly related to the federal government's very strict marketing and advertising rules. While the government justified these rules as necessary to protect youth from promotion, questions have been raised by both academics and industry participants about the appropriate level of regulation in this area. As noted by Bowel et al,

> The remarkably high level of regulatory detail makes compliance virtually impossible without legal advice or the ability of a person to otherwise parse thousands of words of legalese. . . . An unregulated market is not the answer, but imposing micro-regulations results in higher costs and other consequences. Brands enjoy little opportunity to build trust with customers

---

48 Michael Armstrong, "Legal Cannabis Market Shares During Canada's First Year of Recreational Legalization" (2021) 88 International Journal of Drug Policy, DOI: <>https://doi.org/10.1016/j.drugpo.2020.103028> at 7

49 Bowal et al, *supra* note 6, at 703–703

50 *Ibid* at 718: The authors note that the average price per gram in Canada in 2019 was $9.99 (legal cannabis) vs. $6.40 (black market cannabis). They also noted that similar supply limitations did not exist in the United States, where states like Oregon regularly report overabundances of inventory

51 De Koning & McArdle, *supra* note 19, at 371–372

56 *Provincial Implementation*

at points of sale. Craft producers struggle to inform prospective customers about their product specialties.[52]

This issue was raised by several of the cannabis industry leaders surveyed for this book. As one industry leader stated,

> The ability to put basically nothing on a package at all makes it very difficult when you go into a store to distinguish 'do I want this or do I want that?'. They can't even tell you certain things about the product. . . . It's difficult to target consumers one brand over another . . . so there's certainly marketing and promotion things that could be changed that would actually benefit the industry and also benefit the government by virtue of helping to further drive people away from the illicit market.[53]

Another industry leader laments the fact that marketing restrictions are actively driving smaller companies out of the market:

> There's no way to market and build that affinity with the consumer. . . . It's impossible for these guys to compete. . . . What we're seeing in a retail space right now is a little bit of a race to the bottom and a race for economies of scale. . . . What's sad is that the small mom and pop shops run by these independent entrepreneurs that are very passionate about educating their consumer base and trying to drive value for them won't survive. You just can't.[54]

The marketing issue is given an added layer of (rather ironic) context when considered alongside the fact that most provinces chose regulatory schemes that very closely resemble their regulation of alcohol, an industry rife with marketing and promotion. This irony was not lost on one study participant, who noted:

> The number one thing I'd like to see improved upon would be . . . marketing regulations and some of the rules around the prescriptive regulations with respect to people seeing it in the store or not having minors be able to come into the store if they're accompanied with a parent. You know, try to be more progressive, just like liquor has evolved over the days, try to make it more socially acceptable and stop making the barriers there so the stigma can start to go away.[55]

Academic evaluations of the marketing issue have come to similar conclusions: "Canada's restrictions on retail promotions (little advertising, no free samples, etc.) presumably made it harder for new stores to stimulate local demand".[56]

---

52 Bowal et al, *supra* note 6, at 718
53 Participant R, *supra* note 45
54 Participant K, *supra* note 24
55 Participant S, *supra* note 25
56 Armstrong, *supra* note 47, at 4

A third Canada-wide trend pertains to the availability (or lack thereof) of provincial data on legal cannabis implementation. Armstrong notes that most provincial governments have been very secretive about their pricing policies, making it difficult to discern average retail prices or make effective comparisons to the illicit market.[57] This lack of information is frustrating, given that "Provincial cannabis agencies have the most information about recreational sales, especially where they operate all the stores; but despite public ownership, public mandates, and public attention, most provide minimal public disclosure".[58] Moreover, every province's designated agency (such as Alberta Gaming, Liquor and Cannabis, or Ontario's Ontario Cannabis Store) is already reporting monthly sales to Health Canada, and, as such, the material is readily available.[59] This data could provide crucial bases for analysis and comparison, helping both regulators and other interested stakeholders (including academics) better understand the market and shape their reforms accordingly. It is worth noting that similar data is extensively collected and shared in U.S. states (particularly those that were first movers/leaders in the legalization movement sweeping across the country), allowing for sales to be broken down all the way to store level (Washington) or by county (Colorado).[60] This has led some to conclude that there is "an almost generalized absence of provincial will to assess their cannabis legalization policies [and thus] there is insufficient research to draw satisfactory conclusions on the impact of legalization".[61] This is particularly concerning given the early stage of legal cannabis implementation, as major questions still exist about whether legalization as a whole is meeting its goals and objectives. These questions include:

> Do models that include greater emphasis on private retail and economic development veer close to highly commercialized cannabis markets and, if so, what might the implications be for cannabis consumption and demand, and ultimately public health? On the other hand, while strictly government-controlled sales might ostensibly seem more in line with public health, what if such systems fail to replace illicit markets, especially for certain products?[62]

Absent the appropriate and necessary data, these questions remain largely unanswered, greatly stunting further evaluation and analysis of provincial regulatory regimes.

---

57 Armstrong, *supra* note 48, at 3

58 *Ibid* at 8

59 Michael Armstrong, "Canada's Provinces and Territories Should Disclose Cannabis Data to Support Research" (2021) 193:10 CMAJ 341 at 341

60 *Ibid*

61 Gabriel Levesque, "Cannabis Legalization in Canada. Case studies: British Columbia, Ontario and Quebec" (2020), online (pdf): *French Monitoring Centre for Drugs and Drug Addiction* <>https://en.ofdt.fr/BDD/publications/docs/ASTRACAN_Levesque-EN.pdf> at 70

62 Tara Marie Watson et al, "Early-Stage Cannabis Regulatory Policy Planning Across Canada's Four Largest Provinces: A Descriptive Overview" (2019) 54:10 Substance Use & Misuse 1691 at 1699

58 *Provincial Implementation*

The final Canada-wide trend to be discussed stems from the complete lack of social justice and social equity provisions in the federal Cannabis Act, with academics and cannabis industry leaders commenting on barriers to access that exist in the provincial implementation of cannabis legalization. Chapter 4 discusses several jurisdictions that proactively pre-empted this issue by building social justice and social equity provisions (i.e. dedicated licenses for equity applicants, financial assistance and advice, automatic expungements of records, etc.) into their legalization legislation.[63] Considering how closely the provinces have followed federal guidelines for marketing and advertising, it seems at least plausible that the inclusion of social justice and social equity provisions in the federal legislation would have had an impact on provincial implementation. One major way that this has had an impact on market entry in the provinces has been in relation to the "legacy market", i.e. businesses that operated dispensaries prior to legalization. There is a wealth of entrepreneurial experience and cannabis-specific expertise present in this "legacy market" that remains on the outside looking in. As noted by De Koning and McArdle,

> Many entrepreneurs with substantial experience in the cannabis industry developed that experience in the illegal market; others did not have ready access to sufficient capital during what was often a lengthy and uncertain regulatory approval and licensing process. Those individuals seeking to transition from the illegal to the legal market, a stated goal of policy and regulatory reform, faced difficulty in doing so, as a conviction for a drug-related offence would bar them from eligibility for a license.[64]

One industry participant noted observing this issue in two different provinces: "We have issues with not only just the retail side in places like Alberta and in places like Ontario where it prevents somebody from participating in the space if they have a previous conviction but then also on the cultivation side as well".[65] That participant also went on to argue that inadequate consideration of social equity and the legacy market is actively countering the government's own stated objective of eliminating the illicit market.[66] It is thus fair to argue that, absent any further direction from the federal government, provinces themselves should implement social equity provisions (as has occurred in several U.S. states and

---

63 These include, but are not limited to: Arizona (Ch. 4.4.2); California (Ch. 4.4.3); Connecticut (Ch. 4.4.5); Illinois (Ch. 4.4.6); Massachusetts (Ch. 4.4.8); Montana (Ch. 4.4.10); New Jersey (Ch. 4.4.12); New York (Ch. 4.4.14); and Virginia (Ch. 4.4.17)

64 De Koning & McArdle, *supra* note 19, at 370

65 Participant A, *supra* note 23

66 *Ibid*: "It doesn't mean that they're going to cease participating in the cannabis space just because they're not allowed to participate in the legal space and I think this idea that the government had of putting in these regulations and not considering that there is an industry that existed decades before they came into power and that can continue to exist . . . even post legalization I think it's to their detriment"

Provincial Implementation   59

other jurisdictions) that would allow those most disproportionately affected by cannabis criminalization better access to the legal cannabis market.

Finally, before moving on to a discussion of the differences, peculiarities, challenges and successes of each specific province, it should be noted that there were some common trends in how provinces went about implementing cannabis legalization. Each province established online retail sales of cannabis, though it has since been noted that the percentage of online sales sharply declined after the opening of retail stores and remains low.[67] Each province leaned heavily on the institutions, processes, and policies from their alcohol and tobacco regimes, handing over authority for the distribution of cannabis to their well-established liquor control boards and generally basing their cannabis retail models on their approaches to selling alcohol.[68] Moreover, while the specific design of each province's distribution and retail framework will be discussed below, it has been observed that "Wholesale distribution is both a government monopsony (where the government is the only buyer of goods or services) and a government monopoly (where the government is the only seller of goods or services) in every province but Saskatchewan".[69] The COVID-19 pandemic has been argued to have had "minimal impacts on the expansion of legal cannabis retail stores in Canada, with record numbers of stores opening during the pandemic period".[70] Moreover, in almost all provinces, "non-medical cannabis retail sales were officially declared an essential service in those jurisdictions that made such declarations or were treated as such in most other jurisdictions".[71] Despite these commonalities, massive discrepancies in certain areas of policy implementation still exist. For example, one study suggests that during the final quarter of 2020, Alberta had opened 149 stores (per million residents), with Ontario (17.5 per million), Quebec (6.69 per million), and several other provinces well below the Canadawide average (38.65).[72] While more recent statistics show that this gap is closing,[73] the analyses in the section below explain each province's specific approach to

---

67 Armstrong, *supra* note 59, at 3: For instance, the percentage of legal recreational sales occurring online was 43.4% in October 2018 but had dropped to 5.9% just a year later in September 2019

68 Wesley, *supra* note 9, at 541

69 De Koning & McArdle, *supra* note 19, at 371

70 Daniel Myran et al, "How Has Access to Legal Cannabis Changed Over Time? An Analysis of the Cannabis Retail Market in Canada 2 Years Following the Legalization of Recreational Cannabis" (2021) Drug and Alcohol Review, DOI: <DOI:10.1111/dar.13351> at 6

71 "Cannabis Retail During COVID-19" (January 2021), online (pdf): *Canadian Centre on Substance Use and Addiction* #x003C;www.ccsa.ca/sites/default/files/2021-01/CCSA-COVID-19-Cannabis-Retail-Policy-Brief-2021-en.pdf>: Newfoundland, Prince Edward Island and Ontario saw stores close for short periods of time (one to three months) before being allowed to re-open with physical distancing measures in place. Online sales continued during these periods of time

72 Armstrong, *supra* note 47, at 3

73 Jan Conway, "Number of Cannabis Stores in Canada as of June 2021, by Region" (17 September 2021), online: *Statista* #x003C;www.statista.com/statistics/1035996/number-of-cannabis-stores-by-region-canada>

60 Provincial Implementation

legalization implementation with an eye towards understanding differences that exist in provincial cannabis markets across the country.

3.4 Provincial Implementation of Cannabis Legalization in Ontario

The story of Ontario's provincial implementation of cannabis legalization provides for an excellent example of how political regime change can have an immense impact on regulatory outcome. The province's previous Liberal government (then led by Kathleen Wynne) had planned to create a market model employing a retail monopoly based on the provincial liquor system, only to be replaced by the current Premier Doug Ford's conservative government that instead shifted focus to licensing private businesses to create a network of retail stores.[74] In the initial leadup to the legalization rollout, Ontario decided to cap retail cannabis licenses at 25, despite receiving 17,230 expressions of interest.[75] The initial cap on licenses has been described as "absurdly low given the size of Ontario's population and the heightened interest among private businesses".[76] This cap on retail locations, in a province with the largest population in Canada, has also arguably contributed to the continuing operation of illegal dispensaries.[77] This concern was echoed by a cannabis industry leader, who stated, "Why is Ontario still allowing illicit retail stores to operate? Like you talk about getting rid of the illicit market but yet I got a café down the street from me still selling cannabis on a regular basis".[78] Moreover, there has been comprehensive academic and industry criticism of the province's decision to award the initial 25 licenses via a "lottery" system. This system allowed anyone without a criminal record to apply for a license, having only to pay a $75 application fee, regardless of the absence of past experience in cannabis, retailing or access to capital.[79] This lottery system was the subject of intense criticism from cannabis industry leaders. Said one industry participant:

> In Ontario, a week before they were going to start accepting applications they announced they were going to do a lottery instead and only give out twenty-five [licenses] to start and everyone's saying I spent this money on leases, I've spent building up stores, applications are a week away what are you talking about?[80]

Another industry leader referred to the lottery as a "clumsy process" and indicated that it was likely counter-intuitive to the government's stated goal of

---

74 De Koning & McArdle, *supra* note 19, at 385
75 Ben-Ishai, *supra* note 30, at 228
76 De Koning & McArdle, *supra* note 19, at 385
77 *Ibid* at 236
78 Participant K, *supra* note 24
79 De Koning & McArdle, *supra* note 19, 385
80 Participant R, *supra* note 45

combatting the black market.[81] This concern was valid. The initial 25 license winners were announced on January 12, 2019, giving them less than three months to open their stores by April 1, 2019.[82] By the time that date arrived, only nine of the twenty-five initial licensees were ready to open their doors to the public.[83]

Other aspects of Ontario's initial and subsequent implementation have also been criticized by both academics and cannabis industry leaders. It has been suggested that the province's rollout also suffered from "inadequate coverage based on geographical distribution".[84] This suggestion was supported by this industry leader, who stated,

> They really made a quagmire of legalization in Ontario. . . . Distance requirements between stores is a massive issue that you're seeing in the city and that's why you're getting these pockets and clusters of stores and unfortunately you're gonna see a lot of good entrepreneurs lose their stores.[85]

Another industry leader echoed this sentiment: "The Government of Ontario could have done a better job with respect to trying to space the stores out a bit more. I've got some stores that literally have eight to ten stores all within a stone's throw of me all selling the same product which is kind of foolish".[86] Yet another industry leader focused blame for this issue squarely on the province's Alcohol and Gaming Commission (AGCO).[87] The lack of broader retail access across the province has been suggested as one explanation for greater purchase of cannabis from illegal dealers, with Ontario standing in stark contrast to a province like Alberta (where retail access was high and the largest drop in purchasing from dealers was found).[88] The problematic lottery process, minimal retail rollout (by comparison to other provinces), and inadequate geographic distribution in Ontario have led to a situation where

> Ontarians were less likely to purchase dried flower from a legal source than dried flower purchasers in all provinces except Manitoba, after adjusting for price and other covariates. . . . By September 2019, the legal and non-medical

---

81 Participant S, *supra* note 25: "Having a lottery process just isn't an effective tool to be able to get commerce to open up and to really combat the black market"

82 De Koning & McArdle, *supra* note 19, at 385

83 Ben-Ishai, *supra* note 30, 246

84 De Koning & McArdle, *supra* note 19, 378

85 Participant A, *supra* note 23

86 Participant S, *supra* note 25

87 Participant K, *supra* note 24: "The AGCO is the governing body that's authorizing store openings and they don't look at a real estate map and say, 'Oh well there's already ten stores in this one hundred meter cluster maybe an eleventh store doesn't make sense'. They don't look at it with reason"

88 Andrew Hathaway, Greggory Cullen & David Walters, "How Well Is Cannabis Legalization Curtailing the Illegal Market? A Multi-wave Analysis of Canada's National Cannabis Survey" (2021) 55:2 Journal of Canadian Studes 307 at 328

62 *Provincial Implementation*

market had only 13% of the total cannabis market share in Ontario, the lowest across the provinces.[89]

After two rounds of the lottery process, "a more conventional private market approach took place by March 2020".[90] The removal of store limits in April 2020 allowed the number of stores per capita to more than double and, "As of 31 May 2021, there were 776 stores authorized to open, resulting in stores per capita in Ontario (6.2 per 100 000) overtaking the national average (3.7 per 100 000) at 2 years".[91]

The size and significance of Ontario's population and consumer cannabis market meant that these initial growing pains had a ripple effect throughout the country. As noted by De Koning and McArdle, "For Canada's policy, as a whole, this delay has dampened the growth of the legal production of cannabis, as licensed producers had to limit production without access to the large Ontario market".[92] A cannabis industry leader further reinforced this point:

> Ontario represents close to 40 percent of cannabis sales to the end consumer across the whole country. . . . Every time something happens with the OCS or they close their doors for a month that screws every single producer in the country because more than 40 percent of their revenue is attributed to this province.[93]

This viewpoint is significant, not only because it speaks to the broader national importance of Ontario's market, but because it also notes what many have argued is a significant design flaw in the province's cannabis implementation. The Ontario Cannabis Store (OCS) is a crown agency solely owned by the province, providing the only source of online retail sales and, crucially, acting as the wholesaler of legal recreational cannabis.[94] The problem created by this regulatory scheme was described by one industry leader:

> The bigger hold up seems to be the Ontario Cannabis Store which is the provincial wholesaler and just seems to be unnecessary. Private retail can't have a website and can't have e-commerce, can't do direct delivery but the government can and the government that sells it through e-commerce and

---

89 Elle Wadsworth et al, "Cannabis Flower Prices and Transitions to Legal Sources After Legalization in Canada, 2019–2020" (2022) 231 Drug and Alcohol Dependence, DOI: <>https://doi.org/10.1016/j.drugalcdep.2021.109262> at 5

90 Levesque, *supra* note 61, at 21

91 Myran et al, *supra* note 70, at 7

92 De Koning & McArdle, *supra* note 19, at 386

93 Participant K, *supra* note 24

94 "About Us" (n.d.), online: *Ontario Cannabis Store* <https://ocs.ca/pages/about-us>

Provincial Implementation   63

direct delivery is also the wholesaler that sells to stores. Like it just makes no sense.[95]

As noted by another cannabis industry leader, businesses in the cannabis space are effectively competing against their only wholesaler, creating obvious conflicts and logistical issues.[96] Another industry leader also questioned the value added by the OCS:

> The OCS wants their cut. For what, what do they do? They pay a bunch of government employees three hundred plus grand a year to come up with strategy. They've siphoned through more than four CEOs in less than a year. There's zero leadership and zero accountability at that organization.[97]

It thus seems that Ontario may need to give some thought to regulatory system reform moving forward, as the current system is requiring industry participants to engage in some absurd regulatory workarounds.[98] Moreover, concerns with distance requirements and saturation in certain areas will also need to be addressed, as it appears that this problem has recently also spread to the province's northern regions.[99] The province appears to have recovered somewhat from its disastrous first years in the industry. Ontario recently surpassed Alberta in terms of the number of stores (613 to 599) but still lags far behind in per capita stores (13.5 stores per 100,000 people in Alberta vs. 4.1 stores per 100,000 people in Ontario).[100]

95 Participant R, *supra* note 45
96 Participant S, *supra* note 25: "[The OCS] is our only wholesaler, so we compete against our only wholesaler. Their business model has really tried to compete against retail. . . . There's a lot of supply chain and logistics things they have to contemplate that just isn't where it needs to be as of today. They need to learn how to manage whether they go direct from LP to retailers or consumers or do you have this kind of middle man body [the OCS] that floats in all kinds of channels that may not make strategic sense"
97 Participant K, *supra* note 24
98 Participant R, *supra* note 24: "Unfortunately it seems like the politics of things got in the way and you have this wholesaler and it starts manifesting itself in ridiculous ways. . . . Canopy can have a retail store in Smith Falls but the legislation requires it to buy the cannabis from the OCS, so the OCS has created a system where Canopy's cultivation facility will have a designated storage area that's technically OCS property. . . . You can just set the product aside on the warehouse floor and we'll buy it and we'll sell it back to you on paper and then you can put it in your store. . . . The whole point is that if you're doing all of this just to get around what's in the legislation, let's just change the legislation and get rid of the ridiculousness of the whole thing"
99 Erik White, "With Dozens of Pot Shops Popping Up Across Northern Ontario, Legal Weed Market Could Be at Saturation Point" (24 January 2022), online: *CBC News* #x003C;www.cbc.ca/news/canada/sudbury/cannabis-market-northern-ontario-1.6321293>
100 Solomon Israel, "Ontario Overtakes Alberta to Lead Canada in Legal Cannabis Stores" (17 December 2021), online: *MJBiz Daily* <https://mjbizdaily.com/ontario-overtakes-alberta-to-lead-canada-in-legal-cannabis-stores/>

64 *Provincial Implementation*

As it moves towards addressing this gap in the future, the province would do well to consider the myriad of issues and industry concerns noted above.

3.5 Provincial Implementation of Cannabis Legalization in Alberta

In theory, Alberta implemented a similar model to Ontario's eventual model under the Ford conservative government, with the province controlling online sales and wholesale distribution to private retailers, overseen by Alberta Gaming, Liquor and Cannabis (AGLC).[101] In practice, the actual implementation of legal cannabis has occurred in a remarkably different manner. First and foremost, the AGLC did not place a limit on the number of retail cannabis licenses that can be issued, opting instead to only require that no person or entity hold more than 15% of the total retail cannabis licenses in the province.[102] This prompted one industry leader to state, "Alberta in terms of the retail licensing makes sense. They seem to have gotten it right sort of right off the bat".[103] It should nonetheless be pointed out that the above nationwide supply shortage trend also had its own specific impact in Alberta. Supply shortages caused the AGLC to issue a temporary moratorium on new license issuance, but, "Despite that moratorium, Alberta led the nation in the total number of retail stores established in the first year of the legal market".[104] This is perhaps unsurprising given the province's cultural and political pro-business history,[105] but the impact of less regulation is nonetheless stark in comparison to the situation in Ontario discussed above. Alberta has been characterized as a province that did well by having many stores relative to its population.[106] Moreover, the province's less restrictive regulatory approach to issuing retail licenses has meant that its "market was relatively well-served in its initial stages".[107] Myran et al argue that "Two years post-legalisation, Alberta, the province with the highest per capita legal cannabis stores, had 24 times more stores per capita than Quebec, the province with the fewest".[108] It is subsequently suggested that the less regulated, private retail system in the province has accelerated the move from an illicit to a legal, non-medical cannabis market, thus capturing "a higher proportion of the total market".[109] In another contrast to Ontario,

---

101 "Alberta Cannabis Framework and Legislation" (n.d.), online: *Government of Alberta* #x003C;www.alberta.ca/cannabis-framework.aspx>
102 Ben-Ishai, *supra* note 30, at 247
103 Participant R, *supra* note 45
104 De Koning & McArdle, *supra* note 19, at 377
105 Watson et al, *supra* note 62, at 1698: "With the exception of a current government monopoly on online sales, this model of cannabis regulation is consistent with the high degree of commercialization found in the province's approach to alcohol regulation, which has entailed fully private alcohol retail sales since 1994"
106 Armstrong, *supra* note 48, at 8
107 De Koning & McArdle, *supra* note 19, at 377
108 Myran et al, *supra* note 70, at 6
109 *Ibid* at 7

"The data suggest that the relatively diffuse nature of Alberta's brick-and-mortar retail store network served the market fairly well, as per-capita and total sales in Alberta were quite high relative to other provinces".[110] It thus appears that Alberta has not suffered from the same issue of "clustered" retailed stores that occurred in Ontario. Alberta has not been totally immune to growing pains, with provincial restrictions on transferring product between stores apparently preventing "chains from efficiently managing their stock and ensuring the right product mix for their local customer demographic".[111] Nonetheless, one study suggests that Alberta's implementation has so far been a success in combatting the illicit market, with users in the province "significantly less likely to purchase from a dealer post-legalization".[112] One of the province's biggest cities, Edmonton, hopes to further continue this trend by drastically reducing the business license fees for cannabis retail shops in 2022.[113] Another significant change is on the horizon: The Government has announced that it will no longer engage in online sales, opting instead to further privatize its model and allow its current 744 retail license holders (and any future bricks-and-mortar retailers) to engage in online sales that will begin on March 8, 2022.[114]

3.6 Provincial Implementation of Cannabis Legalization in Quebec

There are no two provinces that have had a more opposite implementation of cannabis legalization than Quebec and Alberta. Quebec had strong stakeholder endorsement of a public-health oriented approach that would prioritize health and safety over commercial interests.[115] A focus on the protection of public health dominated the legislative process, and, as a result, the province implemented a retail market that is entirely managed through crown corporations.[116] The Société des alcools du Québec (SAQ), which oversees the provision of alcohol in the province, became the provincial wholesale distributor of cannabis, setting up a subsidiary for the provincial retail of cannabis (The Société québécoise du cannabis, or SQDC).[117] While Quebec has a reputation for progressive social policy in other areas, its approach to cannabis has been argued to be the most restrictive

---

110 De Koning & McArdle, *supra* note 19, at 377
111 *Ibid* at 375
112 Hathaway, Cullen & Walters, *supra* note 88, at 320
113 Dustin Cook, "High Business Licence Fees for Edmonton Cannabis Retail Shops to Be Slashed by 90 Percent in 2022" (18 August 2021), online: *Edmonton Journal* <https://edmontonjournal.com/news/local-news/edmonton-cannabis-store-licence-fees-to-drop-by-90-per-cent-in-2022-prompting-tax-levy-increase>
114 Janet French, "Alberta Stores Preparing as Online Cannabis Sales to Go Private in March" (21 February 2022), online: *CBC News* #x003C;www.cbc.ca/news/canada/edmonton/alberta-cannabis-online-sales-private-1.6357872>
115 Watson et al, *supra* note 62, at 1696
116 De Koning & McArdle, *supra* note 19, 387
117 *Ibid*

66 Provincial Implementation

in Canada as: 1) the province prohibits the home cultivation of the substance, despite the fact that this was made legal under the federal law; 2) the province has the highest minimum legal age (21) for cannabis consumption; and 3) the Coalition Avenir Quebec (CAQ) government has prohibited the consumption of cannabis in public and has previously suggested that it may limit cannabis possession amounts to 15 grams (half of what is allowed federally).[118] This restrictive approach has had a number of implications for the legal cannabis rollout in Quebec. One study suggests that product choice in Quebec is minimal compared to other provinces.[119] This, of course, leads to concerns that consumers may turn to the illicit market when a preferred product of choice is not otherwise available. Product access is also minimal relative to other provinces, as the province has severely constrained both the number of licensed producers and the number of retail stores allowed to open.[120] In this sense, Quebec and Alberta sit entirely opposite on two divergent sides of a spectrum, with the latter province accounting for 24 times more stores per capita than the former.[121] A recent study suggested that jurisdictions adding more stores get substantial increases in legal sales but limited increases in prevalence, suggesting that a province like Quebec could increase access without necessarily contributing to increased use.[122] If the province decides to maintain its restrictive approach to implementation, it may continue to be subject to a criticism that

> restricting access to legal avenues for cannabis possession has the unintended consequence of driving consumers to the grey or black market. The entrepreneurs in other provinces may target Quebecois consumers given the ease of cross-provincial shopping, while black market dealers continue to operate within the province, using well-established illicit business models.[123]

Some news reports suggest that the black market is continuing to thrive in the province, particularly through online sales.[124] The province's restrictive approach has also extended to medical cannabis. Quebec has the lowest amount of medical prescriptions in the country (21, 692), prompting further concerns that the government's strict regulations for healthcare professionals are further re-directing

---

118 Benoit and Levesque, *supra* note 10

119 Levesque, *supra* note 61, at 23: The SQDC reports that around 200 products were available in branch or online for 2019–2020. In Ontario, the OCS instead reported no less than 1,567 items available during the same year

120 De Koning & McArdle, *supra* note 19, at 387: A retail store to population ratio is estimated to be around one retail outlet for every 500, 000 Quebec residents

121 Myran et al, *supra* note 70, at 6

122 Armstrong, *supra* note 48, at 5

123 De Koning & McArdle, *supra* note 19, at 388

124 Thomas Quinn, "The Black Market for Cannabis and Mushrooms Is Alive and Well Online" (12 May 2021), online: *CULT MTL* <https://cultmtl.com/2021/05/black-market-cannabis-and-mushrooms-alive-and-well-online-edibles-sqdc-quebec-websites-sales-mail-order-websites/>

Provincial Implementation 67

sales towards the black market.[125] Quebec has remained stubbornly committed to its home cultivation ban. After a 2019 superior court decision found the ban unconstitutional, the government launched an appeal that was successful before the Quebec Court of Appeal.[126] The issue thus seems destined for the Supreme Court, with a potential landmark ruling on Canadian federalism and cannabis implementation the likely outcome.

3.7 Provincial Implementation of Cannabis Legalization in British Columbia

Similar to Alberta, the province of British Columbia (BC) does not limit the overall number of retail cannabis licenses that can be issued but does place a limit on any individual entity holding more than the maximum of eight licenses.[127] Unlike Alberta (or any other province), British Columbia operates a hybrid public-private system that mirrors its regulation of alcohol. Under this system, the BC Liquor Distribution Branch (LDB) oversees cannabis online sales and retail sales through government-run stores, while the Liquor and Cannabis Regulation Branch oversees the licensing of private retail stores.[128] The province has a unique history with pre-existing medical dispensaries and a well-established "legacy market", and, as such, it has been suggested that,

> In BC, both total sales and per capita sales numbers suggest that the legal market was both underserved by the number of retail outlets and that the conversion rate of customers purchasing from illegal black market outlets to legal outlets lagged.[129]

As the province has attempted to transition to legal cannabis implementation, entrepreneurs in the legal space struggled to compete with the variety and cost of cannabis products available elsewhere. As noted by De Koning and McArdle,

> The differences in prices were particularly challenging: In the early stages of legalization, price and selection issues reflected both the expenses of Health Canada's regulation of licensed producers, including stringent quality controls and the operational hiccups of the provincial distribution operations. To make matters worse for the entrepreneurs running licensed stores, BC

---

125 Catherine Paradis, "More Than 2 Years After Legalization, Quebec's Cannabis Industry Lags Behind" (4 April 2021), online: *CBC News* #x003C;www.cbc.ca/news/canada/montreal/quebec-cannabis-industry-profits-provinces-1.5975350>

126 David Brown, "Court of Appeal Sides with Quebec on Home Grow Ban, Next Step Is Supreme Court" (3 September 2021), online: *Stratcann* <https://stratcann.com/2021/09/03/court-of-appeal-sides-with-quebec-on-home-grow-ban-next-step-is-supreme-court/>

127 Ben-Ishai, *supra* note 30, at 247

128 Watson et al, *supra* note 105, at 1698

129 De Koning & McArdle, *supra* note 19, at 377–378

68 Provincial Implementation

Cannabis Online sold directly to consumers at a price 30% lower than they could afford to match and also offered more variety than they could.[130]

Moreover, some entrepreneurs seeking to transition into the regulated market have indicated that the long and arduous licensing process may be actively discouraging market entry.[131] Figures supplied by the province to Statistics Canada have also indicated a disproportionate share of unlicensed cannabis production dominating the market ($1.24 billion for unlicensed compared with $765 million licensed in 2019).[132] Despite the province's unique issues (largely stemming from its robust pre-legalization legacy market), its provincial implementation has been categorized as a "less restrictive model that is more favourable to the cannabis industry than Ontario or Quebec".[133] Also, to its credit, the province has recently taken steps to bring those in the illegal grey market under the umbrella of legal sales. The cannabis business transition initiative program provides financial and organizational assistance to illegal producers to help them transition to the formal economy, and it has been argued that "this strategy could tackle the problem of transition at its source".[134] Other provinces should also take note of the government's "B.C. Indigenous cannabis project", launched on January 18, 2022, with an eye towards further promoting cannabis businesses with Indigenous ownership.[135]

3.8 Provincial Implementation of Cannabis Legalization in Saskatchewan

Both academics and cannabis industry leaders have recognized the success of various aspects of Saskatchewan's legal cannabis implementation. Saskatchewan is the only province in Canada where a provincial wholesaler is not acting as an intermediate between producers and retailers.[136] Instead, the province empowered its Liquor and Gaming Authority (SLGA) to regulate the wholesale and retail of cannabis

---

130 *Ibid* at 382

131 Angela Jung & Bhinder Sajan, "Why Are British Columbians Still Buying Pot on the Black Market 1 Year After Legalization?" (17 October 2019), online: *CTV News* <https://bc.ctvnews.ca/why-are-british-columbians-still-buying-pot-on-the-black-market-1-year-after-legalization-1.4643258>

132 Megan Turcato, "B.C.'s Unlicensed Cannabis Producers Brought in $1.24B in 2019" (24 June 2020), online: *Global News* <https://globalnews.ca/news/7099004/unlicensed-cannabis-revenue-2019/>

133 Levesque, *supra* note 61, at 27

134 *Ibid* at 48

135 Maya Stano, Emma Hobbs & Lauren Mar, "British Columbia Launches the BC Indigenous Cannabis Project" (1 February 2022), online: *Lexology* #x003C;www.lexology.com/library/detail.aspx?g=5ee3fb29-03a2-4c10-bf3b-05434b3ce745>

136 Levesque, *supra* note 61, at 42

done entirely by private companies in an "open market system".[137] Per capita data suggests that the ratio of retail outlets to population has been fairly high in Saskatchewan.[138] The province first took a phased approach to the issuing of licenses, allowing for 51 in the first stage and placing no limits on the number of licenses that a person or entity can possess.[139] In clear contrast to the above described "clumsy" lottery process in Ontario, Saskatchewan pre-qualified applicants in a formal process before the lottery and followed up with a further process to ensure that applicants drawn were in compliance with regulatory standards.[140] As a result, Saskatchewan's implementation was ahead of the curve compared to other provinces in a number of ways, including: 1) the province avoided operational delays in the opening of retail outlets and was open for business on the first day of legal sales – October 17, 2018; 2) retailers in the province had no issue accessing cannabis stock in the early phase of legalization, despite the supply chain issues that plagued the rest of the country; and 3) the province was also ahead of the "second wave" of legalization (i.e. that of edible products), with edibles stocked in stores before Christmas while other provinces struggled to deal with the added step of government distribution.[141] As a result, Saskatchewan's laws have been described as providing for "clear procedures and responsibilities . . . that would be a good exemplar for other provinces to consider".[142] Cannabis industry leaders echoed this favourable evaluation of Saskatchewan's implementation. As noted above,[143] Saskatchewan appears to be a leading province when it comes to incentivizing Indigenous owners and partners. Another industry leader provided this positive evaluation:

> I think the provincial model in Saskatchewan is the most optimal one. I can send a product directly from the Licensed Producer to a retail store to get to the end consumer. Aside from a small excise tax that is paid to the province there's no middle man. The middle man just clouds and interferes with the process.[144]

As a result of its unique approach to legal cannabis implementation, it has been suggested that cannabis prices in 2022 are more or less on par with the illicit market, which certainly bodes well for legalization's stated policy goal of eliminating said market.[145]

---

137 "Cannabis Legalization" (n.d.), online: *Saskatchewan Liquor and Gaming Authority* #x003C;www.slga.com/faqs#group-4-15>
138 De Koning & McArdle, *supra* note 19, at 377
139 Ben-Ishai, *supra* note 30, at 229
140 De Koning & McArdle, *supra* note 19, at 383
141 *Ibid*
142 Ben-Ishai, *supra* note 30, at 251
143 Participant R, *supra* note 45
144 Participant K, *supra* note 24
145 Ian Duffy, "How Saskatchewan Cannabis Prices Have Plummeted" (11 February 2022), online: *Global News* <https://globalnews.ca/news/8614408/saskatchewan-cannabis-prices-market-saturated/>

70 Provincial Implementation

3.9 Provincial Implementation of Cannabis Legalization in Manitoba

Manitoba's approach to legal cannabis implementation evidences an interesting (and perhaps contradictory) blend of a more restrictive, public-health oriented approach (similar to Quebec) with a less restrictive, private retail model (similar to Alberta and Saskatchewan). Similar to Quebec, the province has considered lowering possession amounts and has banned home cultivation, leading academic commentators to argue that Manitoba's laws "do not respect the spirit of the federal law (stop criminalizing cannabis consumption, fight the organized crime market) and perhaps even totally contradict it (criminalization of personal cultivation, restriction of legal possession quantities)".[146] As was the case in Quebec, the move to ban home cultivation is before the Manitoba courts, led by private citizen Jessie Lavoie and supported by seven legal experts.[147] On the other hand, Manitoba's decisions in other areas of implementation are far more in line with its more business-friendly neighbours in the prairies. Like Alberta, the province controls distribution and vests authority with its Liquor, Gaming and Cannabis Authority (LGCA) to oversee licenses to private retail stores that engage in bricks-and-mortar and online retail sales.[148] Similar to Saskatchewan, initial license lotteries pre-qualified applicants, leading to a (relatively restrained) selection of four companies to initially head up the province's rollout.[149] The government subsequently held another lottery aimed at ensuring access in more remote communities, hoping to achieve a previously stated goal of combating the black market by ensuring that 90% of the province's population was within a 30-minute drive of a cannabis store.[150] Similar to both Alberta and Saskatchewan, a less restrictive regulatory approach to issuing retail licenses allowed Manitoba to maintain a good ratio of retail outlets to population and serve its market well in the early years of legalization.[151] As was the case in Alberta, it has been suggested that users in Manitoba are significantly less likely to purchase cannabis from an illicit dealer than in other provinces.[152] This trend is likely to continue given the future possibility of increased cannabis delivery access. Manitoba and Saskatchewan are the only provinces where licensed cannabis shops can deliver products through third-party companies, and the country's first-ever on-demand cannabis delivery

---

146　Benoit & Levesque, *supra* note 10

147　Simon Stones, "Manitoba Man Challenges Province's Recreational Cannabis Growing Ban" (29 January 2021), online: *CTV News* <https://winnipeg.ctvnews.ca/manitoba-man-challenges-province-s-recreational-cannabis-growing-ban-1.5288491>

148　"Buying Cannabis in Manitoba" (n.d.), online: *Liquor, Gaming and Cannabis Authority of Manitoba* <https://lgcamb.ca/cannabis/>

149　De Koning & McArdle, *supra* note 19, at 384

150　*Ibid* at 383

151　*Ibid* at 377

152　Hathaway, Cullen & Walters, *supra* note 88, at 320

app, The Half Circle, launched in Winnipeg in late December 2021.[153] The province has been commended for its speed and flexibility in dealing with third-party app cannabis delivery services, which have been pointed to as an example of the public-private partnership that is core to Manitoba's approach.[154]

3.10 Provincial Implementation of Cannabis Legalization in Canada's Eastern Provinces

New Brunswick, Nova Scotia, Newfoundland and Labrador, and Prince Edward Island make up the country's eastern provinces. These provinces have been grouped together in this analysis, not only because of their geographic, political, and cultural proximities, but also because of the relative similarities of their cannabis regulatory schemes. All four provinces instituted government monopolies for cannabis wholesale. This reflected the model of alcohol distribution in the provinces, but New Brunswick quickly realized that the model did not work in their province, losing $12 million dollars in the first six months of business.[155] As a result, the province tried to change to a "concessionaire model", maintaining provincial authority over regulation while allowing a private business to operate its system with the following features: 1) cannabis distribution is still a monopoly, but companies were invited to submit bids to run the system for 20 years under a renewable, long-term monopoly model; 2) the provincial government acts strictly as a regulator and not an operator; and 3) the model relies on close monitoring by government regulators to ensure compliance with contractual commitments, regulations and standards of service.[156] After eliciting only eight responses through its Request for Proposal (RFP) process, the province decided against changing its model in March 2021 and instead retained its government monopoly model.[157] Facing increased concerns that black market dispensaries are thriving, the province has recently suggested that it may consider amendments that allow it to license private retailers to operate under the provincial umbrella.[158] If New Brunswick, Nova Scotia or Prince Edward Island consider moving towards licensing private retailers in the future, they may look to the close neighbour experience of Newfoundland. The province was the only one out of the four provinces to allow licenses for private brick and mortar retail stores. While

153 Kathryn Tindale, "On-Demand Cannabis Delivery App Launches in Manitoba" (14 December 2021), online: *Mugglehead* <https://mugglehead.com/on-demand-cannabis-delivery-app-launches-in-manitoba/>
154 De Koning & McArdle, *supra* note 19, at 384
155 *Ibid* at 388
156 *Ibid* at 389
157 Jennifer Vienneau, "News Release: Cannabis NB Retail Model Will Be Retained, RFP Discontinued" (19 March 2021), online: *Government of New Brunswick* <https://www2.gnb.ca/content/gnb/en/departments/finance/news/news_release.2021.03.0214.html>
158 Marie Sutherland, "Private Cannabis N.B. Stores Coming to Province to Combat Black Market" (30 November 2021), online: *CBC News* #x003C;www.cbc.ca/news/canada/new-brunswick/cannabis-nb-retail-outlets-expand-1.6268261>

72   Provincial Implementation

there is sparse data on these provinces (particularly in comparison to Quebec, Alberta and Ontario), it appears as though Newfoundland's private retail store system has led to greater store access. For example, in the final quarter of 2020, Newfoundland was the only eastern province with an average number of stores above the overall Canadian average (41.29 stores per million residents).[159] Nova Scotia (21.76), Prince Edward Island (29.58) and New Brunswick (29.88) were all below the Canadian average of 38.65.[160] A recent study suggested that Newfoundland's model has been performing well, ending the 2021 fiscal year with $52 million in sales, a 36% increase from the previous year.[161]

There are a few other unique regulatory aspects that stand out in the eastern provinces. For example, Nova Scotia was the only Canadian province to allow cannabis and liquor sales in the same premises, making it the only province whose cannabis and liquor operations are fully integrated into the same organization.[162] As such, given the unique nature of this approach and the commonly stated objective of provinces to not encourage cannabis use, future research might usefully look at whether the co-availability of cannabis and alcohol in the same location had an impact on consumption and public health. The most recently available figures suggest that cannabis sales in the province have increased as prices have dropped nearly 40% since legalization in 2018.[163] As such, future research into Nova Scotia's market could also focus on the connection between price and consumption. Finally, those looking for a case study on how to effectively combat the black market may also wish to look further at the (albeit small sample) example of Prince Edward Island. While the province's population and market are small compared to pretty much every other province in the country, it has been argued that Prince Edward Island "opened ample stores for its small market, offered relatively low prices and avoided most of the dry product shortages. Thus, by September 2019, legal recreational products represented 70% of the province's consumption".[164] Further analysis of the province's more recent performance was hindered by a lack of available data, again underscoring the need for greater data collection and transparency across all provinces.

3.11 Conclusion: Is a Course Correction Necessary?

As discussed earlier in this chapter, much more research on provincial implementation will need to be done (and released) in order to discern whether the

---

159 Armstrong, *supra* note 47, at 3

160 *Ibid*

161 "Newfoundland Cannabis Sales Top 35% Growth, Rising to CA$52 Million" (17 December 2021), online: *MJBIZDaily* <https://mjbizdaily.com/newfoundland-cannabis-sales-grow-35-annually-to-52-million/>

162 Wesley & Murray, *supra* note 11, at 1090

163 Jack Julian, "Legal Marijuana Prices Have Dropped 40% in Nova Scotia Since 2019" (15 November 2021), online: *CBC News* #x003C;www.cbc.ca/news/canada/nova-scotia/legal-marijuana-prices-dropping-nslc-1.6243347>

164 Armstrong, *supra* note 59, at 8

stated objectives of legalization (i.e. protection of public health and elimination of the black market) are being effectively balanced. This section has shown that some provinces (Alberta) are on the far end of that spectrum towards black market elimination, while others (Quebec) have implemented very restrictive cannabis regimes with an eye towards protecting public health. The optimal balance, which may lie somewhere in between, will become much clearer with the passage of time and the collection of greater amounts of data. With that said, one nationwide problem with provincial implementation (market concentration) in need of a course correction would require a coordinated effort across all provincial governments. As noted by Levesque, three of the biggest stakeholders (Aphria, Canopy Growth and Aurora) now account for more than 60% of the market and "an oligopoly for the selling of a product like this one is not good news for any stakeholder in legalization, whether it is the other companies, regulatory agencies, public health experts or users".[165] As one cannabis industry leader noted:

> Look at the stats. Look at the amount of cannabis consumers vs. what Canopy is growing. Like just one LP has more supply now for two years than all of the others combined that can service the cannabis market. It's absolutely ridiculous. . . . What's going to end up happening is one of two things: they're [smaller producers] all going to go bankrupt, or they're all going to sell to the big guys and it's going to be a market that's controlled by the big players like it is in alcohol, you know Labatt and Molson.[166]

Taking these statistics and arguments into account, the following course correction suggested by Levesque seems to be as necessary as it is reasonable: "Governments should resort to mechanisms favouring the smallest producers. These mechanisms should in particular cover the accompaniment of small stakeholders (including illegal market actors), the valuation of their products and the fiscal means to redistribute capital within the market".[167]

Armstrong, Michael, "Canada's Provinces and Territories Should Disclose Cannabis Data to Support Research" (2021) 193:10 CMAJ 341

Armstrong, Michael, "Legal Cannabis Market Shares During Canada's First Year of Recreational Legalization" (2021) 88 International Journal of Drug Policy, DOI: <https://doi.org/10.1016/j.drugpo.2020.103028>

Armstrong, Michael, "Relationships Between Increases in Canadian Cannabis Stores, Sales and Prevalence" (2021) 228 Drug and Alcohol Dependence, DOI: <https://doi.org/10.1016/j.drugalcdep.2021.109071>

Ben-Ishai, Stephanie, "Bankruptcy for Cannabis Companies: Canada's Newest Export?" (2020) 27:2 University of Miami International and Comparative Law Review 226

---

165 Levesque, *supra* note 61, at 70
166 Participant K, *supra* note 24
167 Levesque, *supra* note 61, at 70

74 *Provincial Implementation*

Benoit, Maude & Levesque, Gabriel, "What Can Cannabis Legalisation Teach Us About Canadian Federalism?" (2019), online: *Fifty Shades of Federalism* <http://50shadesoffederalism.com/policies/what-can-cannabis-legalisation-teach-us-about-canadian-federalism/>

Bowal, Peter, Kisska-Schulze, Kathryn, Haigh, Richard & Ng, Adrienne, "Regulating Cannabis: A Comparative Exploration of Canadian Legalization" (2020) 57:4 American Business Law Journal 677

Brown, David, "Court of Appeal Sides with Quebec on Home Grow Ban, Next Step Is Supreme Court" (3 September 2021), online: *Stratcann* <https://stratcann.com/2021/09/03/court-of-appeal-sides-with-quebec-on-home-grow-ban-next-step-is-supreme-court/>

Canadian Centre on Substance Use and Addiction, "Cannabis Retail During COVID-19" (January 2021), online (pdf): *Canadian Centre on Substance Use and Addiction*<www.ccsa.ca/sites/default/files/2021-01/CCSA-COVID-19-Cannabis-Retail-Policy-Brief-2021-en.pdf>

Constitution Act, 1867 (UK), 30 & 31 Vict, c 3, Reprinted in RSC 1985, App II, No 5, s 91

Conway, Jan, "Number of Cannabis Stores in Canada as of June 2021, by Region" (17 September 2021), online: *Statista* <www.statista.com/statistics/1035996/number-of-cannabis-stores-by-region-canada>

Cook, Dustin, "High Business Licence Fees for Edmonton Cannabis Retail Shops to Be Slashed by 90 Percent in 2022" (18 August 2021), online: *Edmonton Journal* <https://edmontonjournal.com/news/local-news/edmonton-cannabis-store-licence-fees-to-drop-by-90-per-cent-in-2022-prompting-tax-levy-increase>

Crosby, Andrew, "Contesting Cannabis: Indigenous Jurisdiction and Legalization" (2019) 62:4 Canadian Public Administration 634

De Koning, Alice & McArdle, John, "Implementing Regulation in an Emerging Industry: A Multiple-Province Perspective" (2021) 55:2 Journal of Canadian Studies 362

Duffy, Ian, "How Saskatchewan Cannabis Prices Have Plummeted" (11 February 2022), online: *Global News* <https://globalnews.ca/news/8614408/saskatchewan-cannabis-prices-market-saturated/>

French, Janet, "Alberta Stores Preparing as Online Cannabis Sales to Go Private in March" (21 February 2022), online: *CBC News* <www.cbc.ca/news/canada/edmonton/alberta-cannabis-online-sales-private-1.6357872>

Government of Alberta, "Alberta Cannabis Framework and Legislation" (n.d.), online: *Government of Alberta* <www.alberta.ca/cannabis-framework.aspx>

Hathaway, Andrew, Cullen, Greggory & Walters, David, "How Well Is Cannabis Legalization Curtailing the Illegal Market? A Multi-wave Analysis of Canada's National Cannabis Survey" (2021) 55:2 Journal of Canadian Studies 307

Israel, Solomon, "Ontario Overtakes Alberta to Lead Canada in Legal Cannabis Stores" (17 December 2021), online: *MJBiz Daily* <https://mjbizdaily.com/ontario-overtakes-alberta-to-lead-canada-in-legal-cannabis-stores/>

Julian, Jack, "Legal Marijuana Prices Have Dropped 40% in Nova Scotia Since 2019" (15 November 2021), online: *CBC News* <www.cbc.ca/news/canada/nova-scotia/legal-marijuana-prices-dropping-nslc-1.6243347>

Jung, Angela & Sajan, Bhinder, "Why Are British Columbians Still Buying Pot on the Black Market 1 Year After Legalization?" (17 October 2019), online: *CTV News* <https://bc.ctvnews.ca/why-are-british-columbians-still-buying-pot-on-the-black-market-1-year-after-legalization-1.4643258>

Levesque, Gabriel, "Cannabis Legalization in Canada. Case Studies: British Columbia, Ontario and Quebec" (2020), online (pdf): *French Monitoring Centre for Drugs and Drug Addiction* <https://en.ofdt.fr/BDD/publications/docs/ASTRACAN_Levesque-EN.pdf>

Liquor, Gaming & Cannabis Authority of Manitoba, "Buying Cannabis in Manitoba" (n.d.), online: *Liquor, Gaming and Cannabis Authority of Manitoba* <https://lgcamb.ca/cannabis/>

MJBiz Daily, "Newfoundland Cannabis Sales Top 35% Growth, Rising to CA$52 Million" (17 December 2021), online: *MJBIZDaily* <https://mjbizdaily.com/newfoundland-cannabis-sales-grow-35-annually-to-52-million/>

Myran, Daniel, Staykov, Emiliyan, Cantor, Nathan, Taljaard, Monica, Quach, Bradley, Hawken, Steven & Tanuseputro, Peter, "How Has Access to Legal Cannabis Changed Over Time? An Analysis of the Cannabis Retail Market in Canada 2 Years Following the Legalization of Recreational Cannabis" (2021) Drug and Alcohol Review, DOI: <https://doi.org/10.1111/dar.13351>

Ontario Cannabis Store, "About Us" (n.d.), online: *Ontario Cannabis Store* <https://ocs.ca/pages/about-us>

Paradis, Catherine, "More Than 2 Years After Legalization, Quebec's Cannabis Industry Lags Behind" (4 April 2021), online: *CBC News* <www.cbc.ca/news/canada/montreal/quebec-cannabis-industry-profits-provinces-1.5975350>

Quinn, Thomas, "The Black Market for Cannabis and Mushrooms Is Alive and Well Online" (12 May 2021), online: *CULT MTL* <https://cultmtl.com/2021/05/black-market-cannabis-and-mushrooms-alive-and-well-online-edibles-sqdc-quebec-websites-sales-mail-order-websites/>

Saskatchewan Liquor and Gaming Authority, "Cannabis Legalization" (n.d.), online: *Saskatchewan Liquor and Gaming Authority* <www.slga.com/faqs#group-4-15>

Stano, Maya, Hobbs, Emma & Mar, Lauren, "British Columbia Launches the BC Indigenous Cannabis Project" (1 February 2022), online: *Lexology* <www.lexology.com/library/detail.aspx?g=5ee3fb29-03a2-4c10-bf3b-05434b3ce745>

Stones, Simon, "Manitoba Man Challenges Province's Recreational Cannabis Growing Ban" (29 January 2021), online: *CTVNews* <https://winnipeg.ctvnews.ca/manitoba-man-challenges-province-s-recreational-cannabis-growing-ban-1.5288491>

Sutherland, Marie, "Private Cannabis N.B. Stores Coming to Province to Combat Black Market" (30 November 2021), online: *CBC News* <www.cbc.ca/news/canada/new-brunswick/cannabis-nb-retail-outlets-expand-1.6268261>

Tindale, Kathryn, "On-Demand Cannabis Delivery App Launches in Manitoba" (14 December 2021), online: *Mugglehead* <https://mugglehead.com/on-demand-cannabis-delivery-app-launches-in-manitoba/>

Train, Andrew & Snow, Dave, "Cannabis Policy Diffusion in Ontario and New Brunswick: Coercion, Learning, and Replication" (2019) 62:4 Canadian Public Administration 549

Turcato, Megan, "B.C.'s Unlicensed Cannabis Producers Brought in $1.24B in 2019" (24 June 2020), online: *Global News* <https://globalnews.ca/news/7099004/unlicensed-cannabis-revenue-2019/>

Vienneau, Jennifer, "News Release: Cannabis NB Retail Model Will Be Retained, RFP Discontinued" (19 March 2021), online: *Government of New Brunswick* <https://www2.gnb.ca/content/gnb/en/departments/finance/news/news_release.2021.03.0214.html>

Wadsworth, Elle, Driezen, Pete, Pacula, Rosalie & Hammond, David, "Cannabis Flower Prices and Transitions to Legal Sources After Legalization in Canada,

2019–2020" (2022) 231 Drug and Alcohol Dependence, DOI: <https://doi.org/10.1016/j.drugalcdep.2021.109262>

Watson, Tara Marie, Hyshka, Elaine, Bonato, Sarah & Rueda, Sergio, "Early-Stage Cannabis Regulatory Policy Planning Across Canada's Four Largest Provinces: A Descriptive Overview" (2019) 54:10 Substance Use & Misuse 1691

Wesley, Jared, "Beyond Prohibition: The Legalization of Cannabis in Canada" (2019) 62:4 Canadian Public Administration 533

Wesley, Jared & Murray, Kyle, "To Market or Demarket? Public-Sector Branding of Cannabis in Canada" (2021) 53:7 Administration & Society 1078

White, Erik, "With Dozens of Pot Shops Popping Up Across Northern Ontario, Legal Weed Market Could Be at Saturation Point" (24 January 2022), online: *CBC News* <www.cbc.ca/news/canada/sudbury/cannabis-market-northern-ontario-1.6321293>

4 Status of Drug Legalization in Other Federalist Constitutional Democracies

This chapter provides a comprehensive account of cannabis (and wider drug) prohibition and legalization in jurisdictions around the world. Jurisdictions are grouped into the broad categories of Commonwealth Jurisdictions,[1] European Countries,[2] Latin American nations,[3] and several states within the United States.[4] The chapter proceeds with alphabetical ordering and thus avoids presenting one jurisdiction before another simply because of a subjective assessment of that jurisdiction's significance. Jurisdictions from Asian, African, and Middle Eastern regions are not discussed due to space constraints, lack of available (English language in particular) academic and documentary material, and lack of sufficient bases for comparative analysis (i.e. few federalist democracies and legal systems that are incomparable to Canada's common-law system). This chapter's analyses of 40 jurisdictions uncovers several trends that may be relevant for future drug policy reform discussions in Canada. Where space allows, this relevance is noted in this chapter, with further analyses of lessons Canada can learn from a comparative scan of relevant jurisdictions occurring in Chapter 5.[5] Academics, policy-makers, interested stakeholders, and individual citizens from these jurisdictions will also benefit from current information pertaining to the status of drug policy in their given jurisdiction.

4.1 Commonwealth Jurisdictions

4.1.1 Australia

As a federated nation comprised of the Commonwealth of Australia and eight states and territories, Australia provides for an interesting case study on drugs, as

1 Chapter 4.1
2 Chapter 4.2
3 Chapter 4.3
4 Chapter 4.4
5 Chapter 5.3

DOI: 10.4324/9781003200741-4

78 *Drug Legalization in Other Democracies*

"responses to illicit drug offences are largely the remit of states and territories".[6] As a result, much innovation has occurred across the country, largely driven by alternative diversionary programs implemented at the state level. While some small-scale initiatives (drug treatment courts, prosecution diversions) exist or have existed in different provinces across Canada, most of the country's responses to drug use stem from the federal government's jurisdiction in criminal law matters. An early example of "bottom up" regulatory change is South Australia's 1987 introduction of the Cannabis Expiation Notice, which "effectively decriminalized the use, possession and cultivation of cannabis for personal use, and enabled infringement notices for simple cannabis offences defined as possession of up to 100 grams of cannabis".[7] The Australian Capital Territory (ACT) and Northern Territory (NT) introduced similar civil penalty schemes for cannabis possession and cultivation for personal use in 1992 and 1996, respectively. These measures were indicative of a broader trend towards the use of diversionary approaches across the country: "Alternatives to arrest are deemed 'mainstream' and policy endeavours are focused on expanding drug diversion and/or the removal of criminal penalties for the use and possession of all illicit drugs".[8] More recently, two significant developments pertaining to cannabis policy liberalization have occurred. First, as of January 31, 2020, the ACT has passed amendments to its state legislation that allows for the exemption of criminal liability for those aged 18 and over to possess up to 50 grams of cannabis and grow up to two cannabis plants per person.[9] The legislation was met with concerns that it may be challenged by the federal government because of a direct conflict with federal laws on cultivation and possession, but in February 2021, the country's Prime Minister confirmed that the commonwealth would not intervene to overturn the law, stating "States will make their own decisions according to their own priorities".[10] Early evidence from the ACT experiment is encouraging – there have been no notable increases in cannabis use or impaired driving charges – and it seems likely that other states may follow suit, continuing a trend seen in the past with the Cannabis Expiation Notice.[11] Other states enacting similar legislation, coupled with increased levels of support for cannabis legalization,[12] could

---

6 Caitlin E. Hughes, "The Australian Experience and Opportunities for Cannabis Law Reform" in Tom Decorte, Simon Lenton & Chris Wilkins, eds, *Legalizing Cannabis: Experiences, Lessons and Scenarios* (London: Routledge, 2020) 337 at 337

7 *Ibid*

8 *Ibid* at 362

9 "Drugs and the Law" (8 October 2020), online: *Australian Capital Territory Policing* #x003C;www.police.act.gov.au/safety-and-security/alcohol-and-drugs/drugs-and-law>

10 Emily Ledger, "A Year on from Australian Capital Territory Cannabis Legalization" (1 Feburary 2021), online: *Canex* <https://canex.co.uk/a-year-on-from-australian-capital-territory-cannabis-legalisation/>

11 *Ibid*

12 Don Weatherburn, Sergey Alexeev & Michael Livingston, "Changes in and Correlates of Australian Public Attitudes Toward Illicit Drug Use" (2021) Drug and Alcohol Review, DOI: <https://doi.org/10.1111/dar.13426>

Drug Legalization in Other Democracies 79

potentially prompt changes to the country's federal legislation in the not too distant future. One federal party (the Green Party) has already made recreational cannabis legalization part of its platform.[13]

The second significant development pertaining to cannabis policy liberalization in Australia occurred in 2016 when the federal government passed the Narcotic Drugs Amendment Act.[14] That legislation enabled a range of cannabis-based products to be prescribed medicinally, with government-approved manufacturers and distributors providing products to licensed pharmacies for dispensing.[15] By 2020, more than 30,000 official approvals had been issued, allowing patients to access more than 100 different cannabis-based products.[16] When compared to the early years of Canada's (ineffective) medical legalization, these numbers represent significant progress. Further market evaluations paint a similarly optimistic picture. One study noted that Australia's medical cannabis market has grown three times year on year and estimates that 2021 sales will be in excess of $150 million dollars.[17] Nonetheless, some studies have suggested that a large proportion of medical cannabis users are obtaining their supply outside of the government-regulated system, primarily because they did not know a medical practitioner that was willing to prescribe (47.8% of respondents) or because medical cannabis was too expensive (18.4% of respondents).[18] It has been suggested that

> Until medical cannabis products are licensed as medicines with the TGA [Therapeutic Goods Administration], and subsidized under the Australian Pharmaceutical Benefits Scheme, it seems likely that the cost of unlicensed cannabis-based products will continue to force many people to source their medical cannabis illicitly.[19]

Australia's Therapeutic Goods Administration announced regulatory changes in late 2021 that should help address some of these issues, including simplified requirements around becoming an authorized prescriber.[20]

---

13 "Legalise Cannabis" (17 November 2021), online: *Australian Greens* <https://greens.org.au/campaigns/legalise-it>

14 Australia, *Narcotic Drugs Amendment Act* 2016, No 12

15 Nicholas Lintzeris et al, "Medical Cannabis Use in the Australian Community Following Introduction of Legal Access: The 2018–2019 Online Cross-Sectional Cannabis as Medicine Survey" (2020) 17:37 Harm Reduction Journal at 38

16 *Ibid*

17 "Australian Medicinal Cannabis Market: Patient, Product and Pricing Analysis" (August 2020), online (pdf): *Fresh Leaf Analytics* < https://freshleafanalytics.com.au/wp-content/uploads/2020/09/FreshLeaf-Analytics-Q3-2020.pdf>

18 Lintzeris et al, *supra* note 15, at 44

19 *Ibid* at 46

20 Anastasia Tsirtsakis, "Changes to Medicinal Cannabis Prescribing Pathways" (23 November 2021), online: *NewsGP* <https://www1.racgp.org.au/newsgp/clinical/changes-to-medicinal-cannabis-prescribing-pathways>

80 *Drug Legalization in Other Democracies*

4.1.2 Jamaica

For many people in Canada, the United States, and other Western liberal democracies, cannabis has long been as associated with Jamaican culture as the music of cultural icon Bob Marley. It would thus likely surprise many in these countries to learn that cannabis use and possession were criminalized in the country until 2015. This changed with the 2015 passage of the Dangerous Drug Amendment Act, which made consequential amendments to various aspects of Jamaica's cannabis laws, including: 1) allowing for the possession of two ounces or less of cannabis, with the only potential penalty being a small fine and no risk of arrest, prosecution, or criminal record; 2) establishing 18 as the legal age for possession of cannabis; 3) providing exemptions to all cannabis laws for those who use it for religious purposes as a sacrament in adherence to the Rastafarian faith; 4) allowing for personal cultivation up to a maximum of five cannabis plants per household; and 5) establishing a legal medical market to be overseen by the Cannabis Licensing Authority, which was put in charge of regulating the licensing for production and distribution of medical cannabis.[21] Under the Jamaican medical system, applicants can apply for cultivation, processing, transport, retail, and research and development licenses.[22] It is argued that this legislative reform was made possible "by the growing agitation in wider society, as was evident in the ganja civil society groups, with several groups of ganja growers, lobbyists, community organizers, and academics making public their views of support for more liberal ganja laws in Jamaica".[23]

The legislative reform has been met with criticism. One comprehensive academic survey of over 200 cannabis interest groups suggests that 81% of these groups do not believe that the right legislation was enacted.[24] Several factors were expressed as justification for this belief, including: 1) scepticism expressed by 72% of respondents about the sufficiency of the Cannabis Licensing Authority; 2) concerns about the licensing process and rigid fee structures faced by cannabis farmers, growers and processors; and 3) a widespread belief that the decriminalization model does not adequately address the continuing prevalence of the illicit cannabis market.[25] Subsequent studies have noted that despite large amounts of foreign investment in the medical cannabis sector, more regulatory reform is needed to protect the domestic industry and help facilitate the transition

---

21 Jamaica Ministry of Justice, "Fact Sheet: Dangerous Drugs (Amendment) Act 2015" (2020), online: <https://moj.gov.jm/news/dangerous-drugs-amendment-act-2015-fact-sheet>

22 Vicki J. Hanson, "Cannabis Policy Reform: Jamaica's Experience" in Tom Decorte, Simon Lenton & Chris Wilkins, eds, *Legalizing Cannabis: Experiences, Lessons and Scenarios* (London: Routledge, 2020) 375 at 383

23 *Ibid* at 379

24 Machel A. Emanuel, Andre Y. Haughton & K'adamawe K'nife, "Policy Analysis and Implications of Establishing the Caribbean Cannabis Economy (CCE): Lessons from Jamaica" (2018) 18:2 Drugs and Alcohol Today 99 at 104

25 *Ibid* at 104–105

of small-scale illegal cultivators into the legal regime.[26] The Jamaican model has also been criticized for not adequately allowing Rastafarians the opportunity to gain economic benefits from the industry, despite a long history of persecution under the previous laws.[27] The cumulative effect of these various concerns leads to the suggestion that, at least in the first six years since the passage of the 2015 legislative reforms, "the economic gains of the reforms, and the intended impact on social equity, have yet to materialize".[28] Severe weather systems in 2021 – heavy rains followed by an extended period of drought – had significant impacts on Jamaica's supply, with some reports additionally suggesting that COVID-19 curfews preventing traditional farming practices are also to blame for a lack of product.[29] Given what has been said above, it appears that some form of legislative or regulatory reform will be necessary in the years to come.

4.1.3 New Zealand

The prohibition of drugs in New Zealand is provided for by the 1975 Misuse of Drugs Act, which places various drugs into one of three classes (A, B, and C) and allows for potential imprisonment terms for possession ranging from three to six months depending on the class.[30] The law also provides for penalties for trafficking and cultivation, with cannabis cultivation potentially carrying a maximum penalty of seven years (by indictment) or two years (by summary conviction).[31] This is despite the fact that, according to a recent study, New Zealand has one of the highest cannabis use rates in the Western world.[32] Moreover, despite the criminal prohibitions noted above, enforcement focus on cannabis has substantially eased over the last decade, with less than 2000 arrests reported in 2017.[33] Following the 2017 national election, draft parameters for recreational cannabis legalization were established, and it appeared likely that the country would move

---

26 Marta Rychert, Machel A. Emanuel & Chris Wilkins, "Foreign Investment in Emerging Legal Medicinal Cannabis Markets: The Jamaica Case Study" (2021) 17:38 Globalization and Health at 47

27 Randy Goldson, "Ganja Struggles: Rastafari and the Contestation for Cannabis Rights in Jamaica" (2020) 55:4 Journal of Ecumenical Studies 569 at 593

28 Marta Rychert, Machel A. Emanuel & Chris Wilkins, "Issues in the Establishment of a Therapeutic Cannabis Market Under Jamaica's Dangerous Drugs Amendment Act 2015" (2020) 86 International Journal of Drug Policy at 8

29 Sharlene Hendricks & Dànice Coto, "Jamaica Faces Marijuana Shortage as Farmers Struggle" (5 Feburary 2021), online: *ABC News* <https://abcnews.go.com/International/wireStory/jamaica-faces-marijuana-shortage-farmers-struggle-75710269>

30 "Illicit Drugs – Offences and Penalties" online: *New Zealand Police* #x003C;www.police.govt.nz/advice/drugs-and-alcohol/illicit-drugs-offences-and-penalties>

31 *Ibid*

32 Benedikt Fischer & Chris Bullen, "Emerging Prospects for Non-Medical Cannabis Legalization in New Zealand: An Initial View and Contextualization" (2019) 40 International Journal of Drug Policy at 1

33 *Ibid*

82 *Drug Legalization in Other Democracies*

forward with legislative reform.[34] On October 17, 2020, New Zealand held the world's first national referendum involving a detailed bill for recreational cannabis legalization, with the legalization proposal narrowly defeated by a vote of 50.7% opposed to 48.4% in support.[35] A wide variety of explanations have been put forward as to why the proposal failed, including: 1) better organization and greater funding of the anti-reform campaign versus the pro-legalization campaign; 2) lack of political elite support for legalization, particularly from Prime Minister Jacinda Arden, who refused to disclose how she would vote prior to the referendum; 3) lack of specific evidence on the consequences of legalization, including risks of impaired driving, increased use, and impact on other legal and illegal substances; 4) a public perception that declining rates of arrest for cannabis use reduced the urgency for legalization; and 5) fears about the establishment of a commercial market under legalization.[36] It thus appears that recreational cannabis law reform will not occur any time soon. That said, the country did take steps towards allowing medical cannabis use for people with terminal illness or chronic pain via the passage of the 2018 Misuse of Drugs (Medicinal Cannabis) Amendment Act and subsequently implemented regulations for the medical cannabis scheme in 2020.[37] While these regulations set stringent minimum standards for products that have largely precluded access, there is optimism on the horizon for 2022 as domestic producers have begun to attain licenses.[38]

4.1.4 South Africa

Medical cannabis was legalized in South Africa in 2017 under the Cultivation of Cannabis and Manufacture of Cannabis-Related Pharmaceutical Products for Medical and Research Purposes regulations.[39] As of September 2021, only one medical cannabis prescription had been issued in South Africa,[40] and little to no academic or otherwise publicly available material exists to describe the

---

34 *Ibid* at 2
35 Marta Rychert & Chris Wilkins, "Why Did New Zealand's Referendum to Legalise Recreational Cannabis Fail?" (2021) 40:6 Drug and Alcohol Review at 877
36 *Ibid* at 878–879
37 "Medicinal Cannabis Agency – Background Information" (11 April 2020), online: *Ministry of Health NZ*#x003C;www.health.govt.nz/our-work/regulation-health-and-disability-system/medicinal-cannabis-agency/medicinal-cannabis-agency-background-information>
38 Carmen Doran, "Medicinal Cannabis Industry Not in Delivery Phase" (30 December 2021), online: *Scoop* #x003C;www.scoop.co.nz/stories/GE2112/S00155/medicinal-cannabis-industry-now-in-delivery-phase.htm>
39 "Cultivation of Cannabis and Manufacture of Cannabis-Related Pharmaceutical Products for Medicinal and Research Purposes" (November 2019), online (pdf): *South African Health Products Regulatory Authority* <https://sahpra.org.za/wp-content/uploads/2020/01/93b0b4262.44_Cannabiscultivation_v2_Nov2019.pdf>
40 Patricia Miller, "First Medical Cannabis Prescription Issued in South Africa" (14 September 2021), online: *Cannabis & Tech Today* <https://cannatechtoday.com/first-medical-cannabis-prescription-issued-in-south-africa/>

operation of this system. By contrast, there is a wealth of material on the topic of recreational cannabis, largely due to a landmark court ruling. In September 2018, South Africa's Constitutional Court found that Sections 4(b) and 5(b) of the Drugs and Drug Trafficking Act (1992) and Section 22A(9)(a)(1) of the Medicines and Related Substances Control Act were unconstitutional because they criminalized the use or possession in private (or cultivation in a private place) of cannabis for personal purposes.[41] The ruling effectively decriminalized these activities, with the Court arguing that it would be for parliament to decide the amount for personal possession and any further legislative reform, fueling speculation that calls for full legalization would be strengthened.[42] In the years since the ruling, this speculation has crystallized into a reality. In August 2021, South Africa's government revealed that it is working on a "master plan" for cannabis legalization that it believes will create as many as 25,000 jobs and a $1.9 billion USD cannabis industry.[43] Included within the plan's list of priorities is the signing of the Cannabis for Private Purposes Bill into law within the 2022/23 financial year.[44] Some of the key aspects of the legislation, which is a direct legislative response to the Constitutional Court judgment, are as follows: 1) it provides for expungements of minor criminal convictions; 2) it provides for stiff penalties, up to 15 years in prison, for those who sell cannabis to minors; and 3) it allows for a possession limit of 600 grams of cannabis per individual and also allows for home cultivation.[45] As of late 2021, specific details pertaining to the commercialization of the cannabis industry have yet to be revealed.[46] It has been suggested that 2022 will be something of a "make or break" year for the legal cannabis industry, with numerous regulatory issues in need of resolution.[47]

41 South Africa, *Minister of Justice and Constitutional Development and Others v Prince* [2018] ZACC 30
42 Charles Parry, Bronwyn Myers & Jonathan Caulkins, "Decriminalisation of Recreational Cannabis in South Africa" (2019) 392:10183 The Lancet 1804 at 1805
43 Paul Burkhardt, "South Africa Unveils US$1.9 Billion Cannabis Industry Plan" (25 August 2021), online: *Financial Post* <https://financialpost.com/cannabis/cannabis-business/south-africa-crafts-strategy-for-1-9-billion-cannabis-industry>
44 "New Cannabis Rules Proposed for South Africa- to Be Introduced Within Next 2 Years" (13 April 2021), online: *Business Tech* <https://businesstech.co.za/news/lifestyle/482625/new-cannabis-rules-proposed-for-south-africa-to-be-introduced-within-next-2-years/>
45 Sipho Sebele, "South Africa's Cannabis Bill Is Widely Unpopular – Here's Why" (2 September 2021), online: *Mugglehead Magazine* <https://mugglehead.com/south-africas-cannabis-bill-is-widely-unpopular-heres-why/>
46 Siseko Maposa, "Opinion: Siseko Maposa: The Complexities of SA's Cannabis Policy-More Integration Needed" (22 December 2021), online: *News24* #x003C;www.news24.com/news24/columnists/guestcolumn/opinion-siseko-maposa-the-complexities-of-sas-cannabis-policy-more-integration-needed-20211222>
47 Brett Hilton-Barber, "Pointers for the SA Cannabis Industry in 2022" (4 January 2022), online: *Cannabiz Africa* #x003C;www.cannabiz-africa.com/sa-cannabis-industry-2022/>

84 *Drug Legalization in Other Democracies*

4.1.5 United Kingdom

The 1971 Misuse of Drugs Act[48] allows for penalties for possession (as well as trafficking) of various drugs that vary depending on whether the drug in question is categorized as class A, B, or C. Cannabis was moved to class C in 2001,[49] dropping the penalty for possession to a maximum of two years, but was re-classified as a class B drug in 2009, increasing the maximum penalty for possession to five years.[50] Despite the harsh penalties, it is estimated that over 4.7 million people consume cannabis in the U.K., creating a black market economy estimated at £6 billion.[51] While the current conservative government has indicated little interest in cannabis policy reform, it seems as though there is support for more liberal initiatives in various parts of the United Kingdom. A growing number of police forces have been choosing to forego traditional criminal penalties in favour of "community resolutions" or fines, and, as a result, there has been a significant drop in offences for cannabis possession (160,733 in 2010/11 compared with 110,085 in 2019/20).[52] Moreover, there is widespread public support for legal cannabis, with one 2021 study showing that 52% of the population supports legalization while only 17% strongly opposes it.[53] A comprehensive and lengthy study by a coalition of academics, lawyers, civil society organizations, young people, and community stakeholders also adds an important social justice element to the conversation, noting that: 1) black people were stopped and searched for drugs at more than nine times the rate of white people; 2) black people were convicted of cannabis possession at nearly twelve times the rate of white people, despite lower rates of self-reported use; and 3) while arrests from drug searches halved for white people between 2010/11 and 2016/17, rates remained consistent for black people.[54] It is thus unsurprising that jurisdictions within the United Kingdom are considering, or have implemented, significant reform measures. According to the Scottish Drugs Form, the Scottish National Party recently backed the decriminalization of all drugs at a party conference, and the country's Health and Social Care Committee has released a report that urges

---

48 United Kingdom, *Misuse of Drugs Act* 1971, c 38

49 Alan Travis, "Cannabis Laws Eased in Drug Policy Shakeup" (24 October 2001), online: *The Guardian* #x003C;www.theguardian.com/society/2001/oct/24/drugsand alcohol>

50 Johnny Connolly, "Cannabis Again Reclassified in the UK" (1 January 1970), online: *Drugs and Alcohol* #x003C;www.drugsandalcohol.ie/12158/>

51 Liam O'Dowd, "Is the UK Any Closer to Legalizing Cannabis?" (4 January 2022), online: *Leafie* #x003C;www.leafie.co.uk/articles/will-the-uk-legalise-cannabis/>

52 Grahame Allen & Richard Tunnicliffe, "Drug Crime: Statistics for England and Wales" (23 December 2021), online (pdf): *United Kingdom House of Commons Library* <https://researchbriefings.files.parliament.uk/documents/CBP-9039/CBP-9039.pdf>

53 "Daily Question: 06/04/2021" (6 April 2021), online: *YouGov* <https://yougov.co.uk/topics/politics/survey-results/daily/2021/04/06/fcf4a/3>

54 Michael Shiner et al, "The Colour of Injustice: 'Race', Drugs and Law Enforcement in England and Wales" (31 January 2019), online (pdf): *Release* #x003C;www.release.org.uk/publications/ColourOfInjustice>

Drug Legalization in Other Democracies 85

decriminalization of drug possession for personal use from a criminal offence to a civil matter.[55] Closer to home, in London, mayor Sadiq Khan is reportedly developing a 2022 pilot scheme to implement a diversionary program in three London boroughs that would divert youth under 25 found in possession of small quantities of cannabis away from criminal sanctions and towards classes or counselling.[56] While neither the mayor of London nor the Scottish Parliament has the power to modify the United Kingdom's drug policy, Boris Johnson's conservative government may find that inaction is no longer a tenable policy response as pressures for reform mount in various parts of the United Kingdom.

While recreational drug and cannabis reform has remained stubbornly stagnant in the United Kingdom, some substantial developments have occurred in the country's medical cannabis sector. In 2018, Cannabis-Based Products for Medicinal Use (CBPMs) were rescheduled into Schedule 2 of the Misuse of Drugs Regulations 2001,[57] making them available for prescription in certain limited circumstances.[58] In the years since, both academic studies and media reports have comprehensively criticized the operation of the medical cannabis system. A 2021 VICE investigation reported that the production of medical cannabis in the United Kingdom has risen by almost 700% over the last five years.[59] This was further confirmed by an International Narcotics Control Board report that suggests the United Kingdom is a "significant manufacturer of pharmaceutical preparations containing cannabis extracts" while "projections made on the basis of available data series indicate that about 320 tons of cannabis were produced in 2019".[60] It is thus unsurprising to see academic criticisms of the system suggesting that while supply and patient demand for medical cannabis is high, access has been extremely minimal.[61] As a result, a large amount of people in the country have turned to illegal cannabis to relieve the symptoms of

---

55 "Westminster Committee Believes UK Should Consider Decriminalization" (23 October 2020), online: *SDF Scottish Drugs Forum* #x003C;www.sdf.org.uk/tag/decriminali sation/>

56 Jessica Elgot, "Sadiq Khan Plans Pilot to 'Decriminalise' Minor Cannabis Offences in London" (4 January 2022), online: *The Guardian* #x003C;www.theguardian.com/society/ 2022/jan/04/sadiq-khan-plans-pilot-to-decriminalise-minor-cannabis-offences>

57 United Kingdom, *The Misuse of Drugs Regulations* 2001, No 3998

58 Steph Hazelgreaves, "The UK's Legalization of Medicinal Cannabis" (24 February 2021), online: *Open Access Government* #x003C;www.openaccessgovernment.org/ the-uks-legalisation-of-medicinal-cannabis-products/104618/>

59 Mattha Busby, "'It's Crazy'- Patients Say the UK's Medical Cannabis System Is Not Working" (6 February 2021), online: *VICE* #x003C;www.vice.com/en/article/z3xmyc/ uk-medical-cannabis-production-prescription>

60 "Report of the International Narcotics Control Board for 2020" (February 2020), online (pdf): *United Nations International Narcotics Control Board* #x003C;www.incb.org/docu ments/Narcotic-Drugs/Technical-Publications/2020/Narcotic_Drugs_Technical_publica tion_2020.pdf> at 48

61 Anne K. Schlag et al, "Medical Cannabis in the UK: From Principle to Practice" (2020) 34:9 Journal of Psychopharmacology 931 at 931–932

86 *Drug Legalization in Other Democracies*

their health conditions.[62] It is argued that a variety of barriers to the prescribing of medical cannabis exist: 1) doctors lack the knowledge and training to confidently prescribe cannabis medicines; 2) guidelines established by the National Institute for Health and Care Excellence (NICE) and the Royal College of Physicians (2018) are restrictive, generally only recommending cannabis as a prescription as a last resort after conventional treatment has failed; and 3) the cost of medical cannabis in the U.K. is currently high; and 4) importation and supply chain issues persist, as the U.K. government has only recently loosened regulations that previously allowed licensing and imports for one patient at a time.[63] As a result of these issues, one 2020 academic study notes that almost no National Health Service (NHS) prescriptions have been issued, and less than a hundred have been made available from private providers at a cost of £1000 a month.[64] A comprehensive comparative analysis of medical systems in other jurisdictions has put forward a number of recommendations for improvement of the U.K. system going forward in the future.[65]

4.2 European Countries

4.2.1 *Czech Republic*

According to the Transnational Institute, the Czech Republic's drug policy is considered modern and pragmatic, focused on evidence-based prevention, harm reduction, treatment, and rehabilitation programs.[66] Penalties for drug trafficking, provisions for diversion of prosecution, and other drug-related offences are found in the country's criminal code, which has been in force since 2010.[67] Drug use is not a criminal offence in the Czech Republic, with possession of small quantities for personal use subject only to a fine not more than the equivalent

---

62 Matej Mikulic, "Topic: Medical Cannabis in the UK" (27 October 2021), online: *Statista* #x003C;www.statista.com/topics/6200/medical-cannabis-in-the-uk/>

63 Schlag et al, *supra* note 61, at 933–934

64 David Nutt et al, "So near Yet So Far: Why Won't the UK Prescribe Medical Cannabis?" (2020) 10:9 BMJ Open at 1

65 Anne K. Schlag, "An Evaluation of Regulatory Regimes of Medical Cannabis: What Lessons Can Be Learned for the UK?" (2020) 3:1 Medical Cannabis and Cannabinoids 76 at 80–82: These include, but are not limited to: 1) the need to provide education, training, and support for physicians and health care professionals; 2) the need for improvement of the evidence base through real-world data collection; 3) the benefits of establishing a medical cannabis office; 4) the importance of effectively calculating demand; 5) the need to clarify costs and insurance; 6) the need to involve patients and stakeholders in decision-making; and 6) the need to address the stigma of medical cannabis so that it can be further accepted by the medical profession

66 Tereza Filipkovà, "Cannabis Policy in the Czech Republic" (22 August 2017), online: *Transnational Institute* #x003C;www.tni.org/en/article/cannabis-policy-in-the-czech-republic>

67 "Czech Republic: Country Drug Report 2017" (2017), online (pdf): *European Monitoring Centre for Drugs and Drug Addiction* #x003C;www.emcdda.europa.eu/system/files/publications/4511/TD0416912ENN.pdf> at 4

Drug Legalization in Other Democracies 87

of 550 euros.[68] A 2014 decision of the country's Supreme Court set the limits for personal possession at 10 grams of cannabis, 1.5 grams of heroin, 1 gram of cocaine, 5 grams of hash, and 4 tablets of ecstasy.[69] The country is far more advanced than Canada in its adoption of harm reduction measures, with nationwide needle and syringe programs operating in all regions of the country, funded through grant systems established at the national and regional levels.[70] Law 221/2013 established a system for the provision of medical cannabis in the country that uses a prescription-based procedure, with the government regulating licensing and specifying that only specific medical practitioners (i.e. not general practitioners) can prescribe medical cannabis.[71] In the early years of the operation of the medical cannabis system, concerns were raised that medical cannabis was cost-prohibitive.[72] Some of these issues have been rectified by recent reforms. In 2020, about 90% of the cost of medical cannabis was being covered by health insurance companies.[73] Moreover, the Czech government relaxed rules around medical cannabis on January 1, 2022, including allowing for medical cannabis to contain three times more THC content than previously allowed.[74] As a result, it is estimated that the number of patients being prescribed medical cannabis grew from 30 in 2015 to 4,370 in 2021 (as of November).[75] In 2021, the lower house of the country's Parliament rejected a proposal that would have further liberalized recreational cannabis production and consumption, including provisions for the possession and carrying of up to 30 grams and home cultivation of up to five plants.[76] This decision came on the same day as the above-noted liberalization of medical cannabis laws, so it appears that the Czech government at present is more focused on providing an accessible and robust medical system than it is any further reform to recreational cannabis laws.

4.2.2 Germany

Germany's population, geographic size, economic strength and political power make it one of the most influential countries within the European Union. As

---

68 *Ibid*
69 Jan Jirička, "Nejvyš 10 gramu konopí. Soud nove stanovil vetší než malé množstyí drog" (9 April 2014), online: *iDNEScz* <www.idnes.cz/zpravy/domaci/nejvyssi-soud-nove-stanovil-vetsi-nez-male-mnozstvi-drog.A140409_102935_domaci_jav>
70 Czech Republic: Country Drug Report, *supra* note 67, at 10
71 Filipková, *supra* note 66
72 *Ibid*
73 Kafkadesk Prague Office, "Czech Republic Rejects Liberalization of Cannabis Use" (12 September 2021), online: *Kafkadesk* <https://kafkadesk.org/2021/01/28/czech-republic-rejects-liberalization-of-cannabis-use/>
74 "Lékaři budou nově léčebné konopí předepisovat pouze electronicky" (30 December 2021), online: *ČeskéNovinycs* #x003C;www.ceskenoviny.cz/zpravy/lekari-budou-nove-lecebne-konopi-predepisovat-pouze-elektronicky/2139190>
75 *Ibid*
76 Kafkadesk Prague Office, *supra* note 73

88 Drug Legalization in Other Democracies

such, it is extremely significant that the country's new coalition government has announced an agreement amongst its three parties to legalize recreational cannabis.[77] In terms of population, Germany would become the largest country in the world to allow the sale of cannabis.[78] Some legal experts have suggested that Germany's decision to legalize may have a wider and more profound impact on the entire continent, including a potential rethink of the European Union's drug laws.[79] The country has not yet released details of the forthcoming legal cannabis system, with the government presently only stating that it will allow for the "controlled sale of cannabis to adults for recreational purposes in licensed shops".[80] At present, the German Narcotic Drugs Act does not differentiate penalties between different types of drugs, and Section 31a of that legislation allows for the possibility of prosecution to be diverted when amounts are minor and intended for personal use.[81] A coordinated and voluntary drug support service aimed at preventing drug dependence has operated for more than 15 years in the country, with around 120 project locations currently located across the country.[82] Medical cannabis has been legal in the country since 2017 as a result of the Cannabis as Medicine Act, which allows for costs of treatment to be reimbursed by health insurance providers and establishes a state-controlled system of production overseen by the German Cannabis Agency.[83] In the early years of this system, it appears that large amounts of people have been accessing medical cannabis. It is estimated that medical cannabis units dispensed in the first ten months grew from 44,000 to 145,000 in 2018.[84] While the number of patients appears to have grown rapidly, it is argued that there are still barriers hindering further rates of increase, including: 1) demand for medical cannabis has exceeded Germany's import capacities; 2) only about 60% of medical cannabis claims are currently reimbursed by health insurance companies; and 3) a sizeable amount

---

77 Guy Chazan, "Germany's Nascent Cannabis Industry Hits New Highs as Legalization Looms" (27 December 2021), online: *Financial Times* #x003C;www.ft.com/content/66016598-7307-4c07-a789-22d3973f2223>

78 *Ibid*

79 Robin Hofmann, "Cannabis Legalization in Germany – the Final Blow to European Drug Prohibition?" (10 January 2022), online: *European Law Blog* <https://europeanlawblog.eu/2022/01/11/cannabis-legalization-in-germany-the-final-blow-to-european-drug-prohibition/>

80 Cecilia Rodriguez, "Germany Moves to Legalize Cannabis, Second Country After Malta in Europe" (28 December 2021), online: *Forbes* #x003C;www.forbes.com/sites/ceciliarodriguez/2021/12/27/germany-moves-to-legalize-cannabis-second-country-after-malta-in-europe/?sh=57261>

81 Heino Stover et al, "Cannabis Regulation in Europe: Country Report Germany" (February 2019), online (pdf): *Transnational Institute* #x003C;www.tni.org/files/publication-downloads/cr_german_10062019.pdf> at 2

82 *Ibid*

83 *Ibid* at 5

84 Jürgen Rehm et al, "Medical Marijuana. What Can We Learn from the Experiences in Canada, Germany and Thailand?" (2019) 74 International Journal of Drug Policy 47 at 49

Drug Legalization in Other Democracies 89

of physicians are still hesitant to prescribe medical cannabis.[85] These issues have already been somewhat addressed by the licensing of German companies to produce cannabis domestically, and it seems plausible that the impending legalization of recreational cannabis may break down some of the stigmatization around the medical use of the substance. Overall, Germany seems poised for a significant liberalization of its cannabis policy heading into 2022. The ramifications of this decision will reverberate across the continent. One economist has estimated that legalization will create nearly 4.7 billion euros annually for the German economy.[86] As noted below, several European countries have already announced intentions to move forward with cannabis legalization. As Germany moves forward towards legalization, it is likely that more European nations will soon follow their lead.

4.2.3 Italy

Italy has experienced significant liberalization of its drug laws in the last decade as a result of both judicial and public activism. A 2014 Constitutional Court decision found a law that did not distinguish between hard and soft drugs unconstitutional and "wiped out a legislation which has been widely recognized as one of the main reasons for the overcrowding of Italian prisons".[87] The ruling reinstated the 1990 "Consolidation of the laws governing drugs and psychotropic substances, the prevention, treatment and rehabilitation of drug addicts", legislation that is far more liberal in several ways, including: 1) it makes a distinction between hard drugs and cannabis, with milder penalties for cannabis; 2) it allows for the abolition of a "threshold" to distinguish between personal use and dealing; and 3) it decriminalizes *all* drug possession (for personal use), with the availability of milder administrative sanctions and easier access to alternative therapeutic measures.[88] More recently, the country's Supreme Court ruled in 2019 that small-scale home cultivation of cannabis for personal use should not be subject to criminal penalties, and, as such, a debate around the wider legalization of recreational cannabis was ignited.[89] As a result, pro-legalization activists turned in more than 630,000 signatures supporting a Spring 2022 referendum

---

85 *Ibid*
86 "Cannabis Legalization Brings the State 4.7 Billion Euros Annually – Around 27,000 Legal Jobs Would Be Created" (16 November 2021), online: *HHU* #x003C;www.dice.hhu.de/startseitennews/studie-cannabislegalisierung-bringt-dem-staat-jaehrlich-47-milliarden-euro-rund-27000-legale-arbeitsplaetze-wuerden-entstehen>
87 "The Italian Supreme Court Abolishes the 2006 Antidrug Legislation" (13 February 2014), online: *IDPC* <https://idpc.net/alerts/2014/02/the-italian-supreme-court-abolishes-the-2006-antidrug-legislation>
88 *Ibid*
89 Patrick Cain, "Italian Court Rules Home-Growing Cannabis Is Legal, Restarting Legalization Debate-National" (27 December 2019), online: *Global News* <https://globalnews.ca/news/6340024/italian-court-rules-home-growing-cannabis-is-legal-restarting-legalization-debate/>

90 *Drug Legalization in Other Democracies*

on cannabis policy reform.[90] Having secured the minimum number of signatures, the referendum proposal will now be sent to the country's Constitutional Court, with a February 15 decision expected to certify the measure for a nationwide vote between April and June 2022. Advocates are confident that the referendum proposed will be approved by the court, as the scope of the proposed reform is relatively limited: cultivation of cannabis would be formally decriminalized, and possession and use would be subject only to fines.[91] Although the referendum does not propose a system of legal and regulated recreational cannabis, a definitive referendum result (along with the growing wave of legalization occurring across the continent) may provide the impetus for Italy's government to engage in further legislative reform. Italy also currently has a relatively unique medical cannabis system. A 2013 Ministerial Decree allows for pharmacies to distribute cannabis products prescribed by a doctor, and, interestingly, in 2014, the Italian Ministry of Defence (in cooperation with the Ministry of Health) began the production of domestic medical cannabis products.[92] The use of the military to produce cannabis is certainly a novel approach. Medical cannabis is prescribed to treat a wide variety of conditions, and, as a result, a recent academic study noted that "Medical cannabis-based prescriptions are constantly increasing in Italy".[93] The existence of a regulated and controlled medical cultivation and distribution infrastructure may benefit the country if it chooses to move further towards commercialized recreational cannabis in the future.

4.2.4 *Malta*

Malta's 2014 Drug Dependence (Treatment not Imprisonment) Act stipulates that a person found in possession of a small amount of drugs for personal use is only subject to a fine (50–100 euros for cannabis and 75–125 euros for other drugs).[94] A 2021 Valentine's Day arrest of a couple in possession of a small amount of cannabis drew media criticism and galvanized momentum for policy reform.[95] Not long after, Malta became the first European country to legalize the cultivation and possession of cannabis for personal use, allowing for possession of up

---

90 Kyle Jaeger, "Italian Officials Certify Signatures for National Marijuana and Psilocybin Referendum" (12 January 2022), online: *Marijuana Moment* #x003C;www.marijuanamoment.net/italian-officials-certify-signatures-for-national-marijuana-and-psilocybin-referendum/>

91 *Ibid*

92 Simona Zaami et al, "Medical Use of Cannabis: Italian and European Legislation" (2018) 22 European Review for Medical and Pharmacological 1161 at 1164

93 Alberto Ramella et al, "Impact of Lipid Sources on Quality Traits of Medical Cannabis-Based Oil Preparations" (2020) 25 Molecules 2986 at 2987

94 "Malta: Country Drug Report 2019" (2019), online (pdf): *European Monitoring Centre for Drugs and Drug Addiction* #x003C;www.emcdda.europa.eu/system/files/publications/11328/malta-cdr-2019.pdf> at 4

95 James Debono, "Cannabis Legalization: There Can Be No Way Forward Without a White Paper" (25 February 2021), online: *MaltaToday* #x003C;www.maltatoday.com.mt/news/national/107856/cannabis_legalisation_no_way_forward_without_white_paper>

Drug Legalization in Other Democracies 91

to seven grams of cannabis and up to four plants at home.[96] The Maltese system will also allow for non-profit cannabis clubs to cultivate the drug for distribution to its members, setting a limit on membership to 500 people with a maximum of seven grams per day and fifty grams per month distributed.[97] The new legislation maintains a prohibition on cannabis consumption in public and also imposes fines between 50–100 for those found in possession of more than seven but less than 28 grams of cannabis.[98] Medical cannabis has been legal in Malta since the 2018 passage of the Production of Cannabis for Medical and Research Purposes Act, which allows for the country's Medicines Authority to issue licenses for the production, importation and distribution of medical cannabis.[99] Patients require a doctor's prescription, and doctors have to show that other treatments were tried and were not successful.[100] While Malta's size, population, economy and political influence pale in comparison to Germany and some of the other countries surveyed below, its reform is nonetheless consequential and appears to be part of a larger European wave towards drug policy liberalization in 2022.

4.2.5 Netherlands

While the Netherlands is often assumed to be the earliest adopter of a legal cannabis system, this view misses important nuances of the actual legal situation of cannabis (and other drugs) in the country. While the sale of recreational cannabis through the system of "coffeeshops" has been tolerated and heavily regulated since the 1970s, all drug-related activities (including cultivation, sale, and possession) are still technically illegal.[101] However, the coffeeshop system has created an often criticized paradox, commonly referred to as the front door back door issue:

> Selling cannabis in coffeeshops is condoned, but subject to strict regulations. Coffeeshops sell cannabis to consumers from their "front door", but of course, this is only possible when the shops are sufficiently supplied. The supply of coffeeshops is commonly known in the Netherlands as the "back

---

96 Daniel Boffey, "Malta to Legalise Cannabis for Personal Use in European First" (13 December 2021), online: *The Guardian* #x003C;www.theguardian.com/society/2021/dec/13/malta-to-be-first-in-europe-to-legalise-cannabis-for-personal-use>

97 *Ibid*

98 Emma Bubola, "Malta Becomes First E.U. Country to Legalize Marijuana" (15 December 2021), online: *The New York Times* #x003C;www.nytimes.com/2021/12/15/world/europe/malta-eu-marijuana-legalize.html>

99 Victor Bercea, "The Legal Situation of Cannabis in Malta" (22 August 2020), online: *StrainInsider* <https://straininsider.com/legal-situation-cannabis-malta/>

100 *Ibid*

101 Henk Van de Bunt & Thaddeus Muller, "The Bankruptcy of the Dutch Cannbis Policy: Time for a Restart" in Hans Nelen & Dina Siegel, eds, *Contemporary Organized Crime: Developments Challenges and Responses*. 2nd ed. (Switzerland: Springer, 2021) at 12

92 *Drug Legalization in Other Democracies*

door". . . . The Dutch policy of tolerance towards coffeeshops does not apply to the back door, but this problem has been ignored for many years.[102]

Police turn a blind eye to the source of the coffeeshop's supply, so long as it's done discreetly and in small amounts, but this nonetheless "leaves coffeeshops in a complicated interface between the illegal production market and the tolerated sale of cannabis to consumers".[103] It has been argued that this approach, devoid of any effort from the national government to regulate supply, has inadvertently contributed to an ongoing process of increased involvement of organized crime in the cannabis industry.[104] Recently, mounting pressure on the government from municipalities, activists, and coffeeshop owners themselves has led to some promise for reform in the form of the 2019 Controlled Cannabis Supply Chain Experiment Act.[105] The legislation allows for an "experiment" that will implement a four-year pilot scheme in 10 cities, through which 79 coffeeshops will be supplied by officially regulated cannabis producers, with an eye towards future legalization of cannabis production.[106] The Netherlands has granted 10 licenses to entities allowing them to grow commercial cannabis to supply the adult-use market, leading some to characterize the recent initiatives as an "incremental approach to legalization"[107] and "a legal experiment that's needed to happen for some time".[108] Ironically, as this supply experiment continues, Amsterdam took steps in 2021 to ban foreign visitors from its coffeeshops.[109] As more European countries move towards recreational cannabis legalization in 2022, the future of reform in the Netherlands remains uncertain.

Often lost in the global notoriety of the Dutch recreational cannabis debate is the country's medical cannabis system. Along with Canada, the Netherlands was one of the first countries to begin a national medical cannabis system in 2003.[110]

---

102 Dirk Korf, "Cannabis Regulation in Europe: Country Report Netherlands" (27 March 2019), online: *Transnational Institute* #x003C;www.tni.org/en/publication/cannabis-regulation-in-europe-country-report-netherlands> at 2

103 *Ibid* at 9

104 *Ibid* at 15

105 Netherlands, *Controlled Cannabis Supply Chain Experiment Act* 2019

106 Peter Cluskey, "High Time: Netherlands Moves to Clean Up Absurd Cannabis Policy" (6 February 2020), online: *The Irish Times* #x003C;www.irishtimes.com/business/innovation/high-time-netherlands-moves-to-clean-up-absurd-cannabis-policy-1.4160217>

107 "The Dutch Cannabis Experiment Is Expanding" (23 December 2021), online: *Cannabis & Tech Today* <https://cannatechtoday.com/the-dutch-cannabis-experiment-is-expanding/>

108 Hilary Bricken, "The Netherlands and Cannabis: Legal Supply Chain Experiment Continues" (23 July 2020), online: *Cannalaw Blog* <https://harrisbricken.com/cannalawblog/the-netherlands-and-cannabis-legal-supply-chain-experiment-continues/>

109 Jon Henley, "Foreign Visitors Face Ban from Amsterdam's Cannabis Cafes" (11 January 2021), online: *The Guardian* #x003C;www.theguardian.com/world/2021/jan/11/foreigners-face-ban-from-amsterdams-cannabis-cafes>

110 Bas de Hoop, Eibert Heerdink & Arno Hazekamp, "Medical Cannabis on Prescription in the Netherlands: Statistics for 2003–2016" (2018) 3 Cannabis and Cannabinoid Research 54 at 54

Drug Legalization in Other Democracies 93

The system, which is overseen by the Office of Medicinal Cannabis (OMC), allows for the provision of medical cannabis to patients by prescription, with the product dispensed by pharmacies. Prior to 2015, medical cannabis was only available in herbal form (dried cannabis flowers), but a subsequent expansion to cannabis oils has led to an enormous increase in prescriptions.[111] It is important to note that the medical system in the Netherlands was largely developed because of concerns associated with the inability of the country's coffeeshop system to supply regulated and quality-controlled cannabis to patients who needed it for therapeutic use.[112] This is the opposite of the trend observed in Canada, where the licensed producer system developed under the medical framework and subsequently greatly contributed to the implementation of the country's recreational cannabis market.[113] Similar to Canada, in the first few years of medical cannabis legalization, views of the OMC and its products were very negative, and barely 600 patients enrolled in the program.[114] This gradually changed over time as doctors gained more knowledge about medical cannabis. The fact that medical cannabis is significantly less expensive than that which is available in coffeeshops likely also played a role.[115] Nonetheless, an October 2021 study found that both medical cannabis sales and patient prescriptions had declined, contributing to a downward trend that began in 2018 when insurance reimbursements were halted in the country.[116] As such, it seems likely that patients have turned to either coffeeshops or the illicit market for their cannabis needs, which adds an additional policy question for the Dutch government to answer once its supply chain experiment has concluded.

4.2.6 Portugal

Many people incorrectly assume that Portugal's historic and groundbreaking decision to decriminalize all drugs in 2001 came out of thin air. In fact, the 2001 decision was the end result of about six years of extensive policy work, including: 1) the 1995 establishment of the "Assessment of Drug Addiction, Consumption and Traffic" Parliamentary Committee; 2) the government's creation of a multi-disciplinary expert group (Commission for a National Drug Strategy), which drafted a guideline for drug policy in 1998; 3) the government's 1999 approval of a National Strategy for the Fight Against drugs; and 4) the initiation

111 _Ibid_ at 55
112 Werner Knöss et al, "Key Elements of Legal Environments for Medical Use of Cannabis in Different Countries" (2019) 62 Bundesgesundheitsbl 855 at 855
113 Chapter 2.3
114 Knöss et al, _supra_ note 112 at 856
115 _Ibid_
116 "Sales of Medical Cannabis in the Netherlands Decline in 2021" (15 October 2021), online: _Prohibition Partners_ <https://prohibitionpartners.com/2021/10/15/sales-of-medical-cannabis-decline-in-the-netherlands-in-2021/>

94   *Drug Legalization in Other Democracies*

of the Portuguese Institute for Drugs and Addiction.[117] As such, by the time decriminalization arrived, the Portuguese system already included a fairly extensive public health institutional framework. The system at the time was, and still is, an incredibly novel approach towards treating drug use and addiction as a public health issue and generally works as follows: 1) each district in the country establishes a dissuasion committee to deal with the administrative offences of those who use drugs in that district; 2) each committee is usually made up of two representatives from the medical sector (physicians, psychologists, social workers, etc.) and a legal expert; 3) people who are found in possession with up to 10 days' worth of an average daily dose of drugs are referred to the committee (without arrest); and 4) the committee considers the type of drug used, addiction status of the user, occasional vs. habitual use of drugs, and the personal/economic circumstances of the user in deciding whether to suspend sanctions or make them conditional on the offender seeking treatment.[118] Alongside this decriminalization, the country invested significantly in harm reduction, treatment and prevention. For example, by 2008, more than half of the country was serviced by publicly funded needle exchange programs.[119] As a result, various metrics have been pointed to as evidence of the policy's success, including: 1) the consumption of drugs has actually decreased since its implementation; 2) the number of HIV cases in drug users also decreased, and the number of deaths by drug overdose stabilized (currently one of the lowest in all of the EU); 3) drug consumption by young adults is remarkably low; 4) fears that Portugal would become a drug tourism destination never materialized; and 5) the number of drug users seeking medical treatment increased.[120] It is thus unsurprising that many (particularly American) academics point to the Portuguese example as an approach to ending the war on drugs.[121]

It should be noted that the Portuguese experiment has had some critics, which was to be expected given the novelty of the country's approach. A small minority of doctors and academics claim that the country's harm reduction measures decrease pressure to stop using drugs.[122] Another criticism points to policy evaluation, noting that the majority of evaluations of the Portuguese policy have been

---

117 Ali Unlu, Tuukka Tammi & Pekka Hakkarainen, "Drug Decriminalization Policy" (September 2020), online (pdf): *Finnish Institute for Health and Welfare* <>http://fileserver.idpc.net/library/drug_decriminalisation_policy_2020_report.pdf> at 56
118 *Ibid* at 57
119 *Ibid*
120 Tiago Cabral, "The 15th Anniversary of the Portuguese Drug Policy: Its History, Its Success and Its Future" (2017) 30 Drug Science, Policy and Law 1 at 1–2
121 Christine Minhee & Steve Calandrillo, "The Cure for America's Opioid Crisis? End the War on Drugs" (2019) 42:2 Harvard Journal of Law and Public Policy 547 at 622: "We watch countries like Portugal and Switzerland benefit from discarding ineffective War on Drugs Policies, and hope that our patchwork of politically facile initiatives will yield the same effect". See also: Brian D. Earp, Jonathan Lewis & Carl L. Hart, "Racial Justice Requires Ending the War on Drugs" (2021) 21:4 The American Journal of Bioethics 4
122 Kathryn Kundrod, "Decriminalization of Drugs in Portugal: A Controversial Experiment for Public Health" (2015) 33 Perspectives on Business and Economics at 2

Drug Legalization in Other Democracies 95

conducted by external stakeholders rather than internal government reports.[123] Nonetheless, overall views of the country's system have been positive, with the country "often cited for leadership in implementing effective, health-driven policies on illicit drug use that include decriminalizing drug possession".[124] Interestingly, in recent years there have been calls for Portugal to further liberalize its laws pertaining to cannabis. Portugal legalized the cultivation, production, import and export, and sale of medical cannabis in 2018, but, as of 2021, only one cannabis-based medicine (Sativex) was being sold in the Portuguese market, and at a relatively high price.[125] This has perhaps fueled broader public advocacy for the legalization of recreational cannabis in the country. Critics lament the fact that medical access is practically unattainable, with virtually all of the country's cannabis use (both medical and non) being supplied by the black market.[126] Advocacy groups were disappointed when their push for legal home cultivation for medicinal use was not included in the 2018 legislation.[127] Portuguese academics have pointed to the models in Canada, Uruguay and several U.S. states to make the case that legalization would remove the largest source of income from organized crime and reduce Portugal's role as one of the main important points of transit for international drug trafficking.[128] It seems as though the Portuguese government has been listening. Proposals for adult-use cannabis legalization were introduced into the Parliament in June 2021.[129] The proposed laws aim to regulate the circuit of cultivation, production and distribution of recreational cannabis with regulations aimed at the state control of authorizations, advertising and pricing and taxation.[130] While the legislation is still pending (having suffered

123 Caitlin Elizabeth Hughes & Alex Stevens, "A Resounding Success or a Disastrous Failure: Re-Examining the Interpretation of Evidence on the Portuguese Decriminalization of Illicit Drugs" (2015) New Approaches to Drug Policies at 138

124 Hakique Virani & Rebecca Haines-Saah, "Drug Decriminalization: A Matter of Justice and Equity, Not Just Health" (2020) 58:1 American Journal of Preventive Medicine 161 at 161

125 Ricardo Rocha, "Three Years of the Portuguese Medical Cannabis Law" (10 November 2021), online: *Mondaq* #x003C;www.mondaq.com/cannabis-hemp/1129956/three-years-of-the-portuguese-medical-cannabis-law>

126 Stephen Chmelewski, "It's Time Portugal: Legalise It" (10 March 2021) online: *The Portugal News* #x003C;www.theportugalnews.com/news/2021-03-10/its-time-portugal-legalise-it/58709>

127 "Portugal Takes a Momentous Step Toward Legal Cannabis-Based Medicine" (2 April 2021), online: *Royal Queen Seeds* #x003C;www.royalqueenseeds.com/blog-portugal-takes-a-momentous-step-toward-legalizing-medical-cannabis-n945>

128 Ricardo Baptista-Leite & Lisa Ploeg, "The Road Towards the Responsible and Safe Legalization of Cannabis Use in Portugal" (2018) 31:2 Acta Med Port 115 at 123

129 Michael Hoban, "Political Parties in Portugal Propose Adult-Use Cannabis Legalization Bills in Parliament" (11 June 2021), online: *Prohibition Partners* <https://prohibitionpartners.com/2021/06/11/political-parties-in-portugal-propose-adult-use-cannabis-legalisation-bills-in-parliament/>

130 Inês Metello & Mariana Ricardo, "Portugal Discusses Draft=Laws to Legalize Cannabis for Personal Use" (9 June 2021), online: *Lexology* #x003C;www.lexology.com/library/detail.aspx?g=c24f0994-b132-4057-a80f-e96f2621e78a>

96 *Drug Legalization in Other Democracies*

delays due to COVID-19 and political instability), media outlets seem confident that Portugal is highly likely to legalize recreational cannabis in 2022,[131] adding another country to the growing wave of cannabis liberalization that is making its way across the continent.

4.2.7 *Spain*

According to Article 36 of the Law on the Protection of Citizens' Security (2015), consumption or minor personal possession of drugs in public places is deemed a non-criminal offence punishable by fines ranging from 600 to 30,000 euros.[132] While public support for legal medicinal cannabis is high (estimated by some studies at 90%), at present medical access to cannabis is extremely limited.[133] This has prompted a May 2021 vote in the Spanish Congress in favour of a proposal that would establish a subcommittee to investigate regulated medical cannabis systems in other countries.[134] While the country lags behind in medical cannabis policy reform, it has been ahead of the curve in recreational cannabis, particularly through a system of cannabis social clubs (CSCs) that first formed in Barcelona in 2001 and to date are estimated to have expanded to between 800 and 1,000 locations nationwide.[135] There has been considerable legal uncertainty as to the operation of these CSCs, with judgements of the country's highest courts finding them illegal but nonetheless acquitting CSC members on legal technicalities.[136] The Spanish system is devoid of nationwide regulations applicable to the activities of CSCs, and there are several peculiarities that have allowed the development of the CSC model in the country: use and possession of cannabis (along with other controlled substances) for personal use is not punishable under Spanish criminal law, with only the commercialization of those substances constituting a criminal offence under Section 368 of the Criminal Code, allowing CSCs to produce cannabis that is distributed on a not for profit basis through a closed circuit of

---

131 "Portugal Is Highly Likely to Legalize Recreational Cannabis" (20 January 2022), online: *Bezinga* #x003C;www.benzinga.com/markets/cannabis/22/01/25124270/portugal-is-highly-likely-to-legalize-recreational-cannabis>. See also: Dario Sabaghi, "These European Countries Could Legalize Cannabis in 2022" (29 December 2021), online: *Forbes* #x003C;www.forbes.com/sites/dariosabaghi/2021/12/29/these-european-countries-could-legalize-cannabis-in-2022/?sh=69687afe2514>

132 "Spain Country Drug Report 2019" (June 2019), online (pdf): *European Monitoring Centre for Drugs and Drug Addiction* #x003C;www.emcdda.europa.eu/publications/country-drug-reports/2019/spain_en> at 5

133 Conor O'Brien, "Spanish Government to Examine Benefits of Legalizing Medical Cannabis" (13 May 2021), online: *Prohibition Partners* <https://prohibitionpartners.com/2021/05/13/spanish-government-to-examine-benefits-of-legalising-medical-cannabis/>

134 *Ibid*

135 Xabier Arana & Oscar Pares, "Cannabis Social Clubs in Spain: Recent Legal Developments" in Tom Decorte, Simon Lenton & Chris Wilkins, eds, *Legalizing Cannabis: Experiences, Lessons and Scenarios* (London: Routledge, 2020) 307 at 307

136 *Ibid* at 315

adult users.[137] Under this ambiguous legal framework, Spain has become one of Europe's main cannabis producers and a hotbed of organized crime activity.[138] Moreover, 2021 court decisions have put the state of Spain's CSCs in question, with activists calling on the federal government to resolve the legal ambiguity and put forward a regulatory framework.[139] Barcelona city authorities and police are in agreement that CSCs reduce street dealing and consumption and are not opposed in principle to the clubs, further underscoring the need for federal regulation.[140] In October 2021, a proposal to legalize cannabis for recreational use was rejected, illuminating deep divisions amongst the parties that make up the government's current ruling coalition.[141] The issue is far from settled: two more proposals on the legalization of cannabis are set to be brought before Congress in 2022.[142]

4.2.8 Switzerland

Switzerland is a federalist state comprised of the confederation, 26 cantons and over 2,000 municipalities, each of which has a certain level of freedom regarding the implementation of policies and, as such, the country has been considered a model case of power-sharing.[143] During the 1980s and 1990s, intravenous heroin use and the transmission of HIV and AIDS became a major crisis in Switzerland, leading many cantons and cities to develop harm reduction measures (such as needle exchanges, methadone substitution programs and heroin prescription centres) and eventually culminating in harm reduction becoming a pillar of national drug policy.[144] It is through the lens of this paradigm shift towards an alternative

---

137 Tom Decorte et al, "Regulating Cannabis Social Clubs: A Comparative Analysis of Legal and Self-Regulatory Practices in Spain, Belgium and Uruguay" (2020) 43 International Journal of Drug Policy 44 at 46

138 Stephen Burgen, "Span Become Cannabis Hub as Criminals Fill Tourism Void" (11 October 2020), online: *The Guardian* #x003C;www.theguardian.com/society/2020/oct/11/spain-becomes-cannabis-hub-as-criminals-fill-tourism-void>

139 Cecilia Rodriguez, "No More Cannabis Tourism in Barcelona? Court Overturns Regulations on 'Clubes Cannábicos'" (21 July 2021), online: *Forbes* #x003C;www.forbes.com/sites/ceciliarodriguez/2021/07/27/the-end-of-barcelonas-cannabis-tourism-court-overturns-regulations-on-clubes-cannbicos/?sh=2156832a272d>

140 Stephen Burgen, "Barcelona Cannabis Clubs Face Closure in New Legal Setback" (27 July 2021), online: *The Guardian* #x003C;www.theguardian.com/society/2021/jul/27/barcelona-cannabis-clubs-face-closure-in-new-legal-setback>

141 Xosé Hermida, "Spain's Socialist Party Votes Against Legalizing Cannabis for Recreational Use" (20 October 2021), online: *El Pais* <https://english.elpais.com/spain/2021-10-20/spains-socialist-party-votes-against-legalizing-cannabis-for-recreational-use.html>

142 *Ibid*

143 Simon Anderfuhren-Biget et al, "Swiss Cannabis Polices" in Tom Decorte, Simon Lenton & Chris Wilkins, eds, *Legalizing Cannabis: Experiences, Lessons and Scenarios* (London: Routledge, 2020) 323 at 323

144 Frank Zobel, "Cannabis Regulation in Europe: Country Report Switzerland" (17 March 2019), online: *Transnational Institute* #x003C;www.tni.org/en/publication/cannabis-regulation-in-europe-country-report-switzerland> at 2–3

98 *Drug Legalization in Other Democracies*

treatment of all drugs that cannabis reform in the country must be considered. In 2008, Swiss citizens voted on a ballot initiative and a referendum on the same day, curiously approving a referendum that fully institutionalized harm reduction as an overall drug policy strategy while rejecting a cannabis legalization initiative by a significant margin (63%).[145] In 2012, in response to a remarkably diverse treatment of cannabis-use offences across Switzerland's cantons, the federal Parliament adopted a limited reform that decriminalized adult cannabis use through an administrative fine of 100 Swiss francs.[146] The fines associated with this legislative reform would be ruled unconstitutional by the country's federal court in 2017, when it decided that possession of less than ten grams of cannabis was no longer punishable, neither by a fine nor any other punishment.[147] Subsequent attempts to legalize cannabis and provide for the regulation of its cultivation, production and sale, including a parliamentary initiative introduced by the Green Party in 2017, failed.[148] Ironically, in comparison to the bottom-up approach that has driven legalization in several U.S. states, the Swiss system of direct democracy and power-sharing has actually provided for a "major challenge to build a coalition that is large enough to win the necessary votes in Parliament or among citizens".[149] That said, it appears as though Switzerland is on the verge of major recreational cannabis use reform as it heads into 2022. The Social Security and Health Commission of the Council of States (a parliamentary committee) argued in 2021 that cannabis should be regulated in the country and, as a result, the government is in the process of drafting a law that would legalize the production, cultivation, trade and consumption of both medical and recreational cannabis.[150] There is still a long way to go before the legislation becomes a reality, as the new law has not yet been written and will require acceptance by both parliament and the Council of States. That said, some of the country's political parties appear supportive of the plan.[151] Coupled with neighbouring Germany's move towards recreational cannabis legalization, reform seems likely in the coming years.

4.3 Latin America

4.3.1 *Argentina*

Argentina's 1989 Law 23737 allowed for drug possession to be punished with imprisonment of one to six years and a fine, while Article 14 of the Law provided

---

145 *Ibid* at 4
146 Anderfuhren-Biget et al, *supra* note 143, at 326
147 *Ibid*
148 Zobel, supra note 144, at 7
149 Anderfuhren-Biget et al, *supra* note 143, at 330
150 "Switzerland to Legalise Recreational and Medical Cannabis Usage" (19 October 2021), online: *The Local* #x003C;www.thelocal.ch/20211019/switzerland-to-legalise-cannabis-production-and-usage/>
151 "Swiss Government Moves Closer to Legalizing Cannabis" (28 October 2021), online: *leNews* <https://lenews.ch/2021/10/28/swiss-government-moves-closer-to-legalising-cannabis/>

Drug Legalization in Other Democracies 99

for the possession of small quantities of drugs for personal use to be subject to either: 1) imprisonment for one month to two years; or 2) replacement of a carceral sentence with detoxification and rehabilitation treatment.[152] Argentina's Supreme Court ruled this provision unconstitutional in the 2009 *Arriola*[153] case, concluding that criminalizing possession of small amounts of marijuana for personal use when no danger or harm is posed to others is a violation of Article 19 of the country's national constitution.[154] The fact that Argentinian Supreme Court rulings do not bind lower courts, coupled with the broad language used in the Court's ruling, has meant that each judge has subsequently been given the authority to determine the quantity and circumstances of possession that qualify as "personal use".[155] As a result, the decision should not be read as decriminalizing the use of marijuana in general, but only that it is unconstitutional to impose criminal penalties on adults who consume small amounts of marijuana in private settings with no harm to others.[156] In the years following the *Arriola* decision, there has been some legislative movement pertaining to the medical and non-medical use of cannabis. In 2017, a law legalizing medical cannabis was passed that has subsequently been criticized for producing regulations so strict that it effectively made the drug inaccessible to patients.[157] It should be noted that a similar trend was observed in the early days of Canada's medical cannabis regime, prompting several legal challenges.[158] In response to these issues, Law 27350 was passed in November 2020, which, amongst other things, allows patients with a medical prescription to choose between cultivating their own cannabis, getting it from "solidary growers" (similar to caregivers in some U.S. states) or acquiring it through pharmacies.[159] Importantly, the new law also vastly expands the qualifying conditions for medical access (previously restricted to cases of drug-resistant epilepsy only), with physicians now deciding when a patient has a qualifying need.[160] In 2021, President Alberto Fernandez's government published a

152 Argentina, Law No. 23737, Article 14, Sept. 1, 1989, Boletin Oficial [B.O]
153 Corte Suprema de Justicia de la Nación [CSJN] [National Supreme Court of Justice], 25/8/2009, "Arriola, Sebastián y otros / Recursode Hecho" (Arriola Case) (A. 891. XLIV)
154 Graciela Rodriguez-Ferrand, "Decriminalization of Narcotics" (2016), online (pdf): *Law Library of the United States Congress* <https://tile.loc.gov/storage-services/service/ll/llglrd/2016479004/2016479004.pdf> at 39
155 *Ibid*
156 "La Corte no Ordenó la Despenalización General del Consumo de Marihuana" (25 August 2009), online: *Centro de información judicial* <www.cij.gov.ar/nota-2156-La-Corte-no-ordeno-la-despenalizacion-general-del-consumo-demarihuana.html>
157 Daniel Politi, "Argentina to Allow Medicinal Marijuana to Be Grown at Home" (11 December 2020), online: *New York Times* #x003C;www.nytimes.com/2020/11/12/world/americas/argentina-cannabis-marijuana.html>
158 Chapter 2.5
159 Javier Hasse, "Argentina Regulates Medical Cannabis Self-Cultivation, Sales, Subsidized Access" (12 November 2020), online: *Forbes* #x003C;www.forbes.com/sites/javier-hasse/2020/11/12/argentina-regulates-medical-cannabis-self-cultivation-sales-sub sidized-access/?sh=17b4b1841655>
160 *Ibid*

100 *Drug Legalization in Other Democracies*

draft regulatory framework for the development of the country's medical industry, including the proposed creation of a national agency to oversee the cannabis production chain.[161] Matias Kulfas, Minister of Productive Development, has estimated that the new medical system will bring in approximately $500 million USD in domestic sales and $50 million USD in export sales annually.[162] While President Alberto Fernandez has recently stated his opinion that "adult-use cannabis legalization needs to be discussed",[163] there has been no further movement on legislative reform pertaining to recreational cannabis.

4.3.2 Brazil

Brazil made consequential amendments to its drug laws when it passed Law No. 11.343 in August 2006. The legislation "aims to reduce drug use by focusing on education and drug abuse prevention for individual users, while reducing the flow of drugs into and through the country".[164] While the new law does not completely decriminalize drug use and possession, it reduces the punishment for possession of small amounts of illicit drugs for personal consumption to alternative "social educational sentences".[165] Brazilian researchers have argued that the law has been applied repressively, with statistics showing that levels of arrest and incarceration for drug trafficking have been high, even amongst those who were found with small amounts of marijuana and cocaine.[166] While the legislation was touted by supporters as providing for alternative measures and treatment, it has been argued that, in practice, there are very few existing drug rehabilitation programs available to addicts.[167] Moreover, the legislation allows for harsher penalties for drug trafficking, including minimum sentences of three years and a maximum sentence of fifteen years.[168] There are no set quantities that distinguish between personal possession and trafficking, thus leaving this determination up to judges.[169] Since 2015, medical access to cannabis has been allowed, but only

---

161 Hector Gomes, "Cannabis and Hemp to Kickstart Argentina's Economic Recovery?" (16 June 2021), online: *Prohibition Partners* <https://prohibitionpartners.com/2021/06/16/cannabis-and-hemp-to-aid-argentinas-economic-recovery/>

162 *Ibid*

163 El Planteo, "Adult-Use Cannabis Legalization Needs to Be Discussed, Says Argentina's President Alberto Fernàndez" (2 August 2021), online: *yahoo!finance* <https://finance.yahoo.com/news/adult-cannabis-legalization-needs-discussed-194908198.html>

164 Spencer Brown, "The Lowdown on Getting High in Brazil: The Evolution of Brazilian Drug Law" (2008) 14 Journal of the Americas at 425

165 *Ibid*

166 Jaime Amparo Alves & Dina Alves, "Drugs and Drug Control in Brazil" in Anita Kalunta-Crumpton, ed, *Pan-African Issues in Drugs and Drug Control: An International Perspective* (Ashgate Publishing Ltd: England, 2015) 241 at 242

167 *Ibid* at 257

168 Brown, *supra* note 164 at 426

169 *Ibid*

Drug Legalization in Other Democracies 101

to terminally ill patients or those who have exhausted other treatment options.[170] Access was sparse prior to 2019, as cannabis remained listed as a plant that could not be cultivated or imported.[171] In order to address this, the Brazilian Health Regulatory Agency (ANVISA) published regulations in late 2019 that effectively allow the manufacture and importation of specific medical cannabis products while rejecting domestic cultivation.[172] This has again raised concerns that medical cannabis products in Brazil are both incredibly expensive and difficult to procure.[173] Legislation that would legalize cultivation was approved in June 2021 by a congressional committee but is still pending Senate and presidential approval.[174] Reform to any of the country's recreational drug laws is extremely unlikely, as President Jair Bolsonaro re-affirmed his election promise to invest in the war on drugs through a 2019 presidential decree that effectively removes all harm reduction approaches and excludes civil society representatives from the National Drug Policy Council.[175]

4.3.3 Chile

According to the Transnational Institute, Chile's current drug legislation is contained in Law 20.000, which came into force in February 2005 and replaced 1995's Law 19.366.[176] The law allows for personal consumption of any recreational drug but does not establish a threshold for permitted quantities, leaving the distinction between trafficking and consumption up to the discretion of the judge.[177] Imprisonment terms for trafficking can range from 5 to 15 years for large quantities and from 541 days to 5 years for small quantities unless the accused is able to prove that the substance is intended for personal consumption.[178] In 2014,

---

170 Angela Kung & Jùlia Kesselring, "Regulation of Cannabis Products in Brazil" (n.d.), online: *International Bar Association* #x003C;www.ibanet.org/article/DD9E29E5-E25A-4EC0-BE4B-C83EB44EFC69>

171 *Ibid*

172 Alfredo Pascual, "Brazil's New Medical Cannabis Rules Reject Domestic Cultivation, Potentially Setting Up Large Import Market" (4 December 2019), online: *MJBizDaily* <https://mjbizdaily.com/brazil-new-medical-cannabis-rules-reject-domestic-cultivation-potentially-setting-up-large-import-market/>

173 Raphael Tsavkko Garcia, "The Struggle for Medical Marijuana Access in Brazil" (14 December 2020), online: *Filter* <https://filtermag.org/struggle-medical-marijuana-brazil/>

174 Ana Mano, "Cannabis Firms Catch a Whiff of Opportunity in Brazil" (20 August 2021), online: *Reuters*#x003C;www.reuters.com/business/cannabis-firms-catch-whiff-opportunity-brazil-2021-08-20/>

175 Felipe Neis Araujo, "In Brazil, Bolsonaro Continues to Pump Blood to the War on Drugs" (29 January 2021), online: *IDPC* <https://idpc.net/alerts/2021/01/in-brazil-bolsonaro-continues-to-pump-blood-to-the-war-on-drugs>

176 "Overview of Drug Laws and Legislative Trends in Chile" (n.d.), online: *Transnational Institute* #x003C;www.druglawreform.info/en/country-information/latin-america/chile/item/202-chile>

177 *Ibid*

178 *Ibid*

102 *Drug Legalization in Other Democracies*

Chile became the first country in Latin America to cultivate cannabis for strictly medical purposes.[179] The Institute of Public Health is the state agency in charge of issuing authorizations and setting the conditions of cannabis use, with patients holding a prescription able to purchase medical cannabis in authorized places.[180] Chileans voted in favour of a constitutional overhaul following protests in 2019 and 2020, leading some to believe that the new arrangements may have favourable impacts on future cannabis legislative reform.[181] Medical cannabis advocates currently argue that the medical system is plagued by law enforcement overreach and difficulties securing affordable treatment.[182] Following the December 2021 election of new President Gabriel Boric, some media outlets have quoted Boric as saying, "I think we have to legalize self-cultivation and not go further",[183] suggesting little likelihood of wider cannabis policy liberalization in the near future.

4.3.4 Columbia

According to the Transnational Institute, Law 30 (1986), also known as the National Narcotics Statute, has had its repressive stance regarding drug use challenged in the courts several times in the nation's history.[184] In 1994, Colombia's Constitutional Court declared provisions of the law unenforceable, arguing that the right to free development of personality was violated by laws that criminalized personal use and possession of drugs.[185] 2011 brought the enactment of the Citizen Security Law, another piece of legislation that sought to criminalize the use and possession of personal amounts of drugs, but a subsequent ruling of the Constitutional Court once again re-affirmed the decriminalization of personal drug use and possession.[186] In 2019, public cannabis consumption was made legal, prompting some to wonder if the legalization of recreational cannabis

---

179 Kyra Gurney, "Chile Kicks Off Medical Marijuana Program" (30 October 2014), online: *InSight Crime* <https://insightcrime.org/news/brief/chile-latin-america-grow-medical-marijuana/>

180 Luise Arze & Matias Somarriva, "Medical Use" (15 April 2021), online: *CMS: Tax, Law, Future* <https://cms.law/en/int/expert-guides/cms-expert-guide-to-a-legal-roadmap-to-cannabis/chile>

181 Fred Rocafort, "Chile's New Constitution: An Opportunity for Cannabis" (16 June 2021), online: *Cannalaw Blog*<https://harrisbricken.com/cannalawblog/chiles-new-constitution-an-opportunity-for-cannabis/>

182 *Ibid*

183 El Planto, "Chile's New President Gabriel Boric Says He Smoked Marijuana in University, Passes Drug Test Before Election" (21 December 2021), online: *Benzinga* #x003C;www.benzinga.com/markets/cannabis/21/12/24727381/chiles-new-president-gabriel-boric-says-he-smoked-marijuana-in-university-passes-drug-test-before>

184 "Colombia: Re-Criminalization Pending" (n.d.), online: *Transnational Institute:* #x003C;www.druglawreform.info/en/site_content/item/203-colombia>

185 "Ruling C-221 of the 1994 Constitutional Court" (5 May 1994), online: *District Legal Secretariat* #x003C;www.alcaldiabogota.gov.co/sisjur/normas/Norma1.jsp?i=6960>

186 "Judgment C-491/12" (November 2011), online: *Constitutional Court of Columbia* #x003C;www.corteconstitucional.gov.co/relatoria/2012/c-491-12.htm>

Drug Legalization in Other Democracies 103

was on the horizon.[187] However, in 2020, legislative attempts to codify the past reasoning of the Constitutional Court and permit recreational consumption and sales of cannabis at regulated stores failed, prompting some lawmakers to argue that drug cartels will continue to benefit from a system that does not allow the state to take control of production and commercialization.[188] Legislative reforms pertaining to medical cannabis have enjoyed greater success over the last five years. In 2015, medical cannabis was legalized by presidential decree, allowing for the production, manufacture, and sale of medical cannabis through a licensing system overseen by the National Narcotics Council.[189] It is interesting to note that a similar trend of medical cannabis legalization (and expansion) alongside continued recreational prohibition occurred in Canada throughout most of the 2000s.[190] In July 2021, President Ivan Duque again signed a presidential decree, this time lifting a prohibition on the exporting of dried cannabis flower for medical and other industrial purposes.[191] This has led to expectations that the Colombian medical cannabis sector is poised for "liftoff", with both production and licensing costs representing a fraction of the price in the United States and other jurisdictions.[192]

4.3.5 Costa Rica

According to the Transnational Institute, drug use has been decriminalized in Costa Rica since Law 7093 was enacted in 1988, making the personal consumption of drugs subject to an administrative punishment of fines.[193] Further legislative reform came in 2001 with Law 8204, which decriminalized drug use completely and included provisions aimed at facilitating "voluntary treatment".[194] Following an increase in arrests of drug users in 2010 and 2011, the Public

---

187 Javier Hasse, "Public Cannabis Consumption Now Allowed in Columbia: Is Full Marijuana Legalization Next?" (19 June 2019), online: *Forbes* #x003C;www.forbes.com/sites/javierhasse/2019/06/19/colombia-public-cannabis-consumption/?sh=2f09f78429e9>

188 Diana Delgado, "Colombia Shelves Congressional Bill on Cannabis Legalization" (10 November 2020), online: *Cannabis Business Times* #x003C;www.cannabisbusinesstimes.com/article/colombia-shelves-bill-legalize-cannabis/>

189 Paula Carrillo, "A Vendor Displays a Marijuana Plant at a Medical-Products Fair in Bogota, Columbia" (22 December 2015), online: *yahoo!news* #x003C;www.yahoo.com/news/colombia-legalizes-medical-marijuana-171023547.html?ref=gs>

190 Chapter 2.5

191 Nelson Bocanegra, "Colombia Boosts Budding Cannabis Industry by Removing Ban on Dry Flower Exports" (23 July 2021), online: *Reuters* #x003C;www.reuters.com/world/americas/colombia-boosts-budding-cannabis-industry-by-removing-ban-dry-flower-exports-2021–07–23/>

192 Stefano Pozzebon, "With Export Restrictions Eased, Colombia's Medical Cannabis Business Is Poised for Liftoff" (25 October 2021), online: *CNN Business* #x003C;www.cnn.com/2021/10/24/business/legal-cannabis-colombia-export/index.html>

193 "About Drug Law Reform in Costa Rica" (30 August 2014), online: *Transnational Institute* #x003C;www.tni.org/en/publication/about-drug-law-reform-in-costa-rica>

194 *Ibid*

104 *Drug Legalization in Other Democracies*

Prosecutor's office issued two circulars instructing prosecutors to reject all cases of possession for personal use.[195] This policy of decriminalization has more recently been subjected to criticism pointing towards a lack of resources aimed at supporting those with addiction.[196] The absence of adequate treatment resources is compounded by the rampant supply provided for by a completely unregulated illicit market.[197] In 2018, in the case of lawyer and activist Mario Salazar, the Costa Rican Supreme Court decriminalized the cultivation of small personal quantities of cannabis and, in doing so, found that cannabis use was not a threat to public health.[198] Nonetheless, in subsequent years recreational cannabis legalization has not appeared on the political agenda in Costa Rica, though there has been significant movement towards medical legalization. Legislation that would allow for the cultivation, production, and industrialization of (non-psychoactive) cannabis for medicinal use was first introduced in 2019 and has slowly been moving its way through Costa Rica's legislative process.[199] In late December 2021, the Constitutional Chamber of the Supreme Court of Justice notified the Legislative Assembly that the draft law on Cannabis for Medicinal and Therapeutic Use did not present any procedural or substantive unconstitutionalities, effectively greenlighting the legislation for passage in the Legislative Assembly.[200]

4.3.6 Mexico

The legalization of cannabis in Mexico is imminent, despite years of stalled legislative efforts amidst a plethora of significant court decisions. Under Mexican law, five decisions of the Supreme Court set a binding precedent nationally.[201] The first of these decisions occurred back in 2015 when the Mexican Supreme Court accepted an argument that the right to free development of one's personality (similar to that accepted by courts in the jurisdictions noted above) rendered

---

195 *Ibid*
196 Allison Tierney, "The Costa Rica Model: Why Decriminalization of Drug Use Sometimes Isn't Enough" (5 April 2017), online: *VICE* #x003C;www.vice.com/en/article/kbjvax/the-costa-rica-model-why-decriminalization-of-drug-use-sometimes-isnt-enough>
197 *Ibid*
198 Carol Vaughn, "Lawyer and Activist Grows Marijuana on Terrace Overlooking Costa Rica Court House" (3 February 2022), online: *The Costa Rica Star* <https://news.co.cr/lawyer-and-activist-grows-marijuana-on-terrace-overlooking-costa-rica-court-house/82523/
199 David Goldberg, "Medical Cannabis in Costa Rica: A Controversial Alternative Awaiting Legalization" (29 December 2021), online: *The Tico Times* <https://ticotimes.net/2021/12/29/medical-cannabis-in-costa-rica-a-controversial-alternative-awaiting-legalization>
200 "Costa Rican Supreme Court Did Not Find Unconstitutionalities in the Medical Cannabis Legalization Project" (5 December 2021), online: *The Costa Rica News* <https://thecostaricanews.com/costa-rican-supreme-court-did-not-find-unconstitutionalities-in-the-medical-cannabis-legalization-project/>
201 Christopher Ingrahm, "Mexico's Supreme Court Overturns Country's Ban on Recreational Marijuana" (1 November 2018), online: *The Washington Post* #x003C;www.washingtonpost.com/business/2018/11/01/mexicos-supreme-court-overturns-countrys-recreational-marijuana-ban/>

Drug Legalization in Other Democracies   105

the prohibition of cannabis possession and consumption unconstitutional.[202] The fifth and most recent of these judgments came in 2018, meaning that "while cannabis prohibition law nominally remains in place for now (and arrests remain possible), all judges nationally are now bound by the Supreme Court judgment as a defense in the (now much less likely) scenario of prosecutions being brought".[203] Legislative change in response to this judgment has been remarkably slow, leading to pressure from human rights groups, both domestic and foreign. Human Rights Watch has called the legalization of marijuana the "first crucial step towards adopting alternative approaches to drug policy"[204] in a jurisdiction that has suffered high human costs of the global war on drugs. Agoff et al argue that "Legalization will limit arrests and police will have one less way of extorting people".[205] Critics note that despite the legalization of medical cannabis in 2017 and the Supreme Court's 2018 decision, it has taken more than three years for legalization legislation to make any real progress through the legislative process.[206] During this three-year period, "The bill has been passed back and forth between chambers with multiple revisions made in that time with no outwardly visible progress".[207] There were, however, reasons to be optimistic throughout 2021. In March, the Chamber of deputies passed legislation that would allow anyone over the age of 18 to purchase and possess less than 28 grams of cannabis whilst also reducing penalties for up to 200 grams to a fine of $500 and allowing for six plants to be grown at home.[208] The Institute for the Regulation and Control of Cannabis will be in charge of granting licenses for cultivation, processing, sale, research, import, and export and is expected to start granting these licenses within six months of the Mexican president's signing of the law.[209] Before this can happen, the bill must gain approval in the Senate, with late December 2021 reports suggesting that Mexican senators are currently considering the legislation and "expectations are high for its success".[210] Other reports, which note the COVID-19 pandemic as the key reason why legislation was not passed by the end

---

202 Christopher Ingrahm, "Mexico's Supreme Court Rules That Smoking Pot Is a Fundamental Human Right" (5 November 2015), online: *The Washington Post* #x003C;www.washingtonpost.com/news/wonk/wp/2015/11/05/mexicos-supreme-court-rules-that-smoking-weed-is-a-fundamental-human-right/>

203 *Ingrahm, supra* note 201

204 "Mexico: Reform Marijuana Policy" (23 April 2021), online: *Human Rights Watch* #x003C;www.hrw.org/news/2021/04/23/mexico-reform-marijuana-policy>

205 Carolina Agoff et al, "Cultural Stigmatization and Police Corruption" (2021) Drugs: Education, Prevention and Policy Journal, DOI: <10.1080/09687637.2021.2004089> at 8

206 *Ibid* at 3

207 Josh Lee, "Mexico to Vote on Legalization" (9 December 2021), online: *The Paper* <https://abq.news/2021/12/mexico-to-vote-on-legalization/>

208 Vanda Felbab-Brown, "Mexico's Cannabis Legalization, and Comparisons with Colombia, Lebanon, and Canada" (30 March 2021), online: *Brookings* #x003C;www.brookings.edu/blog/order-from-chaos/2021/03/30/mexicos-cannabis-legalization-and-comparisons-with-colombia-lebanon-and-canada/>

209 *Ibid*

210 Lee, *supra* note 207

106 *Drug Legalization in Other Democracies*

of 2021, nonetheless quote various members of Mexico's senate as expecting the law to be passed by April 2022, at the latest.[211] Mexico's ideal climate for cannabis cultivation, as well as its abundance of skilled, affordable labour (due to the widespread prevalence of other kinds of agricultural production), have been cited as factors that are likely to contribute to the success of its cannabis industry.[212] With more than 120 million people, Mexico would represent the largest cannabis market in the world by population and, depending on the regulatory system enacted, could provide a financial lift for an economy that has been deeply affected by the coronavirus pandemic.[213]

4.3.7 *Paraguay*

According to the Transnational Institute, the 1988 Law 1.340 exempted punishment for those in possession of up to a maximum of 2 grams of cocaine or heroin and 10 grams of marijuana for personal consumption.[214] Paraguay is consistently ranked as the biggest supplier of cannabis in South America, with its National Anti-Drug Secretariat estimating that nearly 200,000 farmers in the country depend on marijuana cultivation for survival.[215] One 2019 report estimated that the country had produced 40,000 tons of cannabis in that year.[216] While the country legalized medicinal cannabis in 2007, a regulatory system was not established until 2018 and applications for licenses did not begin to be accepted until September 2019.[217] In February 2020, the country granted its first 12 licenses, taking what is argued to be a "novel approach by allowing only pharmaceutical

211 Mattha Busby, "Here's Why Marijuana Still Isn't Legal in Mexico (but could be soon)" (15 December 2021), online: *Leafly* #x003C;www.leafly.ca/news/politics/heres-why-marijuana-still-isnt-legal-in-mexico-but-could-be-soon

212 "This Company Is the One and Only Authorized to Commercialize CBD and CBG in Mexico" (15 December 2021), online: *Financial Post* <https://financialpost.com/business-trends/this-company-is-the-one-and-only-authorized-to-commercialize-cbd-and-cbg-in-mexico>

213 Oscar Lopez, "Mexico Set to Legalize Marijuana, Becoming World's Largest Market" (19 March 20210), online: *The New York Times* #x003C;www.nytimes.com/2021/03/10/world/americas/mexico-cannabis-bill.html>

214 "Paraguay: Decriminalization" (n.d.), online: *Transnational Institute* #x003C;www.druglawreform.info/en/country-information/latin-america/paraguay/item/206-paraguay>

215 Sarah Friedman, "Paraguay Grows It, Brazil Takes It . . . Will New Cannabis Laws Change Anything?" (2021), online: *CBD testers* <https://cbdtesters.co/2020/09/22/paraguay-brazil-cannabis/>

216 Katie Jones, "US Announcement Against Corrupt Paraguay Official May Signal Shift" (9 April 2021), online: *InSight Crime* <https://insightcrime.org/news/corruption-crackdown-us-acts-against-corrupt-paraguay-officials>

217 Alfredo Pascual, "Paraguay to Open Application Process for Medical Cannabis Production Licenses in October" (16 September 2019), online: *MJBizDaily* <https://mjbizdaily.com/paraguay-to-open-application-process-for-medical-cannabis-production-licenses-in-october/>

laboratories to apply for licenses".[218] These licensed producers will be required to donate 2% of their production to the state, which will distribute the drug, free of cost, to qualifying patients, although it is expected that it might be years until this production begins.[219] It has been suggested that by granting licenses to well-established pharmaceutical companies rather than to poor farmers that grow illegal marijuana, the government missed an opportunity to solve two problems at once.[220] There is currently no reason to expect any legislative reform or further liberalization of laws pertaining to recreational cannabis in Paraguay.

4.3.8 Peru

According to the Transnational Institute, a variety of drugs are not subject to punishment when possession is deemed to be for personal use. More specifically, Article 299 of the country's Criminal Code allows for personal use possession of two grams of cocaine, eight grams of marijuana, one gram of opium or two-hundred and fifty milligrams of ecstasy.[221] Nonetheless, it is estimated that 60% of detentions on drug charges are related to use or simple possession, and the Peruvian government's strategy of supply reduction and forced eradication has largely been seen as a failure.[222] Like Paraguay, there is no reason to expect legislative reform in relation to recreational drug use, but there have been some notable developments in regard to medical cannabis legalization. A 2017 police raid uncovered a cannabis laboratory run by a therapeutic association called Searching for Hope, a group of mothers who had been treating their sick children with cannabis oil.[223] Subsequently, multiple protests occurred demanding the legalization of cannabis for medicinal purposes, resulting in the 2017 enactment of Law No. 30681.[224] Two years later, the Peruvian government issued regulations pertaining to the medical cannabis system, establishing licenses for research, wholesale import, and production, whilst mandating that only public institutions and

218 Alfredo Pascual, "Paraguay Issues First 12 Medical Cannabis Production Licenses" (25 February 2020), online: *MJBizDaily* <https://mjbizdaily.com/paraguay-issues-first-12-medical-cannabis-production-licenses/>

219 *Ibid*

220 Max Radwin, "Paraguay Shakes Up Drug Policy with First Medical Cannabis Licenses" (16 March 2020), online: *InSight Crime* <https://insightcrime.org/news/brief/paraguay-medical-cannabis/>

221 "Peru: Decriminalization" (n.d.), online: *Transnational Institute* <http://druglawreform.info/en/country-information/latin-america/peru/item/207-peru>

222 *Ibid*

223 Dan Collyns, "Peru Legalizes Medical Marijuana in Move Spurred by Mother's Home Lab" (20 October 2017), online: *The Guardian* #x003C;www.theguardian.com/world/2017/oct/20/peru-marijuana-cannabis-legal-terminally-ill-children>

224 Nikolás Salazar & Cindy Salvador, "Market Development of the Cannabis in Peru" (20 February 2020), online: *ECOVIS* #x003C;www.ecovis.com/global/market-development-of-the-cannabis-in-peru/>

108 *Drug Legalization in Other Democracies*

registered and certified pharmaceutical laboratories would be allowed to apply.[225] By 2021, activists were arguing that insufficient access was still forcing chronically ill patients to acquire products from an unregulated parallel market.[226] Following additional protests and lobbying efforts by the Searching for Hope group, the Peruvian government passed further reforms in July 2021 that will allow cultivation by patient-run associations.[227] Patients who are registered with the country's National Register of Patients Using Cannabis can now form associations that can apply for licenses to grow, process, transport and store cannabis for medical purposes.[228]

4.3.9 Uruguay

Uruguay is arguably the outlier in Latin America (perhaps even the world) when it comes to its historical drug policy. This was true well before the country became the world's first jurisdiction to legalize recreational cannabis in 2013. Uruguay never criminalized the possession of drugs for personal consumption, and decriminalization of possession for personal use was formally introduced (in 1974) and later updated in 1998 with Law 17.016.[229] The 1998 amendments were particularly important, as they allowed for personal possession and use (minimum amounts determined by a judge) to be prosecuted without the threat of imprisonment.[230] The country's outlier status was solidified when it famously passed Law 19.172 in December 2013, which effectively gave the state control over all aspects (cultivation, production, distribution, etc.) of a legal recreational cannabis system.[231] Uruguay's cannabis legalization has differed from that of Canada (and several U.S. states) in several significant ways. First, unlike the for-profit commercial models that have been adopted in several U.S. states, Uruguay has instead preferred a state-run, non-commercial regulatory system through

---

225 "Peru's New Cannabis Law Opens the Doors for Big Business" (22 October 2021), online: *BizLatin Hub* #x003C;www.bizlatinhub.com/perus-new-cannabis-law-opens-doors-big-business/>

226 Carla Samon Ros, "Peru's Chronically Ill Seeking Right to Grow Cannabis for Medicinal Use" (19 January 2021), online: *La Prensa Latin Media* #x003C;www.laprensalatina.com/perus-chronically-ill-seeking-right-to-grow-cannabis-for-medicinal-use/>

227 Caitlin Donohue, "Mothers Are the Reason Peru Just Expanded Medical Cannabis Legalizing Laws" (n.d.), online: *Merry Jane* <https://merryjane.com/news/mothers-are-the-reason-peru-just-expanded-medical-cannabis-legalization-laws>

228 Kathryn Tindale, "Peru Allows Medical Cannabis Cultivation by Patient Associations" (6 August 2021), online: *Mugglehead* <https://mugglehead.com/peru-allows-medical-cannabis-cultivation-by-patient-associations/>

229 "Uruguay: Overview of Drug Policy, Drug Law and Legislative Trends in Uruguay" (n.d.), online: *Transnational Institute* <http://druglawreform.info/en/country-information/latin-america/uruguay/item/5667-uruguay#2>

230 *Ibid*

231 Hannah Laqueur et al, "The Impact of Cannabis Legalization in Uruguay on Adolescent Cannabis Use" (2020) 80 International Journal of Drug Policy, <DOI: 10.1016/j.drugpo.2020.102748< at 1

which the government controls all large-scale production, requires registration, and limits weekly quantities that a user may purchase.[232] Moreover, while much of the cannabis reform in U.S. states has been achieved through popular referendum and citizens' initiatives, Uruguay's legalization was delivered through a top-down effort from the country's President and his ruling party.[233] This was despite the fact that, at the time of enactment, legalization was opposed by more than 60% of Uruguay's citizens, in stark contrast to positive Canadian public attitudes towards legalization when the Cannabis Act was passed.[234] Whereas the "Liberal Party won the 2015 federal election based on a platform that included cannabis legalization",[235] in Uruguay, "neither activists, nor public opinion, nor a party's mandate towards its electorate played a decisive role in introducing to topic into the public's agenda".[236] Another stark difference is the method of distribution. While the Canadian government downloaded the responsibility for retail sales to each province, Uruguay's system allows for citizens to acquire cannabis through three specific means: home cultivation, cannabis social clubs, or pharmacies.[237]

Unsurprisingly, given Uruguay's status as the first jurisdiction to legalize cannabis, there is a wealth of commentary on the strengths and weaknesses of the country's system. It has been argued that the 2013 legislation was implemented at a "slow but deliberate pace", including the following important regulatory steps: 1) a May 2014 presidential decree that set purchasing limits at 10 grams per week and stipulated that only citizens and residents over the age of 18 could choose one (and only one at a time) method of accessing legal cannabis; 2) the 2014 registration of home-growers and social clubs; 3) the 2015 framework allowing physicians to dispense medical cannabis; 4) the 2015 selection of two companies (out of more than twenty applicants) to grow cannabis for sale in pharmacies; and 5) the July 19, 2017 launch of recreational sales in 16 pharmacies across the country.[238] In the years that followed, several challenges emerged, including: 1) many Uruguayan banks, threatened with the risk of withdrawal of major American financial institutions from their business, notified pharmacies that they would effectively be forced to close their accounts; 2) supply issues, stemming from the above-noted banking issues and production issues at one of the Government's only two authorized cultivators; 3) issues related to enforcement, with limited manpower to monitor compliance with rules aimed at home

---

232 *Ibid*
233 *Ibid* at 2
234 *Ibid*
235 Rosario Queirolo, "Uruguay: The First Country to Legalize Cannabis" in Tom Decorte, Simon Lenton & Chris Wilkins, eds, *Legalizing Cannabis: Experiences, Lessons and Scenarios* (London: Routledge) 116 at 117
236 *Ibid* at 116
237 Laqueur et al, *supra* note 231, at 2
238 John Hudak, Geoff Ramsey & John Walsh, "Uruguay's Cannabis Law: Pioneering a New Paradigm" (March 2018), online (pdf): *Center for Effective Public Management at Brookings* #x003C;www.brookings.edu/wp-content/uploads/2018/03/gs_032118_uruguaye 28099s-cannabis-law_final.pdf> at 5–6

110 *Drug Legalization in Other Democracies*

cultivation and social clubs; 4) the problem of cannabis tourism, which further compounds the above-noted enforcement issue; and 5) limited access to (and high costs of) medical cannabis products, due to stringent requirements and restrictions.[239] Despite these challenges, a number of successes and strengths of Uruguay's system have been identified. It has been suggested that more than half of cannabis consumers in the country are accessing the product through legal means, which represents a significant reduction in the illicit market.[240] Moreover, there have been almost no reports of incidents between legal users and the police, and home growers and social clubs have reportedly "experienced certainty and predictability about how the regulations work and what they must do in order to operate under the law".[241]

In more recent years, appraisals of Uruguay's system have been mixed. One academic study has suggested that Uruguay's non-commercial model has not resulted in the increases in adolescent cannabis use that have been observed in other jurisdictions.[242] In 2020, the former head of the Uruguayan national drug agency, Diego Olivera, heralded the recreational cannabis market as a "tangible success", noting that new production licenses granted at the end of 2019 would likely ease supply issues.[243] Others question whether one of the policy's stated objectives – public security – has been met, noting that crime and violence in the country have not diminished and that the homicide rate, particularly amongst criminals, has increased.[244] Concerns around banking persist, although it is hoped that this will be alleviated as cannabis policy reform continues to sweep across the United States.[245] It should also be noted that banking was identified as one of the early challenges for Canadian cannabis industry leaders looking to establish operations, and it seems that this challenge has dissipated as more banks have become willing to enter the cannabis industry.[246] The tourism challenge faced by Uruguay may also soon be addressed through legislation, as both the Secretary General of the National Drugs Board and the Deputy Tourism Minister have recently suggested that legislation allowing for tourist consumption (with higher prices) is on the horizon and will likely dramatically increase the size of Uruguay's market.[247] With less than five years having elapsed since Uruguay launched recreational

---

239 *Ibid* at 9–15
240 Queirolo, *supra* note 235, at 123
241 *Ibid* at 125
242 Laqueur et al, *supra* note 231, at 7
243 Alfredo Pascual, "Three Years in, Uruguay's Recreational Cannabis Market 'Tangible' Success" (17 December 2021), online: *MJBizDaily* <https://mjbizdaily.com/3-years-after-legalization-uruguays-recreational-cannabis-market-tangible-success/>
244 Queirolo, *supra* note 235, at 125
245 Sarah Friedman, "Uruguay Was the First Country to Legalize Cannabis- How Are They Doing Now?" (2020), online: *CBD Testers* <https://cbdtesters.co/2020/04/26/uruguay-was-1st-country-to-legalize-cannabis-how-are-they-doing-now/>
246 Chapter 2.7
247 Ken Parks, "Uruguay Wants to Open Pot Market to Tourists: Cannabis Weekly" (13 September 2021), online: *Bloomberg* #x003C;www.bloomberg.com/news/articles/2021-09-13/uruguay-wants-to-open-pot-market-to-tourists-cannabis-weekly>

Drug Legalization in Other Democracies 111

sales, much future research is still needed before determining whether or not the country's cannabis experiment has been an overall success.

4.4 United States

The United States Federal Government's "War on Drugs" is discussed in earlier chapters of this book.[248] There is no shortage of academic literature that discusses the failure of the United States' historically punitive drug policy, particularly in light of the mass incarceration of its (disproportionately minority) citizens and an ongoing opioid crisis that continues to claim the lives of thousands of Americans on a yearly basis.[249] Space precludes a full discussion of these issues. The analyses below focus instead on what is a growing wave of cannabis (and in some cases, wider drug) policy liberalization initiated at the state level throughout the country. Nonetheless, it is important to first note the complicated constitutional arrangements within the U.S. federal system that have allowed individual states to engage in drug policy liberalization, even though federal law still heavily prohibits cannabis and other drugs. As is noted by Pardo,

> Cannabis policy in the United States remains unguided, with states continuing to drive changes. . . . Without robust policy guidance from federal authorities, states are stitching their own legal and regulatory patchwork for the supply and use of non-medical cannabis within the remaining legal bounds imposed by federal law.[250]

In 2009, the Obama Administration released the "Ogden Memorandum", a policy memorandum in relation to medical cannabis prohibition that directed federal authorities to focus on high-level targets such as organized criminals and drug

---

248 Chapter 2.3
249 For a small sample of the substantial and comprehensive academic discussion of these topics, see: Minhee & Calandrillo, *supra* note 121; Earp, Lewis & Hart, *supra* note 121; Virani & Haines-Saah, *supra* note 124; Daniel Patten, "The Mass Incarceration of Nations and the Global War on Drugs: Comparing the United States' Domestic and Foreign Drug Policies" (2016) 43:1 Social Justice 85; Michael Tonry, "Race and the War on Drugs" (1994) 1 University of Chicago Legal Forum 25; Joseph Kennedy, Isaac Unah & Kasi Wahlers, "Sharks and Minors in the War on Drugs: A Study of Quantity, Race and Drug Type in Drug Arrests" (2018) 52 University of California Davis Law Review 729; Kenneth B. Nunn, "Race, Crime and the Pool of Surplus Criminality: Or Why the 'War on Drugs' Was a 'War on Blacks'" (2002) 6 The Journal of Gender, Race & Justice 381; Katherine Fornili, "Racialized Mass Incarceration and the War on Drugs" (2018) 29:1 Journal of Addictions Nursing 65; Lawrence Bobo & Victor Thompson, "Unfair by Design: The War on Drugs, Race, and the Legitimacy of the Criminal Justice System" (2006) 73:2 Social Research 445
250 Bryce Pardo, "The Uneven Repeal of Cannabis Prohibition in the United States" in Tom Decorte, Simon Lenton & Chris Wilkins, eds, *Legalizing Cannabis: Experiences, Lessons and Scenarios* (London: Routledge, 2020) 11 at 11

traffickers.[251] In 2013, further guidance on recreational cannabis was provided through the Cole memorandum, which "stipulated that states could implement their adult-use access laws if they adhered to guidelines and fashioned a strict regulatory system".[252]

The principles of federalism (particularly the Tenth Amendment's anti-commandeering rule) have been pointed to by legal scholars as the counterbalance that "precludes the federal government from forcing states to enact coexistent, or even complementary, controlled substances laws, or from requiring state officers to enforce federal drug laws within the state".[253] As a result,

> Most states in the U.S. are adopting a commercial, regulatory framework under the hanging cloud of federal prohibition. It is unclear how or when the federal government will repeal cannabis prohibition, let alone how these markets and state regulatory authorities will react.[254]

As of 2022, the Biden government had yet to implement campaign promises pertaining to federal decriminalization and rescheduling of cannabis under the Controlled Substances Act but has nonetheless continued to allow states to implement policy reform without federal intervention.[255] As a result, and as is evidenced thoroughly by the analyses below, there has been an immense wave of cannabis (and wider drug) policy reform making its way across various states in the U.S. in recent years. There have also been some significant developments that suggest a potential for future changes at the federal level in 2022 and beyond, including: 1) the June 2021 introduction of the first-ever congressional bill to decriminalize possession of all illicit drugs;[256] 2) the July 2021 unveiling of draft Senate legislation by Senate Majority leader Chuck Schumer (Cannabis Administration and Opportunity Act) that would federally deschedule cannabis, expunge prior convictions and maintain states' authority to set their own cannabis policies;[257] and 3) repeated (but ultimately failed) 2021 attempts to pass the Secure and Fair (SAFE)

---

251 *Ibid* at 14

252 *Ibid* at 15

253 Jason Brandeis, "Ravin Revisited: Alaska's Historic Common Law Marijuana Rule at the Dawn of Legalization" (2015) 32:2 Alaska Law Review 309 at 319

254 Pardo, *supra* note 250, at 33

255 Kyle Jaeger, "After One Year as President, Biden's Marijuana Promises Remain Unfulfilled" (20 January 2022), online: *Marijuana Moment* #x003C;www.marijuanamoment.net/after-one-year-as-president-bidens-marijuana-promises-remain-unfulfilled/>

256 Kyle Jaeger, "First-Ever Congressional Bill to Decriminalize All Drugs Announced Ahead of Nixon Drug War Anniversary" (15 June 2021), online: *Marijuana Moment* #x003C;www.marijuanamoment.net/first-ever-congressional-bill-to-decriminalize-all-drugs-introduced-ahead-of-nixon-drug-war-anniversary/>

257 Kyle Jaeger, "Here Are the Full Details of the New Federal Marijuana Legalization Bill from Chuck Schumer and Senate Colleagues" (14 July 2021), online: *Marijuana Moment* #x003C;www.marijuanamoment.net/here-are-the-full-details-of-the-new-federal-marijuana-legalization-bill-from-chuck-schumer-and-senate-colleagues/>

Drug Legalization in Other Democracies 113

Banking Act, which would greatly ease banking restrictions facing the cannabis industry.[258] Given the extremely partisan nature of the country's federal politics at present and heading into a primary election year, it is remarkably difficult to foresee the future of these specific efforts in the years to come. That said, sweeping drug policy reform initiatives occurring at the state level across the country (discussed below), combined with the movement towards drug policy reform at the federal level noted above, suggest that it may very well be time to declare Nixon's "War on Drugs" over.

4.4.1 Alaska

For nearly forty years, cannabis regulation in Alaska was dictated by a significant decision of the state's Supreme Court in *Ravin v. State*.[259] The court in that case decided that cannabis was not sufficiently harmful to justify a state law that infringed an adult's fundamental right to privacy, particularly within the home where an individual's privacy receives special protection.[260] Following the decision, the Alaska state legislature decriminalized cannabis and, in 1982, removed any civil or criminal penalty for in-home use or possession of up to four ounces of cannabis.[261] In 1990, Alaska voters passed a ballot measure that recriminalized all cannabis possession, but this too was eventually overturned in 2001 by the Alaska Court of Appeals.[262] The 2006 passage of legislation that banned all cannabis use and possession once again put the precedent established in *Ravin* directly in conflict with the statute.[263] In 2014, an initiative entitled "An Act to Tax and Regulate the Production, Sale and Use of Marijuana" (known as Ballot Measure 2) passed with 53% of the vote, resulting in important changes: 1) possession for personal use amounts changed to a maximum of one ounce and three flowering plants; 2) possession rights extended beyond the home, allowing for the lawful transportation of marijuana; 3) specific guidance was given for home grow operations, requiring them to be in private, secure and concealed locations; 4) public use of cannabis became a non-criminal offence punishable only by a fine of up to $100; and 5) a commercial system for the production and sale of cannabis was established.[264] The medical use of cannabis was legalized by Alaskan voters in 1998, but that legislation did not make provision for the development of a commercial system, has been expanded minimally in subsequent years, and currently

---

258 Ben Adlin, "Here Are the Best Marijuana Psychedelics and Drug Policy News Stories of 2021" (30 December 2021), online: *Marijuana Moment* #x003C;www.marijuanamoment. net/here-are-the-biggest-marijuana-psychedelics-and-drug-policy-news-stories-of-2021/>
259 537 P. 2d 494 (Alaska 1975)
260 Brandeis, *supra* note 253, at 312–313
261 *Ibid* at 313
262 *Ibid*
263 *Ibid* at 314
264 *Ibid* at 321–322

114 *Drug Legalization in Other Democracies*

serves a very small number of registered patients.[265] A recent study found that recreational cannabis sales grew in Alaska during the COVID-19 pandemic.[266] While the recreational industry flourished in the first few years after the implementation of Ballot Measure 2, in late 2021, reports have raised concerns that the flat excise tax structure placed on cultivators, an over-saturation of retailers and the rigidity of licensing are causing many cannabis businesses to fail.[267]

4.4.2 Arizona

Both medical and recreational cannabis legalization came to Arizona by virtue of citizens' initiatives. In 2010, medical cannabis was authorized through Proposition 203, which passed by a slim margin of 50.13% of the vote.[268] The features of Arizona's medical system are: 1) patients must have a listed debilitating medical condition such as cancer, HIV/AIDS, glaucoma, multiple sclerosis (or one of several others); 2) registered patients can possess up to 2.5 ounces of cannabis; 3) patients can apply to cultivate up to 12 plants; 4) a 2019 legislative change requires dispensaries to have all medical cannabis tested by third-party laboratories and; 5) a 2019 Arizona Supreme Court judgement ruled that concentrates, edibles, and other infused products are legal under the state's medical cannabis law.[269] Recreational cannabis is a more recent development, born out of a 2020 voter initiative (Proposition 207) that passed by a 60% to 40% margin and immediately resulted in recreational sales in January 2021.[270] Key features of the recreational system are: 1) adults 21 and over can possess up to one ounce of cannabis and cultivate up to six plants in their residences; 2) sales are subject to a 5.6% sales tax and a 16% excise tax; and 3) people previously convicted of low-level cannabis offences are permitted to file petitions to have their criminal records cleared and expunged.[271] It has been suggested that the pre-existing medical system allowed the recreational system to be implemented quickly and keep up with a surge in demand.[272] It appears as though the state also benefitted from generous licensing that allowed 73 out of more than 100 dual licenses to be approved on the

---

265 *Ibid* at 314–316
266 Gillian Schauer et al, "Cannabis Sales Increase During COVID-19: Findings from Alaska, Colorado, Oregon, and Washington" (2021) 98 International Journal of Drug Policy
267 Zachariah Hughes, " 'No One's Having a Ton of Fun': Many Alaska Cannabis Businesses Are Struggling and Failing" (30 November 2021), online: *Anchorage Daily News* #x003C;www.adn.com/alaska-marijuana/2021/11/30/no-ones-having-a-ton-of-fun-many-alaska-cannabis-businesses-are-struggling-and-failing/>
268 "Arizona's Adult-Use Cannabis Market Opens Up and Expungement Policies Take Effect" (21 July 2021), online: *Marijuana Policy Project* #x003C;www.mpp.org/states/arizona/>
269 *Ibid*
270 *Ibid*
271 *Ibid*
272 Valeriya Safronova, "How Arizona Won the Weed Legalization Race" (1 April 2021), online: *The New York Times* #x003C;www.nytimes.com/2021/03/29/style/arizona-marijuana-legalization.html>

Drug Legalization in Other Democracies 115

first day of recreational sales.[273] In the first ten months of 2021, medical and recreational cannabis programs in the state have generated more than $1.1 billion dollars in sales (approx. $641 million in medical cannabis and $466 million in recreational cannabis).[274]

4.4.3 California

The Marijuana Policy Project succinctly condenses more than 20 years of cannabis policy reform in California into several key historical moments: 1) voters approve the Compassionate Use Act in 1996, allowing for the medical use of cannabis; 2) California's legislature expands the state's medical cannabis law to allow patients to cultivate cannabis in 2003; 3) California's legislature enacts a licensing and regulatory system for medical cannabis businesses in 2015; 4) voters approve a 2016 ballot initiative legalizing adult-use recreational cannabis and establishing a regulated cannabis market; 5) In 2017, the licensing and regulatory system for medical cannabis businesses was paired with the regulatory system being developed for recreational cannabis, under the umbrella of a single agency; and 6) In 2018, the first legal sales of adult-use recreational cannabis began.[275] Of particular importance was Proposition 64, the 2016 ballot initiative that legalized adult-use recreational cannabis, namely because of its breadth (over 30 pages long) and implications for numerous aspects of the recreational system, including: 1) regulations for testing and quality control of the product; 2) allocation of tax revenues; 3) allocation of authority among state, country and local government entities; 4) regulations for types of licenses and their provision; and 5) limitations on advertising aimed at adolescents.[276] Proposition 64 included numerous social justice provisions that Canada should take note of, including: 1) expungement of criminal records if the offender's conduct is no longer criminal; 2) provisions allowing prior convictions to be adjusted in light of the new legal characterization of the offender's conduct, including a retroactive reduction of an offence from a felony to a misdemeanour; 3) the rejection of a blanket prohibition that previously prevented someone with a prior felony conviction from securing a license; and 4) a provision that gives priority for licenses to applicants who were currently in the cannabis business when the new law was adopted.[277] This wasn't the first

---

273 Bryan McLaren, "How Cannabis Legalization in Arizona Offers a Forecast for Commercial Real Estate in Other Markets" (13 December 2021), online: *Forbes* #x003C;www.forbes.com/sites/forbesbusinesscouncil/2021/12/13/how-cannabis-legalization-in-arizona-offers-a-forecast-for-commercial-real-estate-in-other-markets/>

274 Jim Small, "Arizona Adults Spent $58 Million on Recreational Marijuana in October" (9 December 2021), online: *AZMirror* #x003C;www.azmirror.com/blog/arizona-adults-spent-58-million-on-recreational-marijuana-in-october/>

275 "Cannabis Businesses Essential as Lawmakers Take a Pause" (23 April 2020), online: *Marijuana Policy Project* #x003C;www.mpp.org/states/california/?state=CA>

276 Michael Vitiello, "Marijuana Legalization, Racial Disparity, and the Hope for Reform" (2019) 23:3 Lewis and Clark Law Review 789 at 809–810

277 *Ibid* at 811–812

116 *Drug Legalization in Other Democracies*

time that a voters' initiative in California provided for social justice measures in drug law reform. A 2014 initiative (Proposition 47) "defelonized" drug possession, effectively dropping the crime from a felony to a misdemeanour[278] (a trend subsequently followed by several states discussed below). This broader social justice focus in drug law reform has been curiously and unfortunately absent in Canada.

Despite these promising aspects of the legislation, the actual implementation of adult-use recreational cannabis in California has been widely criticized. While legal cannabis has been selling in record amounts, some experts estimate that 80% to 90% of cannabis sales in the state "still fall into a legal gray zone".[279] One academic study suggests that while California was once a leader in cannabis policy reform (notably when it was the first state to legalize medical cannabis via Proposition 215 in 1996), its regulation was subsequently left to local governments and, as a result, the state has "fallen badly behind".[280] While some reports champion the success of Proposition 64's social justice measures (including the clearing of tens of thousands of cannabis-related conviction records), they nonetheless argue that as 2022 approaches, high taxes have ensured that a large majority of the cannabis being consumed in the state is still coming from the illegal market.[281] A 2021 Forbes article referring to the situation in the state as a "bloodbath" argues that the combination of high taxes and a flood of both legal and illegal supply have basically made it impossible for businesses to prosper.[282] Whether and how the industry will course correct (with or without regulatory reform from the state government) is not the only interesting drug law reform development in the state to watch going into 2022 and beyond. California Senator Scott Wiener currently has two substantial drug policy reform bills under consideration in 2022, one putting forth proposals for state-sanctioned safe consumption sites, and another seeking to decriminalize personal possession of several psychedelics (including

---

278 "Defelonization: Reducing Drug Penalties for Use and Possession from Felonies to Misdemeanors" (n.d.), online (pdf): *Drug Policy Alliance* #x003C;www.nmlegis.gov/handouts/CCJ%20110817%20Item%203%20Drug%20Policy%20Alliance%20-%20Defelonization.pdf>

279 Michael Martin, "5 Years After California Legalized Weed, the Illicit Market Dominates" (7 November 2021), online: *NPR* #x003C;www.npr.org/2021/11/07/1053387426/5-years-after-california-legalized-weed-the-illicit-market-dominates>

280 Sam Kamin, "What California Can Learn from Colorado's Marijuana Regulations" (2017) 49 The University of the Pacific Law Review 13 at 13

281 "Editorial: Californians Overwhelmingly Supported Legalizing Marijuana. Why Is It Still a Mess?" (26 December 2021), online: *Los Angeles Times* #x003C;www.latimes.com/opinion/story/2021-12-26/editorial-californians-overwhelmingly-supported-legalizing-marijuana-so-why-is-it-still-a-mess-five-years-later>

282 Chris Roberts, "'It's Gonna Be a Bloodbath': Epic Marijuana Over Supply Is Flooding California, Jeopardizing Legalization" (31 August 2021), online: #x003C;www.forbes.com/sites/chrisroberts/2021/08/31/its-gonna-be-a-bloodbath-epic-marijuana-oversupply-is-flooding-california-jeopardizing-legalization/?sh=621534147ddb>

psilocybin, MDMA and LSD).[283] As noted in the analyses of other states below, as more states liberalize their cannabis legislation, there has been an accompanying movement in some states towards broader drug policy liberalization.

4.4.4 Colorado

As was the case in California, the legalization of a commercial, recreational cannabis market in Colorado arrived via a ballot initiative (Amendment 64) in 2012.[284] The state legislature subsequently set up a task force that provided 58 recommendations for the development of regulations of the legal cannabis system, which began retail sales in early 2014.[285] Cannabis businesses in the state are subject to regulations from the Colorado Department of Revenue Marijuana Enforcement Division, which, amongst other things, stipulates comprehensive licensing criteria, mandates security measures, including 24-hour surveillance monitoring of plants, and places restrictions on proximity to schools and advertising targeting minors.[286] An (admittedly early) evaluation of the state's regulatory system argued that it was "reasonably transparent, has the ability to respond to issues as they arise, and there is equal access for a range of stakeholders including industry representatives and public health professionals".[287] More recent evaluations have provided conflicting views of the state's recreational cannabis system. One academic study noted that Colorado's system is "rife with inconsistencies, including over-regulation, under-regulation, a lack of standards, and immature verification mechanisms to enforce regulations".[288] The authors argue that this is a result not "of poor government oversight or a lack of proper attention, but rather it stems from the convoluted and multi-faceted nature of the industry which offers inconsistent and sparse data on which to build policy".[289] Another study found that higher use of cannabis has been prevalent since recreational legalization, with Colorado claiming the highest cannabis use in all age groups compared to other U.S. states.[290] A more recent study has suggested that this higher use is likely tied to the commercialization of cannabis in Colorado, where cannabis retail locations

---

283 Kyle Jaeger, "California Senator Says Bill to Legalize Psychedelics Possession Has'50/50' Chance to Pass This Year" (10 January 2022), online: *Marijuana Moment* #x003C;www.marijuanamoment.net/california-senator-says-bill-to-legalize-psychedelics-possession-has-50-50-chance-to-pass-this-year/>

284 Todd Subritzky, Simone Pettigrew & Simon Lenton, "Issues in the Implementation and Evolution of the Commercial Recreational Cannabis Market in Colorado" (2016) 27 International Journal of Drug Policy 1 at 1

285 *Ibid*

286 *Ibid* at 2

287 *Ibid* at 8

288 Dave Yates & Jessica Speer, "Over and Under-Regulation in the Colorado Cannabis Industry – A Data-Analytic Perspective" (2018) 59 International Journal of Drug Policy 63 at 63

289 *Ibid*

290 Jamie Parnes et al, "A Burning Problem: Cannabis Lessons Learned from Colorado" (2018) 26:1 Addiction Research and Theory 3 at 3

118 *Drug Legalization in Other Democracies*

outnumber all McDonald's and Starbucks locations combined by quite a significant margin (1016 registered retail and medical locations combined compared to 392 Starbucks and 208 McDonald's in 2019).[291]

Amidst this backdrop of for-profit market commercialization and reported increased use, the decision of some Canadian provinces to proceed slowly and cautiously with their retail market rollouts stands in stark contrast.[292] The for-profit model implemented in Colorado has produced some remarkable sales figures, with regulators estimating $2.1 billion in combined recreational and medical sales in the state in 2020.[293] The state nonetheless had a busy 2021 legislative session, passing four new laws pertaining to cannabis that will take effect in 2022, including important restrictions on cannabis advertising towards youth and further restrictions on high-potency cannabis concentrates.[294] Another result of this legislative flurry was the creation of the Cannabis Business Office, which will provide loans to social equity licensees for seed capital and ongoing business expenses and make social equity applicants a priority when issuing cannabis licenses.[295] Colorado's governor Jared Polis signed an executive order in 2020 that granted clemency to almost 3,000 people convicted of possessing an ounce or less of cannabis and, towards the end of 2021, further granted 1,351 pardons for convictions of possession of up to two ounces of cannabis.[296] Social justice and social equity measures such as these should be implemented in Canada to address the stark lack of diversity that currently exists in the country's cannabis industry.[297] Canada should also take note of the state's trend towards broader liberalization of drug laws. House Bill 19–1263[298] came into effect in 2020, "defelonizing" (i.e. reclassifying from a felony to a misdemeanour) single-use drug possession for Schedule I and II substances, including heroin, cocaine, ecstasy

---

291 Kevin Sabet, "Lessons Learned in Several States Eight Years After States Legalized Marijuana" (2021) 38 Current Opinion in Psychology 25 at 26

292 Chapter 3.4–3.10

293 A. J. Herington, "Colorado Marijuana Sales Topped $2 Billion Last Year" (30 December 2021), online: *Forbes* #x003C;www.forbes.com/sites/ajherrington/2021/12/30/colorado-marijuana-sales-topped-2-billion-last-year/?sh=34fd23077f22>

294 Hyatt Brownstein, "United States: Changes in Colorado Cannabis Law: What to Expect with Four New Bills" (3 January 2022), online: *Mondaq* #x003C;www.mondaq.com/unitedstates/cannabis-hemp/1146638/changes-in-colorado-cannabis-law-what-to-expect-with-four-new-bills>

295 Moe Clark, "Colorado's New Cannabis Business Office Will Focus on Job Creation, Social Equity" (29 July 2019), online: *Colorado Newsline* <https://coloradonewsline.com/briefs/colorados-new-cannabis-office-social-equity/>

296 Kyle Jaeger, "Colorado Governor Pardons More Than 1,300 People for Past Marijuana Convictions" (30 December 2021), online: *Marijuana Moment* #x003C;www.marijuanamoment.net/colorado-governor-says-new-marijuana-clemency-plan-will-be-announced-within-days/>

297 Chapter 2.7

298 State of Colorado, 72nd G.A., 1st Sess

Drug Legalization in Other Democracies 119

and most other illicit drugs.[299] Significantly, this reform will result in the removal of imprisonment for offences where the limit of four grams is not exceeded and will help those found in possession avoid the rather severe and stigmatized mark of a felony conviction on their criminal record.[300]

4.4.5 Connecticut

According to the Marijuana Policy Project, S.B. 1201 ("An Act Concerning the Equitable and Responsible Regulation of Cannabis") was signed into law by Connecticut governor Edward Lamont in June of 2021.[301] The law has made (or will make) several aspects of recreational cannabis legal in the state, including: 1) as of July 1, 2021, adults over 21 years of age can possess 1.5 ounces of cannabis on their person and up to five ounces in a secure location in their home; 2) state-regulated legal sales are anticipated to begin in May 2022, with 50% of the licenses reserved for equity applicants and 75% of revenue earmarked for equity efforts and community reinvestment; 3) home cultivation will be permitted as of July 1, 2023; and 4) lower-level cannabis records will be expunged.[302] The state is also taking measures to protect its pre-existing medical cannabis market, including requiring dispensaries that want to branch out to recreational sales to submit a "medical preservation plan" to the state Department of Consumer Protection.[303] Connecticut has been operating "one of the most restrictive medical marijuana programs in the country"[304] since 2015. Under this system, pharmacists own and operate dispensaries, with patients requiring an authorization form from a Connecticut-licensed physician in order to register.[305] The state has quickly moved towards its goal of May 2022 legal recreational sales, having already established a Social Equity Council and announcing in early January 2022 that license applications will begin being accepted in February.[306] Lastly, regarding wider

---

299 Óscar Contreras, "Polis Signs Bill 'Defelonizing' Single-Use Drug Possession for Schedule 1 and 2 Substances" (28 May 2019), online: *The Denver Channel.com* <thedenverchannel.com/news/politics/polis-signs-bill-defelonizing-single-use-drug-possession-for-schedule-i-and-ii-substances>

300 Phil Scilippa, "Schedule 1 and 2 Drugs Have Officially Been Defelonized in Colorado" (5 March 2020), online: *edm.com* <https://edm.com/news/schedule-1-2-narcotics-defelonized-colorado>

301 "Connecticut" (n.d.), online: *Marijuana Policy Project* #x003C;www.mpp.org/states/connecticut/>

302 *Ibid*

303 Ginny Monk, "How CT Plans to Protect Medical Marijuana Program as Recreational Use Begins" (15 October 2021), online: *CT Insider* #x003C;www.ctinsider.com/news/article/How-CT-plans-to-protect-medical-marijuana-program-16536544.php>

304 Jesse Vivian, "Dispensing Cannabis" 41:2 US Pharmacist 49 at 50

305 *Ibid*

306 Kyle Jaeger, "Connecticut Marijuana Business License Applications Will Be Accepted Starting Next Month, Officials Announce" (5 January 2022), online: *Marijuana Moment* #x003C;www.marijuanamoment.net/connecticut-marijuana-business-license-applications-will-be-accepted-starting-next-month-officials-announce/>

120   *Drug Legalization in Other Democracies*

drug policy reform, it is worth noting that Connecticut is another state that has also "defelonized" drug possession, passing legislation in 2015 that drops possession of all drugs from a felony to a Class A misdemeanour, allowing the offender to avoid imprisonment under certain circumstances.[307]

4.4.6 Illinois

As a result of the June 2019 passage of the Cannabis Regulation and Tax Act, Illinois has had a state-run and regulated system for recreational cannabis since January 1, 2020.[308] The legislation implemented several consequential changes to the status of cannabis prohibition in the state, including: 1) allowing for the sale of cannabis products in licensed stores, with a 30 gram limit on possession of raw cannabis; 2) providing for the automatic expungement of criminal convictions relating to possession of cannabis up to 30 grams; 3) creating a social equity program that prioritizes equity applications for licenses and provides access to financial resources for start-up costs; and 4) allowing home cultivation for medical cannabis patients with a maximum of five plants per household.[309] In the early years of Illinois' legalization, concerns have been raised about the slow pace of the licensing process, and the legislation's focus on social equity does not yet appear to have materialized in the industry.[310] Various aspects of the state's licensing process are currently the subject of litigation, and market entry for newcomers has thus been put on hold while previous medical cannabis license holders have further consolidated their share of the market.[311] An investigation by the Chicago Tribune suggests that, as of early 2022, only seven companies control 60 of the 110 cannabis stores in the state.[312] The state's 2021 legal cannabis sales were estimated at nearly $1.4 billion dollars, double the amount registered in 2020.[313] One area where the legislation is meeting its promises is in regards to community re-investment. The Cannabis Regulation and Tax Act earmarked nearly 25%

307 Charlie Smart, "Penalties for Drugs" (3 June 2015), online: *PBS* #x003C;www.ctpublic. org/politics/2015-06-03/connecticut-senate-backs-cutting-penalties-for-drugs>
308 "Overview of the Illinois Cannabis Regulation and Tax Act" (n.d.), online: *Marijuana Policy Project* #x003C;www.mpp.org/states/illinois/overview-of-the-illinois-cannabis-regulation-and-tax-act/>
309 *Ibid*
310 Shai Kapos, "Layers, Race and Money: Illinois' Messy Weed Experiment" (18 September 2021), online: *Politico* #x003C;www.politico.com/news/2021/09/18/illinois-weed-experiment-512626>
311 Robert McCopin, "Boom Time for Marijuana Sales in Illinois, as Industry Expands with New Products- but Minority Buisnesses Get Left Behind" (1 January 2022), online: *Chicago Tribune* #x003C;www.chicagotribune.com/marijuana/illinois/ct-illinois-marijuana-2021-review-20220101-6ltav5lghfba3awognltyrzs4m-story.html>
312 *Ibid*
313 Greg Bishop, "Illinois Legal Cannabis Sales Nearly $1.4 Billion in 2021, Double Last Year's Total" (3 January 2022), online: *The Center Square* #x003C;www.thecentersquare. com/illinois/illinois-legal-cannabis-sales-nearly-1-4-billion-in-2021-double-last-years-total/article_dafe48f6–6cc3–11ec-a174-db1ea990d6c7.html>

Drug Legalization in Other Democracies 121

of every cannabis tax dollar collected to go to community groups through the Restore, Reinvest and Renew program. The program's grants fund programs in Illinois communities that have been harmed by violence, excessive incarceration, and economic disinvestment.[314] Mirroring "defelonization" efforts in the states noted above, a 2021 House Bill (3447) that sought to reclassify small amounts of drug possession (up to 3 grams of heroin and 5 grams of cocaine, for example) from a felony to a Class A misdemeanour (maximum one year sentence rather than a possible one to four-year sentence) passed out of the house by a vote of 61–49.[315] The state's Senate did not take up the bill for a vote before the deadline for the 2021 session, but the legislation may be revisited in 2022 and is nonetheless indicative of a move towards broader drug policy reform in states that have implemented legal recreational cannabis.

4.4.7 Maine

According to the Maine State Legislature, "Maine has allowed prescribing, and limited possession, of medical marijuana since 1999 but the law lacked any distribution mechanism and questions arose of noncompliance with federal law and of how patients could legally obtain the prescribed marijuana".[316] Ten years later, Maine voters approved (Question 5) a citizen-initiated bill that significantly improved and expanded Maine's medical cannabis program.[317] Maine thus became the fifth state to provide dispensaries for medical cannabis, and, in 2018, the Maine legislature further expanded the scope of the state's medical cannabis program (removed a list of qualifying conditions and removed a cap on dispensaries effective January 1, 2021).[318] Maine's legalization of recreational possession and cultivation of cannabis, and establishment of a regulated recreational market, also arrived via a citizen's initiative (Question 1) that passed by the narrowest of margins in 2016 (50.26% of the vote, a margin of 3, 995 votes).[319] As a result, adults 21 and over may legally possess up to 2.5 ounces of cannabis (or 5 grams of cannabis concentrate) and are allowed to cultivate up to three mature cannabis plants at home.[320] Almost four years elapsed between the vote on Question 1 and the start of adult-use retail sales, which finally began in October 2020. The delay

---

314 "R3: Restore. Reinvest. Renew" (n.d.), online: <https://r3.illinois.gov/>
315 Sarah Mansur, "Drug-Decriminalization Bill Among Those That Miss Deadline for Illinois Legislature's Session" (2 June 2021), online: *The News-Gazette* #x003C;www.news-gazette.com/news/local/politics/drug-decriminalization-bill-among-those-that-miss-deadline-for-illinois-legislatures-session/article_1ae0007d-c00a-5752-ac4b-d76fd1e92118.html>
316 "Medical Marijuana in Maine" (2 February 2022), online: *Maine State Legislature* <https://legislature.maine.gov/lawlibrary/maines-medical-marijuana-law/9242>
317 "Adult-Use Cannabis Retailers Finally Open for Business in 2020; Voters Approve the State's Legalization Law in 2016" (22 June 2021) online: *Marijuana Policy Project* #x003C;www.mpp.org/states/maine/>
318 *Ibid*
319 *Ibid*
320 *Ibid*

122 *Drug Legalization in Other Democracies*

is largely attributed to interference and opposition from former Governor Paul LePage, who was subsequently replaced by current Governor Janet Mills.[321] The implementation of adult-use recreational sales has remained restrained since it began. As of late 2021, only 47 of Maine's approximately 500 towns had opted in to allow recreational sales.[322] Smaller "mom and pop" operations that serviced the medical market long before recreational cannabis was legalized have argued that new regulations favouring industry giants will effectively push them out of the market.[323] Maine's top cannabis official has also expressed concerns that his office has few tools to prevent medical cannabis from finding its way to the black market.[324] Amidst this slow recreational cannabis rollout, the state has also seen some significant movement on broader drug policy reform in recent years. Legislation that would have decriminalized possession of all illicit drugs (replaced incarceration with a $100 fine) was passed by the House of Representatives in 2021, only to fall by a slim minority in the state Senate.[325] More drug policy reform legislation is scheduled to be debated in 2022, including legislation that would protect people who report drug overdoses from a small set of criminal offences.[326]

4.4.8 Massachusetts

Similar to other states, the large majority of Massachusetts' drug policy reform has come via ballot initiative, with voters approving the decriminalization of possession of small amounts of cannabis in 2008, legalizing cannabis for medical patients with serious health issues in 2012, and legalizing the possession and cultivation of adult-use cannabis (and the establishment of a regulated cannabis

---

321 Kyle Jaeger, "Maine Marijuana Sales Can Finally Begin, Officials Announce Four Years After Voters Legalized It" (14 August 2020), online: *Marijuana moment* #x003C;www.marijuanamoment.net/maine-marijuana-sales-can-finally-begin-officials-announce-four-years-after-voters-legalized-it/>

322 David Marino Jr., "More Than 90% of Maine Towns Still Don't Allow Recreational Marijuana Sales" (20 September 2021), online: *Maine Public* #x003C;www.mainepublic.org/news/2021-09-20/more-than-90-of-maine-towns-still-dont-allow-recreational-marijuana-sales>

323 Mona Zhang, "Maine's Mom and Pop Weed Scene Sweats Corporate 'Gentrification'" (20 June 2021), online: *Politico* #x003C;www.politico.com/news/2021/06/20/maines-fight-over-big-marijuana-493472>

324 David Morino Jr., "There's More Illegal Activity in Maine's Medical Marijuana Market, State's Top Pot Official Says" (10 November 2021), online: *Bangor Daily News* <https://bangordailynews.com/2021/11/10/news/theres-more-illegal-activity-in-maines-medical-marijuana-market-states-top-pot-official-says-joam40zk0w/>

325 Kyle Jaegar, "Maine Senate Defeats Drugs Decriminalization Bill That Cleared the House" (1 July 2021), online: *Marijuana Moment* #x003C;www.marijuanamoment.net/maine-senate-defeats-drug-decriminalization-bill-that-cleared-the-house/>

326 *Ibid*

market) in 2016.[327] Although the 2016 voters' initiative (Question 4) passed with 53.6% of the vote, disagreement in the state legislature delayed the bill from being signed into law until July 28, 2017.[328] Further bureaucratic delays led to licensed sales only beginning in 2018, and there are some reports of license applicants waiting up to 18 months for a decision.[329] While the state's Cannabis Control Commission set up a Social Equity Program (SEP) in 2018 that provides free assistance to individuals interested in entering the industry, critics have argued that it doesn't sufficiently cover high entry costs that can be in the millions.[330] Members of the state Cannabis Control Commission themselves acknowledged that easier access to the industry, particularly through grants for social equity applicants, should be a priority heading into 2022 and beyond.[331] There have certainly been some positives: public health issues foreseen by opponents never materialized, the recreational cannabis industry currently employs over 18,000 workers, and the industry has generated over $2.2 billion dollars in revenue.[332] Moreover, despite what some claim to be "onerous regulations", cannabis delivery companies were able to open in 2021 to help offset the impact of the COVID-19 pandemic.[333] Legislative changes introduced in December 2021 seek to further regulate the industry, including raising the legal age from 21 to 25, introducing new regulations on packaging, and establishing new restrictions on levels of THC content.[334] These are not the only important drug policy reform efforts to watch for in 2022 and beyond. Similar to other states, broader drug policy reform is currently being discussed in the state legislature, including: 1) a proposed bill that would replace criminal penalties for the possession of any controlled substance

327 "Retail Cannabis Sales Exceed $1 Billion; Commission Begins Issuing Delivery Licenses to Social Equity and Economic Opportunity Applicants" (22 June 2021), online: *Marijuana Policy Project* <www.mpp.org/states/massachusetts/>
328 *Ibid*
329 Roesli Arena, "Massachusetts Pot Shops Are a Billion-Dollar Market, but Cannabis Industry Still Faces Hurdles" (2 November 2021), online: *Cape Cod Times* <www.capecodtimes.com/story/business/2021/11/02/pot-shops-billion-dollar-massachusetts-market-cannabis-industry-face-hurdles-cape-cod-retail-medical/6233346001/>
330 *Ibid*
331 Melissa Hanson, "A Milestone Year for the Massachusetts Cannabis Industry Is Ending. What's Next? See Our Q&A with Regulators" (8 December 2021), online: *Masslive* <www.masslive.com/cannabis/2021/12/a-milestone-year-for-the-massachusetts-cannabis-industry-is-ending-whats-next-see-our-qa-with-regulators.html>
332 Dan Adams, "Five Years Later, Legal Marijuana Remains Unfinished Business in Massachusetts" (7 November 2021), online: *Boston Globe* <www.bostonglobe.com/2021/11/07/marijuana/five-years-later-legal-marijuana-remains-unfinished-business-massachusetts/>
333 Spencer Buell, "Why Boston Can't Have Nice Things, Part One Million: Cannabis Cafes" (12 September 2021), online: *Boston Magazine* <www.bostonmagazine.com/news/2021/12/09/massachusetts-cannabis-cafes/>
334 Madeleine Pearce, "Five Years After Massachusetts Voters Approve Marijuana Legalization, Some Lawmakers Seek Increased Restrictions" (8 December 2021), online: *The Berkshire Eagle* <www.berkshireeagle.com/state/massachusetts-marijuana-proposals-in-statehouse-would-increase-restrictions/article_4171f442-56c2-11ec-931d-c71f1d5e0fa4.html>

124 *Drug Legalization in Other Democracies*

with a civil fine of $50 (and an option to forego the fine if the individual enrols in "needs screening" to identify any potential treatment or assistance they require); and 2) a proposed bill that would establish a 10-year pilot program to study the feasibility and effectiveness of safe drug consumption sites.[335]

4.4.9 Michigan

Like several states surveyed in this chapter, Michigan's cannabis policy reform has largely come via voters' initiative. 63% of voters supported the legalization of medical cannabis in 2008, but the law was quickly criticized for not establishing sufficient regulations for businesses providing cannabis to patients.[336] As such, new legislation was passed in 2016 that clarified licensing and regulatory authority, cultivation limits, taxes and fees, and other necessary aspects for a functioning regulatory system.[337] Two years later, Michigan became the 10th state to legalize cannabis for adult recreational use, again through a ballot measure (Proposal 1), allowing adults age 21 and over to possess up to 2.5 ounces of cannabis and providing for home cultivation of up to 12 cannabis plants.[338] Adult-use recreational sales began in December 2019, and the industry has since grown into a (recreational and medical combined) market that produces nearly $2 billion per year in revenue, despite a historic recall in 2021 that affected nearly 60% of the state's cannabis supply.[339] Critics argue that this fast and early explosion of sales largely benefitted large companies and dispensary chain monopolies, and regulators have vowed to focus efforts in 2022 on increasing social equity access to the industry.[340] Broader drug law reform is also progressing alongside recreational cannabis legalization. In late 2021, the state's largest city, Detroit, voted 61% in favour of decriminalizing possession of psychedelic mushrooms, and while possession of this substance is still prohibited under state and federal law, police will

---

335 Kyle Jaeger, "Massachusetts Lawmakers Discuss Drug Decriminalization and Safe Injection Sites at Hearing" (27 September 2021), online: *Marijuana Moment* <www.marijuanamo ment.net/massachusetts-lawmakers-discuss-drug-decriminalization-and-safe-injection-sites-at-hearing/>

336 "Adult-Use Stores Continue to Open; Expungement Bill Awaits Senate Action" (13 January 2020), online: *Marijuana Policy Project* <www.mpp.org/states/michigan/?state=MI>

337 "Michigan's Revised Medical Marijuana Law" (n.d.), online: *Marijuana Policy Project* <www.mpp.org/states/michigan/michigan-s-revised-medical-marijuana-law/>

338 Marijuana Policy Project, *supra* note 336

339 Gus Burns, "Corporatization, Power Struggles and a Historic Recall: Michigan Marijuana's 2021 Growing Pains" (13 January 2022), online: *MLive* <mlive.com/public-interest/2022/01/corporatization-power-struggles-and-a-historic-recall-michigan-marijuanas-2021-growing-pains.html>

340 Sarah Rahal, "How Michigan Marijuana Regulators Are Trying to Prevent a Monopoly of Dispensary Chains" (26 December 2021), online: *The Detroit News* <www.detroitnews.com/story/news/local/michigan/2021/12/27/michigan-cannabis-industry-social-equity-marijuana-entrepreneurs-dispensaries-chains/6336959001/?gnt-cfr=1>

Drug Legalization in Other Democracies 125

effectively not prioritize arrests for possession of them within city limits.[341] While wider drug decriminalization or defelonization is not currently being considered at the state level, Michigan does have a past history of some progressive drug policy reform it could draw on if this becomes a legislative priority. A 2002 package of legislative reforms that repealed mandatory minimum sentences for a variety of drug offences appears to have been successful in reducing crime rates and levels of public expenditure related to drug crime.[342]

4.4.10 Montana

Montana is another state riding the recent wave towards cannabis policy liberalization, again by way of citizens' initiative. In 2020, the state's voters supported two complementary ballot initiatives: Constitutional Initiative 118 sets the legal age for cannabis at 21, and Initiative 190 supports the establishment of a comprehensive system of legalization overseen by the Montana Department of Revenue.[343] The state subsequently passed House Bill 701 in 2021, and, as a result, as of January 1, 2022, recreational cannabis sales (and home cultivation of four plants per household) will begin.[344] The legislation also appointed a special administrative judge and established a dedicated court process specifically to expedite expungements for individuals with prior low-level cannabis offences on their records.[345] The state's medical cannabis history has been a bit more tumultuous. Medical cannabis legalization was first passed by voter initiative in 2004, but a subsequent 2011 law (SB 423) was so restrictive that it led to nearly five years of litigation, resulting in a Montana Supreme Court ruling in 2016 that upheld the legislation and effectively cut 93% of the state's 12, 400 patients off from access to medical cannabis.[346] In November 2016, voters responded to this by supporting another citizens' initiative (I-182) that removed the most restrictive of that law's provisions and further established a regulatory structure for businesses that had previously been absent.[347] While the adult-use recreational system is still in its infancy, it is the pre-existing medical cannabis system doing the heavy lifting. Already established medical dispensaries will be serving the adult-use recreational

---

341 Frances Kai-Hwa Wang, "Detroit Just Decriminalized Psychedelics and 'magic mushrooms.' Here's what that means" (3 November 2021), online: *PBS*<www.pbs.org/newshour/politics/detroit-just-decriminalized-psychedelics-and-magic-mushrooms-heres-what-that-means>

342 "Happy Anniversary, Michigan Reforms: Ten Years After Major Sentencing Reform Victory, Michigan Residents Safer" (1 March 2013), online: *FAMM* <https://famm.org/happy-anniversary-michigan-reforms-ten-years-after-major-sentencing-reform-victory-michigan-residents-safer/>

343 "Adult-Use Cannabis Sales Begin at the Start of 2022!" (3 January 2022), online: *Marijuana Policy Project* <www.mpp.org/states/montana/>

344 *Ibid*

345 *Ibid*

346 "Montana's Rocky Medical Marijuana History" (n.d.), online: *Marijuana Policy Project* <www.mpp.org/states/montana/montanas-medical-marijuana-laws-history/>

347 *Ibid*

126 *Drug Legalization in Other Democracies*

market until the state opens license applications on July 1, 2023.[348] This has led to concerns that medical cannabis users will not be sufficiently supplied, particularly because the large majority of dispensaries have opted to serve both recreational and medical customers.[349] Broader drug policy liberalization is not yet on the horizon in Montana, and the state still allows for up to five years imprisonment for possession of drugs other than cannabis.[350]

4.4.11 Nevada

Citizens' initiatives have almost entirely contributed to Nevada's cannabis policy progress. Medical cannabis arrived in the state after two successful citizens' initiatives in 1998 and 2000, resulting in the 2001 passage of Assembly Bill 453 that exempted medical cannabis from state prosecution and also defelonized possession of up to one ounce of cannabis (to a fine-only misdemeanour).[351] It wasn't until 2013 that the Nevada legislature passed legislation allowing for a regulated system of medical cannabis dispensaries.[352] A subsequent 2016 voter initiative allowed for a legal, recreational cannabis system, with sales for adults 21 and over beginning in July 2017 and maximum possession limits set at one ounce or less.[353] Social justice reform has come largely from the Governor's office, with more than 15,000 pardons issued for low-level cannabis possession offences in 2020.[354] The Governor also signed legislation in June 2020 that barred most employers from requiring pre-employment cannabis drug tests.[355] Nevada also passed legislation in 2021 to allow for cannabis consumption lounges, recognizing that previous laws that limited consumption to private residences largely limited the ability of the recreational market to cater to the city's famous and massive tourism

---

348 Justin Franz, "Recreational Marijuana Is Now Legal in Montana. Here's What You Need to Know" (5 July 2021), online: *MTFP* <https://montanafreepress.org/2021/05/07/legal-cannabis-whats-next-and-what-can-you-do-now/>

349 Justin Franz, "Medical Marijuana Users Brace for Shortages as Montana's Recreational Market Opens" (5 January 2022), online: *KHN* <https://khn.org/news/article/medical-marijuana-users-brace-for-shortages-as-montanas-recreational-market-opens/>

350 Montana Criminal Code, Annotated 2021, Title 45, Ch. 9, Pt. 1, s. 45–9–102

351 State of Nevada Research Library, "AB453–2001" (19 March 2001), online (pdf): <www.leg.state.nv.us/Division/Research/Library/LegHistory/LHs/2001/AB453,2001.pdf>

352 "History of Medical Marijuana in Nevada" (n.d.), online; *The Wright Law Group* <https://wrightlawgroupnv.com/history-medical-marijuana/>

353 "States Increasingly Looking to Nevada as a Model" (5 November 2018), online: *Marijuana Policy Project* <www.mpp.org/states/nevada/?state=NV>

354 Kyle Jaeger, "Nevada Sold More Than $1 Billion in Marijuana in One Year, Officials Report" (13 October 2021), online: *Marijuana Moment* <www.marijuanamoment.net/nevada-sold-more-than-1-billion-in-marijuana-in-one-year-officials-report/>

355 Bill Hutchinson, "Nevada Becomes 1st State to Ban Most Pre-Employment Tests" (12 June 2019), online: *abc News* <https://abcnews.go.com/US/nevada-1st-state-ban-pre-employment-pot-tests/story?id=63656557>

Drug Legalization in Other Democracies 127

industry.[356] By all accounts, the state's cannabis industry seems to be flourishing, with June 2021 figures from the Nevada Cannabis Compliance Board showing yearly sales exceeding $1 billion dollars.[357] The state does not appear to be considering any wider drug policy liberalization at present.

4.4.12 New Jersey

In 2010, New Jersey's former Governor Jon Corzine signed a number of laws on his last day in office, including legislation that made the state the 14th to legalize cannabis for medical purposes.[358] The legislation largely limited medical cannabis use to a small list of specific illnesses, restricted people from growing their own cannabis, carried significant costs for patients, and was not supported by then-incoming Governor Chris Christie.[359] In response to remarkably low enrolment stemming from these issues, Governor Phil Murphy signed new legislation in June 2019 that provided for a number of necessary reforms, including: 1) a significant expansion of the list of qualifying conditions; 2) significantly expanding access by increasing the number of cultivators, retailers, and manufacturers; and 3) creating a Cannabis Regulatory Commission (CRC) to govern the expanded and regulated medical cannabis program.[360] The latter development will be particularly important as the state moves forward towards recreational adult-use cannabis legalization. Following a November 2020 ballot referendum in which New Jersey citizens overwhelmingly approved recreational cannabis legalization, Governor Murphy signed three bills into law on February 19, 2021 that effectively ended arrests and prosecution for cannabis possession in New Jersey and vested the recently formed CRC with the authority to develop rules for adult-use licenses.[361] In August 2021, the CRC released its first set of rules guiding the cultivation, manufacture, and sale of adult-use cannabis, including: 1) prioritizing applications from minority and veteran applicants; 2) flexible application requirements for microbusinesses; and 3) application fees as low as $100. The CRC began accepting licenses for cultivators, manufacturers, and testing

---

356 Geoffrey Lawrence, "Nevada to Allow Tourists to Use Legal Marijuana in Lounges but Restrictive Licensing Problems Remain" (12 October 2021), online: *Reason* <https://reason.org/commentary/nevada-to-allow-tourists-to-use-legal-marijuana-in-lounges-but-restrictive-licensing-problems-remain/>

357 Jaeger, *supra* note 354

358 Clair Heininger, "N.J. Medical Marijuana Law Is Signed by Gov. Corzine" (1 April 2019), online: *NJ.com* <www.nj.com/news/2010/01/medical_marijuana_law_to_take.html>

359 Brent Johnson, "Christie Says Medical Marijuana Programs Are 'a Front for Legalization'" (17 June 2014), online: *NJ.com* <www.nj.com/politics/2014/06/christie_says_medical_marijuana_programs_are_a_front_for_legalization.html>

360 "Jake Honig Compassionate Use Medical Cannabis Act" (2 July 2019), online: *Marijuana Policy Project* <www.mpp.org/states/new-jersey/jake-honig-compassionate-use-medical-cannabis-act/>

361 "N.J. Cannabis Regulatory Commission Adopts Initial Adult-Use Rules" (21 September 2021), online: *Marijuana Policy Project* <www.mpp.org/states/new-jersey/?state=NJ>

128 *Drug Legalization in Other Democracies*

laboratories on December 15, 2021, and retail licenses will begin being accepted on March 15, 2022.[362] On the wider drug policy reform front, a diversionary drug court program originally implemented in 2002 was expanded in 2012 to increase eligibility to a wider spectrum of people.[363] While there are currently no decriminalization or defelonization bills being considered in the state, Governor Murphy did sign a March 2021 bill reclassifying possession of up to an ounce of psilocybin mushrooms as a disorderly person's offence and has suggested that he is "open-minded" to broader drug decriminalization once adult-use recreational cannabis is successfully up and running.[364]

4.4.13 New Mexico

Since 2007, New Mexico doctors have been allowed to prescribe cannabis to seriously ill patients, and, in 2009, the New Mexico Department of Health began accepting applications from nonprofit businesses for the production and distribution of medical cannabis as well as applications for licensed personal production by patients.[365] Regulatory and legislative changes in 2019 greatly expanded both the state's medical cannabis program as well as its list of qualifying conditions.[366] The state also passed legislation to legalize, regulate, and tax adult-use recreational cannabis that came into effect on June 29, 2021.[367] As of that date, adults 21 and older have been able to possess up to two ounces of cannabis and cultivate up to six mature plants, with retail sales expected to begin no later than April 2022.[368] This deadline appears to be in sight: in late December 2021, the Cannabis Control Division of the state Regulation and Licensing Department issued its final rules for manufacturers, retailers, and couriers.[369] During this time, the Regulation and Licensing Department also announced that the first three

---

362 Garrett Rutledge, "Revisiting New Jersey's Cannabis Legalization a Year Later" (28 December 2021), online: *New Jersey Digest* <https://thedigestonline.com/nj/new-jersey-cannabis-legalization/>

363 Victoria Dalton, "What You Should Know About Drug Court in New Jersey" (17 January 2019), online: *NJ.com* <www.nj.com/south-jersey-voices/2015/12/what_you_should_know_about_dru.html>

364 Kyle Jaeger, "New Jersey Governor 'Open-Minded' on Decriminalizing All Drugs" (22 March 2021), online: *Marijuana Moment* <www.marijuanamoment.net/new-jersey-governor-open-minded-on-decriminalizing-all-drugs/>

365 "State Finalizes Medical Marijuana Rules" (9 January 2009), online: *Bisjournals* <www.bizjournals.com/albuquerque/stories/2009/01/05/daily52.html>

366 "Legalization Law Goes into Effect; Sales to Begin No Later Than April 2022" (30 June 2021), online: *Marijuana Policy Project* <www.mpp.org/states/new-mexico/>

367 *Ibid*

368 *Ibid*

369 Robert Nott, "New Mexico Issues Recreational Cannabis Rules" (29 December 2021), online: *Santa Fe News* <www.santafenewmexican.com/news/local_news/new-mexico-issues-recreational-cannabis-rules/article_bbe5e504-6819-11ec-ad3e-97b9eb68c5a2.html>

Drug Legalization in Other Democracies 129

cannabis producer licenses had been awarded.[370] Two New Mexico senators are currently advancing wider drug policy reform initiatives that would defelonize possession of more serious drugs and implement safe injection and consumption sites.[371] The state currently has a Democratic majority and a Democratic governor, which increases the prospects of broader drug policy liberalization heading into 2022.

4.4.14 New York

Cannabis policy reform has developed swiftly in the "Empire State" over the course of the last decade. 2014 legislation authorized the legalization of medical cannabis, giving the state Department of Health an 18-month timeline to establish a regulatory framework through which private cannabis growers were permitted to open up to four dispensaries to distribute the drug to certified patients.[372] The medical cannabis program has since grown exponentially, with 3,489 certifying practitioners servicing 136,915 registered patients as of January 25, 2022.[373] The state first moved to decriminalize cannabis use in 2019, allowing for possession of up to an ounce to be subject to a minimal fine ($50) and, importantly, providing for the automatic expungement of previous cannabis possession arrests and convictions for amounts lesser than the new maximum.[374] On March 31, 2021, the Marijuana Regulation and Taxation Act (MRTA) became law with immediate effect, allowing for legal possession of up to three ounces of cannabis and cultivation of up to three mature plants.[375] The law also provides for: 1) records stemming from legalized conduct to be automatically expunged; 2) the establishment of a state Cannabis Control Board and Office of Cannabis Management to oversee the implementation and regulation of the adult-use cannabis market; 3) the setting of a minimum goal of 50% for licenses to go to social and economic equity applicants; and 4) limits on existing medical cannabis businesses that allow them to convert no more than three of their existing storefronts to

---

370 "New Mexico Approves First Recreational Cannabis Producer Licenses" (17 December 2021), online: *MJBiz Daily* <https://mjbizdaily.com/new-mexico-approves-first-recreational-cannabis-producer-licenses/>

371 Andy Lyman, "Legislators Seek to Reform Drug Laws" (13 January 2021), online: *NM Political Report* <https://nmpoliticalreport.com/2021/01/13/legislators-seek-to-reform-drug-laws/>

372 Jon Campbell, "Cuomo Signs New York's Medical Marijuana Bill" (7 July 2014), online: *USA Today* <www.usatoday.com/story/news/nation/2014/07/07/cuomo-signs-medical-marijuana-bill/12323967/>

373 "Medical Cannabis" (n.d.), online: *New York State Website* <https://cannabis.ny.gov/medical-cannabis>

374 "Decriminalization and Expungement in NY: An Overview of A0850/S06579" (n.d.), online: *Marijuana Policy Project* >www.mpp.org/states/new-york/decriminalization-and-expungement-in-ny-an-overview-of-a0840-s06579/>

375 "New York Becomes 16th State to Legalize Cannabis!" (31 March 2021), online: *Marijuana Policy Project* <www.mpp.org/states/new-york/?state=NY>

130 *Drug Legalization in Other Democracies*

dual-use.[376] Whether the state's adult-use recreational system grows as quickly as its medical system remains to be seen. As of late 2021, more than 40% of the state's municipalities had voted to ban cannabis sales.[377] It has also been suggested that bureaucratic delays and the resignation of Governor Andrew Cuomo might delay the opening of recreational stores well into 2022.[378] The state's Cannabis Control Board chairwoman, Tremaine Wright, recently indicated that recreational sales were most likely to begin sometime between late 2022 and early April 2023.[379] There has also been some movement towards wider drug policy reform in the state. The state Senate is currently considering Bill S1284, which, if enacted, would decriminalize possession of controlled substances and establish a drug decriminalization task force aimed at developing recommendations to treat substance use disorder as a disease rather than a criminal behaviour.[380]

4.4.15 Oregon

Oregon has been a pioneer of cannabis (and wider drug) policy reform for decades, a trend that very much continues today. The state was an early adopter of medical cannabis legalization, with Oregon voters first allowing for possession and cultivation of medical cannabis in 1998, and it has since significantly expanded this program: 1) In 2013, HB 3460 established a state-licensed medical cannabis system; 2) In 2015, SB 460 allowed medical dispensaries to temporarily serve the new adult-use recreational market; and 3) In 2016, HB 404 allowed for out-of-state ownership and investment in the medical cannabis program.[381] Oregon was also the first state to decriminalize cannabis possession back in 1973, and, more recently, its pioneering drug reform efforts continued when voters overwhelmingly passed Measure 110 in 2020, resulting in the decriminalization of possession of small amounts of heroin, methamphetamine, LSD, and other hard drugs.[382] Under the new system, those in possession of these drugs receive

---

376 "New York's Marijuana Regulation and Taxation Act (2021)" (n.d.), online: *Marijuana Policy Project* <www.mpp.org/states/new-york/new-yorks-marijuana-regulation-and-taxation-act-(2021)/>

377 Chris Roberts, "New York Is Already Doing Marijuana Legalization Wrong" (30 December 2021), online: *Forbes* <www.forbes.com/sites/chrisroberts/2021/12/30/new-york-is-already-doing-marijuana-legalization-wrong/>

378 Rachel Smith, "Legal Weed Shops May not Hit in 2022, New York. Here's What We Need to Know" (21 December 2021), online: *The City*<www.thecity.nyc/2021/12/21/22848537/waiting-to-inhale-legal-weed-shops-may-not-hit-nyc-in-2022>

379 Sean Teehan, "New York Cannabis in 2021 in Review: Marijuana Industry Finally Gets Rolling" (29 December 2021), online: *Syracuse* <www.syracuse.com/marijuana/2021/12/new-york-cannabis-in-2021-in-review-marijuana-industry-finally-gets-rolling.html>

380 "Senate Bill S1284" (n.d.), online: *The New York State Senate* <www.nysenate.gov/legislation/bills/2021/s1284>

381 "Oregon Medical Marijuana Laws and Regulations" (n.d.), online: *Americans for Safe Access* <www.safeaccessnow.org/oregon_medical_marijuana_laws>

382 Andrew Selsky, "Oregon First U.S. State to Decriminalize Possession of Hard Drugs" (1 February 2021), online: *CTV News* <www.ctvnews.ca/world/oregon-first-u-s-state-to-decriminalize-possession-of-hard-drugs-1.5291021>

Drug Legalization in Other Democracies   131

a ticket rather than a criminal sanction, with the state putting forward more than $100 million dollars per year in funding for substance abuse treatment centres.[383] The state is logically re-routing the tax revenue from its extremely profitable recreational adult-use cannabis system to fund these public health initiatives.[384] It is estimated that 70 organizations in 26 of Oregon's 36 counties had already received funding as of 2021, with an additional $302 million dollars in funding earmarked for further funding of harm reduction and recovery services in the next two years.[385] The Drug Policy Alliance, a New York-based nonprofit organization that helped fund Ballot Measure 110, is leading initiatives to get wider drug decriminalization measures on the ballot in other states, suggesting that Oregon's leading example may once again spread to several other states in the coming years.[386]

Oregon narrowly missed legalizing adult-use recreational cannabis via ballot Measure 80 in 2012 (53% to 47% opposing), but the issue would soon return to ballots in 2014 via Measure 90, which was approved by voters (56% to 44% approving).[387] As a result, the Control, Regulation, and Taxation of Marijuana and Industrial Hemp Act came into effect on July 1, 2015, establishing: 1) 21 as the legal age for adults to possess up to one ounce of cannabis (outside the home) and up to eight ounces of cannabis (inside the home); 2) gifting provisions that allow adults to gift up to one ounce of cannabis to another adult over the legal age, so long as they are not financially compensated; 3) home cultivation limits of up to four cannabis plants; and 4) the Oregon Liquor Control Commission (OLCC) as the authority to oversee a strictly regulated system of registered cannabis producers, wholesalers, processors, and retailers.[388] While some argue that Oregon's licensing fees (some of the lowest in the country) allow for fewer barriers to market entry for social equity applicants, advocates have argued that

383 Casey Toner, Jared Rutecki & Frank Main, "Oregon's the First State to Ticket Narcotics Users, but Reform Has Yet to Live Up to What Was Promised" (3 December 2021), online: *Chicago Sun Times* <https://chicago.suntimes.com/2021/11/30/22644894/oregon-drug-reform-decriminalization-addictions-help>

384 Scott Akins, "Oregon Just Decriminalized All Drugs- Here's Why Voters Passed This Groundbreaking Reform" (10 December 2020), online: *The Conversation* <https://theconversation.com/oregon-just-decriminalized-all-drugs-heres-why-voters-passed-this-groundbreaking-reform-150806>

385 Matt Sutton, "Drug Decriminalization in Oregon, One Year Later: Thousands of Lives Not Ruined by Possession Arrests, $300 Million+ in Funding for Services" (3 November 2021), online: *DrugPolicy.org* https://drugpolicy.org/press-release/2021/11/drug-decriminalization-oregon-one-year-later-thousands-lives-not-ruined>

386 Sophie Quinton, "Oregon's Drug Decriminalization May Spread, Despite Unclear Results" (3 November 2021), online: *PEW* <www.pewtrusts.org/en/research-and-analysis/blogs/stateline/2021/11/03/oregons-drug-decriminalization-may-spread-despite-unclear-results>

387 "Oregon Legalized Marijuana Initiative, Measure 91 (2014)" (n.d.), online: *Ballotpedia* <https://ballotpedia.org/Oregon_Legalized_Marijuana_Initiative,_Measure_91_(2014)>

388 "Summary of Oregon's Measure 91" (n.d.), online: *Marijuana Policy Project* <www.mpp.org/states/oregon/summary-of-oregons-measure-91/>

132 *Drug Legalization in Other Democracies*

the state should further incorporate social equity into legal provisions.[389] The state's industry has been reactive to changing industry and consumer needs, with various regulations passed in 2021, set to come into force in 2022, including: 1) relaxed rules for licensees to self-distribute products and reduce the time and cost needed to report plant and harvest details; 2) increased purchase limits for consumers from one to two ounces; and 3) allowing for at-home delivery of cannabis products, in response to issues created by the COVID-19 pandemic.[390] Estimates suggest that 80% to 85% of the state's demand for cannabis is met by the legal market, with the OLCC reporting 2021 sales up 6.5% to nearly $1.2 billion dollars during that year.[391]

4.4.16 *Vermont*

Medical cannabis was first legalized in Vermont in 2004 (allowing for home cultivation only), with subsequent legislation significantly expanding qualifying medical conditions in 2007 and the addition of regulated access through medical dispensaries in 2011.[392] Slow, incremental change has continued since then: 1) a 2014 law removed the cap of 1,000 patients who were able to access dispensaries; 2) a 2016 law changed the qualifying condition standard from "severe pain" to "chronic pain"; 3) a 2017 law added an additional dispensary and allowed existing dispensaries to open one additional location each; and 4) a 2020 law shifts oversight of the medical program from the Department of Public Safety (a law enforcement agency) to a newly created Cannabis Control Board.[393] Legislation pertaining to adult-use recreational cannabis also came into effect in 2020, requiring automatic expungement for past cannabis-related possession convictions up to a maximum of two ounces of cannabis and decriminalizing possession of the same amount going forward (subject only to a $100 civil fine).[394] The aforementioned Cannabis Control Board was created in 2020 via bill S.54, legislation that formalized adult-use recreational cannabis legalization and provided for: 1) a robust prioritization of social equity and small-scale cultivator applicants; 2) limits on THC potency; 3) a 20% tax (on retail recreational sales

---

389 Samuel Dewitt, "Achieving Social Equity in the Cannabis industry" (2021) [unpublished], online: *SSRN* <https://papers.ssrn.com/sol3/papers.cfm?abstract_id=3861692> at 6
390 Joelle Jones, "Oregon Changes Cannabis Rules for the New Year" (30 December 2021), online: *Koin* <www.koin.com/news/oregon/oregon-changes-cannabis-rules-for-the-new-year/>
391 Pete Danko, "2021 Cannabis Sales: Border-Crossing Weed Buyers Made This Oregon County No. 1" (4 January 2022), online: *BizJournals* <www.bizjournals.com/portland/news/2022/01/04/2021-oregon-county-cannabis-sales.html>
392 "Vermont Becomes 11th State to Regulate Adult-Use Cannabis Markets; Cannabis Control Board Vows to Create Equitable Marketplace" (10 June 2021), online: *Marijuana Policy Project* <www.mpp.org/states/vermont/>
393   *Ibid*
394 "Vermont Cannabis Expungement and Penalty Reduction Summary" (n.d.), online: *Marijuana Policy Project* <www.mpp.org/states/vermont/vermont-cannabis-expungement-and-penalty-reduction-summary/>

Drug Legalization in Other Democracies 133

only) that would be allocated to substance misuse prevention programming; and 4) a detailed timeline through which licenses for retailers will begin being issued by October 1, 2022.[395] While concerns have been raised about potential supply issues stemming from the state's focus and priority on small-scale growers, the state appears dedicated to taking a slow and cautious approach with its recreational sales rollout.[396] The state has also recently made progress on wider drug policy reform. In early 2022, legislation that would decriminalize possession and distribution of low levels of currently illicit drugs (subject only to a $50 fine) had quickly gained the support of a third of Vermont's house within weeks of its introduction.[397]

4.4.17 Virginia

Virginia has engaged in significant cannabis (and broader drug) policy reform over the course of the last five years. Medical cannabis was first permitted (albeit restrictively) in 2017, with substantial improvements to the system implemented in 2020 and 2021, including: 1) patients are now formally protected from arrest and prosecution for medical cannabis possession; 2) patients with any condition can now purchase cannabis up to a 10 milligram THC dose; 3) whole-plant "botanical" cannabis use was included as a medical treatment; and 4) patients are protected from being disciplined or fired for using medical cannabis away from work.[398] The medical system is nonetheless still quite limited and will take time to grow, as the Board of Pharmacy has so far issued only five approvals to pharmaceutical processers to produce and sell cannabis extracts.[399] Recreational cannabis also has much room to grow in the coming years, as the system is still very much in its infancy. House Bill 2312, passed in 2021, made Virginia the first state in the southern United States to legalize adult-use cannabis.[400] The legislation proposes a system for legal adult-use cannabis that will be taxed and regulated, including: 1) allowing adults 21 and older to possess one ounce of cannabis and/or share the same amount with other adults; 2) allowing adults to securely and discreetly cultivate up to four cannabis plants within their residence; 3) the

---

395 "Summary of S. 54, the Bill to Regulate and Tax Cannabis in Vermont" (n.d.), online: *Marijuana Policy Project* <www.mpp.org/states/vermont/summary-of-s-54-the-bill-to-regulate-and-tax-cannabis-in-vermont/>

396 Andrew Long, "Vermont's Focus on Small Marijuana Growers Could Cause Supply Issues with Adult-Use Rollout" (17 December 2021), online: *MJBiz Daily* <https://mjbizdaily.com/small-marijuana-cultivators-could-cause-supply-issues-in-vermont-adult-use-market/>

397 Kyle Jaeger, "Vermont Lawmakers File Drug Decriminalization Bill with Hopes of Promoting Harm Reduction" (14 January 2022), online: *Marijuana Moment* <www.marijuanamoment.net/vermont-lawmakers-file-drug-decriminalization-bill-with-hopes-of-promoting-harm-reduction/>

398 "Legalization Implementation to Be Considered in 2022" (12 January 2022), online: *Marijuana Policy Project* <www.mpp.org/states/virginia/?state=VA>

399 *Ibid*

400 *Ibid*

134 *Drug Legalization in Other Democracies*

creation of a new Cannabis Control Authority to regulate licenses, including the prioritization of social equity applicants during the first year of license applications (with a percentage of fees waived); and 4) a timeline stipulating that retail sales will not begin before January 1, 2024.[401] Some concerns were raised that the newly elected Republican Governor, Glenn Youngkin, would try to reverse course on the policy reform, but he has confirmed via tweet that he will not seek to repeal the legislation.[402] To the contrary, while it appears that Democratic and Republican senators have some differing views about what the system will look like once set up, several pieces of legislation have already tacitly acknowledged that legalization (in some form) will continue moving forward.[403] Moreover, on the wider drug policy liberalization front, in early 2022, state lawmakers introduced new legislation that would decriminalize possession of small amounts of peyote, ibogaine, or psilocybin.[404] While the future of this drug policy reform is far less foreseeable than the future of cannabis legalization in the state, both are notable and significant departures for a southern (and historically punitive) state, again illustrating the sweeping nature of cannabis (and wider drug) policy reform across the country.

4.4.18 Washington State

The move towards adult-use recreational cannabis legalization in the state of Washington was perhaps unsurprising, as the state was one of the earliest to adopt medical cannabis by way of voter initiative (692) with a resounding majority back in 1998 (59% to 41%).[405] Curiously, the resulting legislation allowed for large amounts of medical cannabis possession but did not explicitly allow dispensaries or set up a regulatory system for cultivation, distribution, or retail. As a result, a multitude of dispensaries proliferated (and were tolerated by law enforcement) in the years leading up to 2011, which resulted in legislation (SB 5073) that would have legalized these dispensaries, had it not been vetoed by the state's then-governor who expressed concerns that state workers could be prosecuted under federal

---

401 "Virginia Cannabis Regulation Law Summary" (n.d.), online: *Marijuana Policy Project* <www.mpp.org/states/virginia/hb-2312/sb-1406-virginia-cannabis-regulation-bill-summary/>
402 Kelly Avellino, "Unfinished Marijuana Legislation Has Hazy Future with Virginia's Political Shift in Power" (23 December 2021), online: *NBC12* <www.nbc12.com/2021/12/23/unfinished-marijuana-legislation-has-hazy-future-with-virginias-political-shift-power/>
403 Jakob Cordes, "First Look: Will Weed Stay Legal in Virginia?" (13 January 2022), online: *ABCNews* <www.wric.com/news/politics/capitol-connection/first-look-will-weed-stay-legal-in-virginia/>
404 Kyle Jaeger, "Virginia Could Decriminalize Psilocybin and Other Psychedelics with Newly Filed Bills" (14 January 2022), online: *Marijuana Moment* <www.marijuanamoment.net/virginia-could-decriminalize-psilocybin-and-other-psychedelics-with-newly-filed-bills/>
405 "November 1998 General Election Results" (n.d.), online: *Washington Secretary of State Website* <www.sos.wa.gov//elections/results_report.aspx?e=10&c=&c2=&t=&t2 = 5&p=&p2=&y=>

law.[406] This changed in 2013 when U.S. Attorney General James Cole provided guidance to U.S. attorneys (mentioned in Chapter 4.4), outlining an expectation that states who had authorized medical and/or recreational cannabis use would implement strong and effective regulatory and enforcement systems.[407] Just one year earlier, voters had approved an initiative (I-502) that legalized possession of up to one ounce of recreational cannabis while leaving cultivation, sale, and gifting illegal and making no consequential changes to the medical system.[408] The initiative, however, did stipulate a December 1, 2013 deadline for recreational sales to be regulated, which meant Washington uniquely first developed a regulated recreational cannabis system despite the fact that medical cannabis legalization had long pre-existed.[409] This situation was reconciled when the recreational and medical cannabis systems were aligned in 2015 through SB 5052 and HB 2136, two pieces of legislation that, taken together, set up a system for the regulated and licensed production, processing and retail sales of medical cannabis that included a tax exemption for qualifying medical patients.[410] The state currently utilizes a "commercial market model comparable to the alcohol and tobacco control regimes . . . although commercial activity is managed by State regulation authorities, cannabis producers and suppliers are profit-seeking entrepreneurs guided by commercial rather than public health initiatives".[411] Nonetheless, academic evaluations of Washington's adult-use system (particularly when compared against Colorado) have referred to it as "cautious", pointing to a lack of vertical integration, no home-growing, retail store caps, higher tax levels, stronger zoning laws, and stricter advertising rules as evidence of a more restrained system.[412] Washington also had a slower rollout than Colorado since it did not allow the aforementioned medical dispensaries to supply cannabis.[413]

Most proponents of Washington's system point to several facts as justification that its system has been successful, including: 1) law enforcement resources being diverted to other priority areas rather than cannabis; 2) Washington's more restrained approach in comparison to Colorado led to fewer of the unintended consequences reported in that state (edible cannabis-induced intoxications, rising use of concentrates, etc.); 3) profits diverted from the black market and tax revenue have been invested into public health and prevention programs; and 4)

---

406 "Medical Marijuana: History in Washington" (n.d.), online: *Washington State Department of Health Website* <www.doh.wa.gov/YouandYourFamily/Marijuana/MedicalMarijuana/LawsandRules/HistoryinWashington>

407 *Ibid*

408 *Ibid*

409 *Ibid*

410 *Ibid*

411 Ivana Obradovic, "From Prohibition to Regulation: A Comparative Analysis of the Emergence and Related Outcomes of New Legal Cannabis Policy Models (Colorado, Washington State and Uruguay)" (2021) 91 International Journal of Drug Policy 1 at 3

412 *Ibid*

413 *Ibid* at 4

136   *Drug Legalization in Other Democracies*

public support for legalization has increased since the time I-502 passed.[414] To be clear, some criticisms have been advanced. Some authors lament the length of time (more than 17 years) it took for medical cannabis to be clearly regulated.[415] Others have noted that the average tax rate (including excise tax and state and local sales taxes) totals 46.2%, which has had the effect of pushing some consumers to the illicit market and has made it difficult for licensed business owners to scale up their operations.[416] The state is indeed receiving an obscene amount of tax revenue from adult-use cannabis sales (estimated at more than $3 billion dollars between 2014 and September 2021), but it does appear that for every $1 billion dollars in revenue collected from sales tax, nearly $600 million dollars is funneled into public health initiatives, including a fund that provides health insurance to low-income families.[417] Washington has also been credited for establishing purchasing limits for certain product types (concentrates, edibles, beverages, etc.) to reduce unintended harm to users.[418] Although studies on the public health impacts of legalization have been mixed, it does not appear as though many of the concerns opponents originally voiced (i.e. increased use, effects on road safety, use of more harmful substances, etc.) have materialized in any significant way.[419] As a result, the state has also proceeded with broader drug law reform on the heels of what appears to have been successful adult-use recreational cannabis legalization. A 2021 Washington State Supreme Court judgment striking down the state's drug possession law has prompted defelonization legislation that makes drug possession of all drugs for personal use a misdemeanour.[420] The new legislation requires police to divert a person's first two offences to treatment before the case can even be made to a prosecutor, with the prosecutor eventually also able to decide whether to divert the case away from the formal criminal justice system. The law will remain in effect for two years, giving lawmakers time to study its effects and eventually decide whether to continue it beyond 2023.[421]

---

414 *Ibid* at 4–5
415 Christopher Cambron, Katarina Guttmannova & Charles B. Fleming, "State and National Contexts in Evaluating Cannabis Laws: A Case Study of Washington State" (2017) 47:1 Journal of Drug Issues 74 at 82
416 "Washington State Adult-Uses Cannabis Generates Huge Impact, but Tax Burden High" (11 January 2022), online: *MJBiz Daily* <https://mjbizdaily.com/washington-state-adult-use-cannabis-generates-huge-impacts-but-tax-burden-high/>
417 "Cannabis Tax Revenues in States that Regulate Cannabis for Adult Use" (n.d.), online: *Marijuana Policy Project* <www.mpp.org/issues/legalization/cannabis-tax-revenue-states-regulate-cannabis-adult-use/>
418 Caislin Firth et al, "How High: Differences in the Developments of Cannabis Markets in Two Legalized States" (2020) 75 International Journal of Drug Policy, DOI: <DOI:10.1016/j.drugpo.2019.102611> at 2
419 Wayne Hall & Michael Lynskey, "Assessing the Public Health Impacts of Legalizing Recreational Cannabis Use: The US experience" (2020) 19 World Psychiatry 179
420 Rachel La Corte & Gene Johnson, "New Washington State Law Makes Drug Possession a Misdemeanor" (13 May 2021), online: *AP News* <https://apnews.com/article/washington-laws-government-and-politics-bf0a8af742fe8053e5d5748125143e84>
421 *Ibid*

Moreover, in early 2022, a pair of state lawmakers introduced legislation that would establish a legal, regulated psilocybin industry available to all adults of legal age.[422] It would thus appear that Washington State is once again poised to be a leader in drug policy liberalization heading into 2022 and beyond.

4.5 Conclusion

The analyses in this chapter represent a comprehensive scan of cannabis (and wider drug) policy reforms in forty jurisdictions from regions around the world. They have standalone value insofar as they have clearly evidenced a global trend towards cannabis policy liberalization. Several jurisdictions with globally significant markets, population size, and political significance have moved towards recreational cannabis legalization, including Mexico, Uruguay, Malta, South Africa, Germany, Portugal, Switzerland and several U.S. states. In several other jurisdictions, cannabis policy liberalization has otherwise occurred through regulated medical cannabis systems and/or decriminalization efforts. Three other trends have been observed across these jurisdictions that are of particular importance for Canada: 1) several jurisdictions have moved towards broader drug policy liberalization through the decriminalization, defelonization, or legalization of illicit substances other than cannabis; 2) several jurisdictions (especially in the United States) have included social justice (pardons) and/or social equity (prioritization of equity applicants, financial assistance, etc.) provisions in their legal cannabis regulatory schemes; and 3) several jurisdictions have implemented public health-oriented drug policies and programs, including syringe exchanges, sanctioned drug consumption sites, etc. As such, there are lessons Canada can and should learn from the comparative liberalization of cannabis (and wider drug) policy that is occurring in jurisdictions around the world.[423]

Adams, Dan, "Five Years Later, Legal Marijuana Remains Unfinished Business in Massachusetts" (7 November 2021), online: *Boston Globe* <www.bostonglobe.com/2021/11/07/marijuana/five-years-later-legal-marijuana-remains-unfinished-business-massachusetts/>

Adlin, Ben, "Here Are the Best Marijuana Psychedelics and Drug Policy News Stories of 2021" (30 December 2021), online: *Marijuana Moment* <www.marijuanamoment.net/here-are-the-biggest-marijuana-psychedelics-and-drug-policy-news-stories-of-2021/>

Adlin, Ben, "Psilocybin Services Would Be Legalized in Washington State Under New Bill" (6 January 2022), online: *Marijuana Moment* <www.marijuanamoment.net/psilocybin-services-would-be-legalized-in-washington-state-under-new-bill/>

---

422 Ben Adlin, "Psilocybin Services Would Be Legalized in Washington State Under New Bill" (6 January 2022), online: *Marijuana Moment* <www.marijuanamoment.net/psilocybin-services-would-be-legalized-in-washington-state-under-new-bill/>

423 Chapter 5.3

138 *Drug Legalization in Other Democracies*

Agoff, Carolina, Fondevila, Gustavo & Sandberg, Sveinung, "Cultural Stigmatization and Police Corruption" (2021) "Drugs: Education" Prevention and Policy Journal, DOI: <https://doi.org/10.1080/09687637.2021.2004089>

Akins, Scott, "Oregon Just Decriminalized All Drugs- Here's Why Voters Passed This Groundbreaking Reform" (10 December 2020), online: *The Conversation* <https://theconversation.com/oregon-just-decriminalized-all-drugs-heres-why-voters-passed-this-groundbreaking-reform-150806>

Allen, Grahame & Tunnicliffe, Richard "Drug Crime: Statistics for England and Wales" (23 December 2021), online (pdf): *United Kingdom House of Commons Library* <https://researchbriefings.files.parliament.uk/documents/CBP-9039/CBP-9039.pdf>

Alves, Jaime Amparo & Alves, Dina, "Drugs and Drug Control in Brazil" in Kalunta-Crumpton, Anita, ed, *Pan-African Issues in Drugs and Drug Control: An International Perspective* (England: Ashgate Publishing Ltd, 2015) 241

Anderfuhren-Biget, Simon, Zobel, Frank, Heeb, Cedric & Savary, Jean-Felix, "Swiss Cannabis Polices" in Decorte, Tom, Lenton, Simon & Wilkins, Chris, eds, *Legalizing Cannabis: Experiences, Lessons and Scenarios* (London: Routledge, 2020) 323

Arana, Xabier & Pares, Oscar, "Cannabis Social Clubs in Spain: Recent Legal Developments" in Decorte, Tom, Lenton, Simon & Wilkins, Chris, eds, *Legalizing Cannabis: Experiences, Lessons and Scenarios* (London: Routledge, 2020) 307

Arena, Roesli, "Massachusetts Pot Shops Are a Billion-Dollar Market, but Cannabis Industry Still Faces Hurdles" (2 November 2021), online: *Cape Cod Times* <www.capecodtimes.com/story/business/2021/11/02/pot-shops-billion-dollar-massachusetts-market-cannabis-industry-face-hurdles-cape-cod-retail-medical/6233346001/>

Argentina, Law No. 23737, Article 14, Sept. 1, 1989, Boletin Oficial [B.O]

Arze, Luise & Somarriva, Matias, "Medical Use" (15 April 2021), online: *CMS: Tax, Law, Future* <https://cms.law/en/int/expert-guides/cms-expert-guide-to-a-legal-roadmap-to-cannabis/chile>

Australia, *Narcotic Drugs Amendment Act* 2016, No 12

Australian Capital Territory Policing, "Drugs and the Law" (8 October 2020), online: *Australian Capital Territory Policing* <www.police.act.gov.au/safety-and-security/alcohol-and-drugs/drugs-and-law>

Australian Greens, "Legalise Cannabis" (17 November 2021), online: *Australian Greens* <https://greens.org.au/campaigns/legalise-it>

Avellino, Kelly, "Unfinished Marijuana Legislation Has Hazy Future with Virginia's Political Shift in Power" (23 December 2021), online: *NBC12* <www.nbc12.com/2021/12/23/unfinished-marijuana-legislation-has-hazy-future-with-virginias-political-shift-power/>

Baptista-Leite, Ricardo & Ploeg, Lisa, "The Road Towards the Responsible and Safe Legalization of Cannabis Use in Portugal" (2018) 31:2 Acta Med Port

Bercea, Victor, "The Legal Situation of Cannabis in Malta" (22 August 2020), online: *StrainInsider* <https://straininsider.com/legal-situation-cannabis-malta/>

Bishop, Greg, "Illinois Legal Cannabis Sales Nearly $1.4 Billion in 2021, Double Last Year's Total" (3 January 2022), online: *The Center Square* <www.thecentersquare.com/illinois/illinois-legal-cannabis-sales-nearly-1-4-billion-in-2021-double-last-years-total/article_dafe48f6-6cc3-11ec-a174-db1ea990d6c7.html>

Bobo, Lawrence & Thompson, Victor, "Unfair by Design: The War on Drugs, Race, and the Legitimacy of the Criminal Justice System" (2006) 73:2 Social Research 445

Boffey, Daniel, "Malta to Legalise Cannabis for Personal Use in European First" (13 December 2021), online: *The Guardian* <www.theguardian.com/society/2021/dec/13/malta-to-be-first-in-europe-to-legalise-cannabis-for-personal-use>

Brandeis, Jason, "Ravin Revisited: Alaska's Historic Common Law Marijuana Rule at the Dawn of Legalization" (2015) 32:2 Alaska Law Review

Bricken, Hilary, "The Netherlands and Cannabis: Legal Supply Chain Experiment Continues" (23 July 2020), online: *Cannalaw Blog* <https://harrisbricken.com/cannalawblog/the-netherlands-and-cannabis-legal-supply-chain-experiment-continues/>

Brown, Spencer, "The Lowdown on Getting High in Brazil: The Evolution of Brazilian Drug Law" (2008) 14 Journal of the Americas

Brownstein, Hyatt, "United States: Changes in Colorado Cannabis Law: What to Expect with Four New Bills" (3 January 2022), online: *Mondaq* <www.mondaq.com/unitedstates/cannabis-hemp/1146638/changes-in-colorado-cannabis-law-what-to-expect-with-four-new-bills>

Bubola, Emma "Malta Becomes First E.U. Country to Legalize Marijuana" (15 December 2021), online: *The New York Times* <www.nytimes.com/2021/12/15/world/europe/malta-eu-marijuana-legalize.html>

Buell, Spencer, "Why Boston Can't Have Nice Things, Part One Million: Cannabis Cafes" (12 September 2021), online: *Boston Magazine* <www.bostonmagazine.com/news/2021/12/09/massachusetts-cannabis-cafes/>

Burgen, Stephen, "Barcelona Cannabis Clubs Face Closure in New Legal Setback" (27 July 2021), online: *The Guardian* <www.theguardian.com/society/2021/jul/27/barcelona-cannabis-clubs-face-closure-in-new-legal-setback>

Burgen, Stephen, "Span Become Cannabis Hub as Criminals Fill Tourism Void" (11 October 2020), online: *The Guardian* <www.theguardian.com/society/2020/oct/11/spain-becomes-cannabis-hub-as-criminals-fill-tourism-void>

Burkhardt, Paul, "South Africa Unveils US$1.9 Billion Cannabis Industry Plan" (25 August 2021), online: *Financial Post* <https://financialpost.com/cannabis/cannabis-business/south-africa-crafts-strategy-for-1-9-billion-cannabis-industry>

Burns, Gus, "Corporatization, Power Struggles and a Historic Recall: Michigan Marijuana's 2021 Growing Pains" (13 January 2022), online: *MLive* <mlive.com/public-interest/2022/01/corporatization-power-struggles-and-a-historic-recall-michigan-marijuanas-2021-growing-pains.html>

Busby, Mattha, "Here's Why Marijuana Still Isn't Legal in Mexico (but Could Be Soon)" (15 December 2021), online: *Leafly* <www.leafly.ca/news/politics/heres-why-marijuana-still-isnt-legal-in-mexico-but-could-be-soon>

Busby, Mattha, " 'It's Crazy'- Patients Say the UK's Medical Cannabis System Is not Working" (6 February 2021), online: *VICE* <www.vice.com/en/article/z3xmyc/uk-medical-cannabis-production-prescription>

Business Tech, "New Cannabis Rules Proposed for South Africa- to Be Introduced Within Next 2 Years" (13 April 2021), online: *Business Tech* <https://businesstech.co.za/news/lifestyle/482625/new-cannabis-rules-proposed-for-south-africa-to-be-introduced-within-next-2-years/>

Cabral, Tiago, "The 15th Anniversary of the Portuguese Drug Policy: Its History, Its Success and Its Future" (2017) 30 Drug Science, Policy and Law

Cain, Patrick, "Italian Court Rules Home-Growing Cannabis Is Legal, Restarting Legalization Debate-National" (27 December 2019), online: *Global News* <https://globalnews.ca/news/6340024/italian-court-rules-home-growing-cannabis-is-legal-restarting-legalization-debate/>

140 *Drug Legalization in Other Democracies*

Cambron, Christopher, Guttmannova, Katarina & Fleming, Charles B., "State and National Contexts in Evaluating Cannabis Laws: A Case Study of Washington State" (2017) 47:1 Journal of Drug Issues

Campbell, Jon, "Cuomo Signs New Tork's Medical Marijuana Bill" (7 July 2014), online: *USA Today* <www.usatoday.com/story/news/nation/2014/07/07/cuomo-signs-medical-marijuana-bill/12323967/>

Carrillo, Paula, "A Vendor Displays a Marijuana Plant at a Medical-Products Fair in Bogota, Columbia" (22 December 2015), online: *yahoo!news* <www.yahoo.com/news/colombia-legalizes-medical-marijuana-171023547.html?ref=gs>

Chazan, Guy, "Germany's Nascent Cannabis Industry Hits New Highs as Legalization Looms" (27 December 2021), online: *Financial Times* <www.ft.com/content/66016598-7307-4c07-a789-22d3973f2223>

Chmelewski, Stephen, "It's Time Portugal: Legalise It" (10 March 2021), online: *The Portugal News* <www.theportugalnews.com/news/2021-03-10/its-time-portugal-legalise-it/58709>

Clark, Moe, "Colorado's New Cannabis Business Office Will Focus on Job Creation, Social Equity" (29 July 2019), online: *Colorado Newsline* <https://coloradonewsline.com/briefs/colorados-new-cannabis-office-social-equity/>

Cluskey, Peter, "High Time: Netherlands Moves to Clean Up Absurd Cannabis Policy" (6 February 2020), online: *The Irish Times* <www.irishtimes.com/business/innovation/high-time-netherlands-moves-to-clean-up-absurd-cannabis-policy-1.4160217>

Collyns, Dan, "Peru Legalizes Medical Marijuana in Move Spurred by Mother's Home Lab" (20 October 2017), online: *The Guardian* <www.theguardian.com/world/2017/oct/20/peru-marijuana-cannabis-legal-terminally-ill-children>

Connolly, Johnny, "Cannabis Again Reclassified in the UK" (1 January 1970), online: *Drugs and Alcohol* <www.drugsandalcohol.ie/12158/>

Contreras, Óscar, "Polis Signs Bill 'Defelonizing' Single-Use Drug Possession for Schedule 1 and 2 Substances" (28 May 2019), online: *The Denver Channel.com* <thedenverchannel.com/news/politics/polis-signs-bill-defelonizing-single-use-drug-possession-for-schedule-i-and-ii-substances>

Cordes, Jakob, "First Look: Will Weed Stay Legal in Virginia?" (13 January 2022), online: *ABCNews* <www.wric.com/news/politics/capitol-connection/first-look-will-weed-stay-legal-in-virginia/>

Corte Suprema de Justicia de la Nación [CSJN] [National Supreme Court of Justice], 25/8/2009, "Arriola, Sebastián y otros/Recursode Hecho" (Arriola Case) (A. 891. XLIV)

Dalton, Victoria, "What You Should Know About Drug Court in New Jersey" (17 January 2019), online: *NJ.com* <www.nj.com/south-jersey-voices/2015/12/what_you_should_know_about_dru.html>

Danko, Pete, "2021 Cannabis Sales: Border-Crossing Weed Buyers Made This Oregon County No. 1" (4 January 2022), online: *BizJournals* <www.bizjournals.com/portland/news/2022/01/04/2021-oregon-county-cannabis-sales.html>

De Hoop, Bas, Heerdink, Eibert & Hazekamp, Arno, "Medical Cannabis on Prescription in the Netherlands: Statistics for 2003–2016" (2018) 3 Cannabis and Cannabinoid Research 54

Debono, James, "Cannabis Legalization: There Can Be No Way Forward Without a White Paper" (25 February 2021), online: *MaltaToday* <www.maltatoday.com.mt/news/national/107856/cannabis_legalisation_no_way_forward_without_white_paper>

Decorte, Tom, Pardal, Mafalda, Queirolo, Rosario, Boidi, Maria, Aviles, Costanza & Franquero, Oscar, "Regulating Cannabis Social Clubs: A Comparative Analysis of Legal and Self-Regulatory Practices in Spain, Belgium and Uruguay" (2020) 43 International Journal of Drug Policy

Delgado, Diana, "Colombia Shelves Congressional Bill on Cannabis Legalization" (10 November 2020), online: *Cannabis Business Times* <www.cannabisbusiness times.com/article/colombia-shelves-bill-legalize-cannabis/>

Dewitt, Samuel, "Achieving Social Equity in the Cannabis Industry" (2021) [unpublished], online: *SSRN* <https://papers.ssrn.com/sol3/papers.cfm?abstract_id=3861692>

Donohue, Caitlin, "Mothers Are the Reason Peru Just Expanded Medical Cannabis Legalizing Laws" (n.d.), online: *Merry Jane* <https://merryjane.com/news/mothers-are-the-reason-peru-just-expanded-medical-cannabis-legalization-laws>

Doran, Carmen, "Medicinal Cannabis Industry not in Delivery Phase" (30 December 2021), online: *Scoop* <www.scoop.co.nz/stories/GE2112/S00155/medicinal-cannabis-industry-now-in-delivery-phase.htm>

Earp, Brian, Lewis, Jonathan & Hart, Carl R., "Racial Justice Requires Ending the War on Drugs" (2021) 21:4 The American Journal of Bioethics 4

Elgot, Jessica, "Sadiq Khan Plans Pilot to 'Decriminalise' Minor Cannabis Offences in London" (4 January 2022), online: *The Guardian* <www.theguardian.com/society/2022/jan/04/sadiq-khan-plans-pilot-to-decriminalise-minor-cannabis-offences>

Emanuel, Machel A., Haughton, Andre Y. & K'nife, K'adamawe, "Policy Analysis and Implications of Establishing the Caribbean Cannabis Economy (CCE): Lessons from Jamaica" (2018) 18:2 Drugs and Alcohol Today 99

European Monitoring Centre for Drugs and Drug Addiction, "Czech Republic: Country Drug Report 2017" (2017), online (pdf): <www.emcdda.europa.eu/sys tem/files/publications/4511/TD0416912ENN.pdf>

European Monitoring Centre for Drugs and Drug Addiction, "Malta: Country Drug Report 2019" (2019), online (pdf): <www.emcdda.europa.eu/system/files/publi-cations/11328/malta-cdr-2019.pdf

European Monitoring Centre for Drugs and Drug Addiction, "Spain Country Drug Report 2019" (June 2019), online (pdf): <www.emcdda.europa.eu/system/files/publications/11353/spain-cdr-2019.pdf>

Felbab-Brown, Vanda, "Mexico's Cannabis Legalization, and Comparisons with Colombia, Lebanon, and Canada" (30 March 2021), online: *Brookings* <www.brookings.edu/blog/order-from-chaos/2021/03/30/mexicos-cannabis-legaliza-tion-and-comparisons-with-colombia-lebanon-and-canada/>

Filipkovà, Tereza, "Cannabis Policy in the Czech Republic" (22 August 2017), online: *Transnational Institute* <www.tni.org/en/article/cannabis-policy-in-the-czech-republic>

Firth, Caislin et al, "How High: Differences in the Developments of Cannabis Markets in Two Legalized States" (2020) 75 International Journal of Drug Policy

Fischer, Benedikt & Bullen, Chris, "Emerging Prospects for Non-Medical Cannabis Legalization in New Zealand: An Initial View and Contextualization" (2019) 40 International Journal of Drug Policy

Fornili, Katherine, "Racialized Mass Incarceration and the War on Drugs" (2018) 29:1 Journal of Addictions Nursing 65

142 *Drug Legalization in Other Democracies*

Franz, Justin, "Medical Marijuana Users Brace for Shortages as Montana's Recreational Market Opens" (5 January 2022), online: *KHN* <https://khn.org/news/article/medical-marijuana-users-brace-for-shortages-as-montanas-recreational-market-opens/>

Franz, Justin, "Recreational Marijuana Is Now Legal in Montana. Here's What You Need to Know" (5 July 2021), online: *MTFP* <https://montanafreepress.org/2021/05/07/legal-cannabis-whats-next-and-what-can-you-do-now/>

Fresh Leaf Analytics, "Australian Medicinal Cannabis Market: Patient, Product and Pricing Analysis" (August 2020), online (pdf): *Fresh Leaf Analytics* <https://freshleafanalytics.com.au/wp-content/uploads/2020/09/FreshLeaf-Analytics-Q3-2020.pdf>

Friedman, Sarah, "Paraguay Grows It, Brazil Takes It . . . Will New Cannabis Laws Change Anything?" (2021), online: *CBD testers* <https://cbdtesters.co/2020/09/22/paraguay-brazil-cannabis/>

Friedman, Sarah, "Uruguay Was the First Country to Legalize Cannabis- How Are They Doing Now?" (2020), online: *CBD Testers* <https://cbdtesters.co/2020/04/26/uruguay-was-1st-country-to-legalize-cannabis-how-are-they-doing-now/>

Goldberg, David, "Medical Cannabis in Costa Rica: A Controversial Alternative Awaiting Legalization" (29 December 2021), online: *The Tico Times* <https://ticotimes.net/2021/12/29/medical-cannabis-in-costa-rica-a-controversial-alternative-awaiting-legalization>

Goldson, Randy, "Ganja Struggles: Rastafari and the Contestation for Cannabis Rights in Jamaica" (2020) 55:4 Journal of Ecumenical Studies

Gomes, Hector, "Cannabis and Hemp to Kickstart Argentina's Economic Recovery?" (16 June 2021), online: *Prohibition Partners* <https://prohibitionpartners.com/2021/06/16/cannabis-and-hemp-to-aid-argentinas-economic-recovery/>

Gurney, Kyra, "Chile Kicks Off Medical Marijuana Program" (30 October 2014), online: *InSight Crime* <https://insightcrime.org/news/brief/chile-latin-america-grow-medical-marijuana/>

Hall, Wayne & Lynskey, Michael, "Assessing the Public Health Impacts of Legalizing Recreational Cannabis Use: The US Experience" (2020) 19 World Psychiatry

Hanson, Melissa, "A Milestone Year for the Massachusetts Cannabis Industry Is Ending. What's Next? See our Q&A with Regulators" (8 December 2021), online: *Massalive* <www.masslive.com/cannabis/2021/12/a-milestone-year-for-the-massachusetts-cannabis-industry-is-ending-whats-next-see-our-qa-with-regulators.html>

Hanson, Vicki J., "Cannabis Policy Reform: Jamaica's Experience" in Decorte, Tom, Lenton, Simon & Wilkins, Chris, eds, *Legalizing Cannabis: Experiences, Lessons and Scenarios* (London: Routledge, 2020) 375 at 383

Hasse, Javier, "Argentina Regulates Medical Cannabis Self-Cultivation, Sales, Subsidized Access" (12 November 2020), online: *Forbes* <www.forbes.com/sites/javierhasse/2020/11/12/argentina-regulates-medical-cannabis-self-cultivation-sales-subsidized-access/?sh=17b4b1841655>

Hasse, Javier, "Public Cannabis Consumption Now Allowed in Columbia: Is Full Marijuana Legalization Next?" (19 June 2019), online: *Forbes* <www.forbes.com/sites/javierhasse/2019/06/19/colombia-public-cannabis-consumption/?sh=2f09f78429e9>

Hazelgreaves, Steph, "The UK's Legalization of Medicinal Cannabis" (24 February 2021), online: *Open Access Government* <www.openaccessgovernment.org/the-uks-legalisation-of-medicinal-cannabis-products/104618/>

Drug Legalization in Other Democracies 143

Heininger, Clair, "N.J. Medical Marijuana Law Is Signed by Gov. Corzine" (1 April 2019), online: *NJ.com* <www.nj.com/news/2010/01/medical_marijuana_law_to_take.html>

Hendricks, Sharlene & Coto, Dànice, "Jamaica Faces Marijuana Shortage as Farmers Struggle" (5 Feburary 2021), online: *ABC News* <https://abcnews.go.com/International/wireStory/jamaica-faces-marijuana-shortage-farmers-struggle-75710269>

Henley, Jon, "Foreign Visitors Face Ban from Ameterdam's Cannabis Cafes" (11 January 2021), online: *The Guardian* <www.theguardian.com/world/2021/jan/11/foreigners-face-ban-from-amsterdams-cannabis-cafes>

Herington, A. J., "Colorado Marijuana Sales Topped $2 Billion Last Year" (30 December 2021), online: *Forbes* <www.forbes.com/sites/ajherrington/2021/12/30/colorado-marijuana-sales-topped-2-billion-last-year/?sh=34fd23077f22>

Hermida, Xosé, "Spain's Socialist Party Votes Against Legalizing Cannabis for Recreational Use" (20 October 2021), online: *El Pais* <https://english.elpais.com/spain/2021-10-20/spains-socialist-party-votes-against-legalizing-cannabis-for-recreational-use.html>

HHU, "Cannabis Legalization Brings the State 4.7 Billion Euros Annually – Around 27,000 Legal Jobs Would Be Created" (16 November 2021), online: *HHU* <www.dice.hhu.de/startseitennews/studie-cannabislegalisierung-bringt-dem-staat-jaehrlich-47-milliarden-euro-rund-27000-legale-arbeitsplaetze-wuerden-entstehen>

Hilton-Barber, Brett, "Pointers for the SA Cannabis Industry in 2022" (4 January 2022), online: *Cannabiz Africa* <www.cannabiz-africa.com/sa-cannabis-industry-2022/>

Hoban, Michael, "Political parties in Portugal propose adult-use cannabis legalization bills in parliament" (11 June 2021), online: *Prohibition Partners* <https://prohibitionpartners.com/2021/06/11/political-parties-in-portugal-propose-adult-use-cannabis-legalisation-bills-in-parliament/>

Hofmann, Robin, "Cannabis Legalization in Germany- the Final Blow to European Drug Prohibition?" (10 January 2022), online: *European Law Blog* <https://europeanlawblog.eu/2022/01/11/cannabis-legalization-in-germany-the-final-blow-to-european-drug-prohibition/>

Hudak, John, Ramsey, Geoff & Walsh, John, "Uruguay's Cannabis Law: Pioneering a New Paradigm" (March 2018), online (pdf): *Center for Effective Public Management at Brookings* <www.brookings.edu/wp-content/uploads/2018/03/gs_032118_uruguaye28099s-cannabis-law_final.pdf>

Hughes, Caitlin Elizabeth, "The Australian Experience and Opportunities for Cannabis Law Reform" Tom Decorte, Simon Lenton & Chris Wilkins, eds, *Legalizing Cannabis: Experiences, Lessons and Scenarios* (London: Routledge, 2020) 337

Hughes, Caitlin Elizabeth & Stevens, Alex, "A Resounding Success or a Disastrous Failure: Re-Examining the Interpretation of Evidence on the Portuguese Decriminalization of Illicit Drugs" (2015) New Approaches to Drug Policies

Hughes, Zachariah, " 'No One's Having a Ton of Fun': Many Alaska Cannabis Businesses Are Struggling and Failing" (30 November 2021), online: *Anchorage Daily News* <www.adn.com/alaska-marijuana/2021/11/30/no-ones-having-a-ton-of-fun-many-alaska-cannabis-businesses-are-struggling-and-failing/>

Hutchinson, Bill, "Nevada Becomes 1st State to Ban Most Pre-Employment Tests" (12 June 2019), online: *abc News* <https://abcnews.go.com/US/nevada-1st-state-ban-pre-employment-pot-tests/story?id=63656557>

Ingrahm, Christopher, "Mexico's Supreme Court Overturns Country's Ban on Recreational Marijuana" (1 November 2018), online: *The Washington Post*

144 *Drug Legalization in Other Democracies*

<www.washingtonpost.com/business/2018/11/01/mexicos-supreme-court-overturns-countrys-recreational-marijuana-ban/>

Ingrahm, Christopher, "Mexico's Supreme Court Rules That Smoking Pot Is a Fundamental Human Right" (5 November 2015), online: *The Washington Post* <www.washingtonpost.com/news/wonk/wp/2015/11/05/mexicos-supreme-court-rules-that-smoking-weed-is-a-fundamental-human-right/>

IDPC, "The Italian Supreme Court Abolishes the 2006 Antidrug Legislation" (13 February 2014), online: *IDPC* <https://idpc.net/alerts/2014/02/the-italian-supreme-court-abolishes-the-2006-antidrug-legislation>

Jaeger, Kyle, "After One Year as President, Biden's Marijuana Promises Remain Unfulfilled" (20 January 2022), online: *Marijuana Moment* <www.marijuanamoment.net/after-one-year-as-president-bidens-marijuana-promises-remain-unfulfilled/>

Jaeger, Kyle, "California Senator Says Bill to Legalize Psychedelics Possession Has '50/50' Chance to Pass This Year" (10 January 2022), online: *Marijuana Moment* <www.marijuanamoment.net/california-senator-says-bill-to-legalize-psychedelics-possession-has-50-50-chance-to-pass-this-year/>

Jaeger, Kyle, "Colorado Governor Pardons More Than 1,300 People for Past Marijuana Convictions" (30 December 2021), online: *Marijuana Moment* <www.marijuanamoment.net/colorado-governor-says-new-marijuana-clemency-plan-will-be-announced-within-days/>

Jaeger, Kyle, "Connecticut Marijuana Business License Applications Will Be Accepted Starting Next Month, Officials Announce" (5 January 2022), online: *Marijuana Moment* <www.marijuanamoment.net/connecticut-marijuana-business-license-applications-will-be-accepted-starting-next-month-officials-announce/>

Jaeger, Kyle, "First-Ever Congressional Bill to Decriminalize All Drugs Announced Ahead of Nixon Drug War Anniversary" (15 June 2021), online: *Marijuana Moment* <www.marijuanamoment.net/first-ever-congressional-bill-to-decriminalize-all-drugs-introduced-ahead-of-nixon-drug-war-anniversary/>

Jaeger, Kyle, "Here Are the Full Details of the New Federal Marijuana Legalization Bill from Chuck Schumer and Senate Colleagues" (14 July 2021), online: *Marijuana Moment* <www.marijuanamoment.net/here-are-the-full-details-of-the-new-federal-marijuana-legalization-bill-from-chuck-schumer-and-senate-colleagues/>

Jaeger, Kyle, "Italian Officials Certify Signatures for National Marijuana and Psilocybin Referendum" (12 January 2022), online: *Marijuana Moment* <www.marijuanamoment.net/italian-officials-certify-signatures-for-national-marijuana-and-psilocybin-referendum/>

Jaeger, Kyle, "Maine Marijuana Sales Can Finally Begin, Officials Announce Four Years After Voters Legalized It" (14 August 2020), online: *Marijuana moment* <www.marijuanamoment.net/maine-marijuana-sales-can-finally-begin-officials-announce-four-years-after-voters-legalized-it/>

Jaeger, Kyle, "Maine Senate Defeats Drugs Decriminalization Bill That Cleared the House" (1 July 2021), online: *Marijuana Moment* <www.marijuanamoment.net/maine-senate-defeats-drug-decriminalization-bill-that-cleared-the-house/>

Jaeger, Kyle, "Massachusetts Lawmakers Discuss Drug Decriminalization and Safe Injection Sites at Hearing" (27 September 2021), online: *Marijuana Moment* <www.marijuanamoment.net/massachusetts-lawmakers-discuss-drug-decriminalization-and-safe-injection-sites-at-hearing/>

Jaeger, Kyle, "Nevada Sold More Than $1 Billion in Marijuana in One Year, Officials Report" (13 October 2021), online: *Marijuana Moment* <www.marijuanamoment. net/nevada-sold-more-than-1-billion-in-marijuana-in-one-year-officials-report/>

Jaeger, Kyle, "New Jersey Governor 'Open-Minded' on Decriminalizing All Drugs" (22 March 2021), online: *Marijuana Moment* <www.marijuanamoment.net/ new-jersey-governor-open-minded-on-decriminalizing-all-drugs/>

Jaeger, Kyle, "Vermont Lawmakers File Drug Decriminalization Bill with Hopes of Promoting Harm Reduction" (14 January 2022), online: *Marijuana Moment* <www.marijuanamoment.net/vermont-lawmakers-file-drug-decriminalization-bill-with-hopes-of-promoting-harm-reduction/>

Jaeger, Kyle, "Virginia Could Decriminalize Psilocybin and Other Psychedelics with Newly Filed Bills" (14 January 2022), online: *Marijuana Moment* <www.mari juanamoment.net/virginia-could-decriminalize-psilocybin-and-other-psychedelics-with-newly-filed-bills/>

Jamaica Ministry of Justice, "Fact Sheet: Dangerous Drugs (Amendment) Act 2015" (2020), online: <https://moj.gov.jm/news/dangerous-drugs-amendment-act-2015-fact-sheet>

Jirička, Jan, "Nejvyš 10 gramu konopí. Soud nove stanovil vetší než malé množstyí drog" (9 April 2014), online: *iDNEScz* <www.idnes.cz/zpravy/domaci/nejvyssi-soud-nove-stanovil-vetsi-nez-male-mnozstvi-drog.A140409_102935_domaci_jav>

Johnson, Brent, "Christie Says Medical Marijuana Programs Are 'a Front for Legalization'" (17 June 2014), online: *NJ.com* <www.nj.com/politics/2014/06/chris tie_says_medical_marijuana_programs_are_a_front_for_legalization.html>

Jones, Joelle, "Oregon Changes Cannabis Rules for the New Year" (30 December 2021), online: *Koin* <www.koin.com/news/oregon/oregon-changes-cannabis-rules-for-the-new-year/>

Jones, Katie, "US Announcement Against Corrupt Paraguay Official May Signal Shift" (9 April 2021), online: *InSight Crime* <https://insightcrime.org/news/corruption-crackdown-us-acts-against-corrupt-paraguay-officials>

Kafkadesk Prague Office, "Czech Republic Rejects Liberalization of Cannabis Use" (12 September 2021), online: *Kafkadesk* <https://kafkadesk.org/2021/01/28/czech-republic-rejects-liberalization-of-cannabis-use/>

Kamin, Sam, "What California Can Learn from Colorado's Marijuana Regulations" (2017) 49 The University of the Pacific Law Review

Kapos, Shai, "Layers, Race and Money: Illinois' Messy Weed Experiment" (18 September 2021), online: *Politico* <www.politico.com/news/2021/09/18/illinois-weed-experiment-512626>

Kennedy, Joseph, Unah, Isaac & Wahlers, Kasi, "Sharks and Minors in the War on Drugs: A Study of Quantity, Race and Drug Type in Drug Arrests" (2018) 52 University of California Davis Law Review 729

Knöss, Werner, Van De Velde, Marco, Sandvos, Catherine & Cremer-Schaeffer, Peter, "Key Elements of Legal Environments for Medical Use of Cannabis in Different Countries" (2019) 62 Bundesgesundheitsbl 855

Korf, Dirk, "Cannabis Regulation in Europe: Country Report Netherlands" (27 March 2019), online: *Transnational Institute* <www.tni.org/en/publication/cannabis-regulation-in-europe-country-report-netherlands>

Kundrod, Kathryn, "Decriminalization of Drugs in Portugal: A Controversial Experiment for Public Health" (2015) 33 Perspectives on Business and Economics

146 *Drug Legalization in Other Democracies*

Kung, Angela & Kesselring, Jùlia "Regulation of Cannabis products in Brazil" (n.d.), online: *International Bar Association* <www.ibanet.org/article/DD9E29E5-E25A-4EC0-BE4B-C83EB44EFC69>

La Corte, Rachel & Johnson, Gene, "New Washington State Law Makes Drug Possession a Misdemeanor" (13 May 2021), online: *AP News* <https://apnews.com/article/washington-laws-government-and-politics-bf0a8af742fe8053e5d57481 25143e84>

Laqueur, Hannah, Rivera-Aguirre, Ariadne, Shev, Aaron, Castillo-Carniglia, Alvaro, Rudolph, Kara, Ramirez, Jessica, Martins, Silvia & Cerda, Magdalena, "The Impact of Cannabis Legalization in Uruguay on Adolescent Cannabis Use" (2020) 80 International Journal of Drug Policy, DOI: <https://doi.org/10.1016/j.drugpo.2020.102748>

Lawrence, Geoffrey, "Nevada to Allow Tourists to Use Legal Marijuana in Lounges but Restrictive Licensing Problems Remain" (12 October 2021), online: *Reason* <https://reason.org/commentary/nevada-to-allow-tourists-to-use-legal-marijuana-in-lounges-but-restrictive-licensing-problems-remain/>

Ledger, Emily, "A Year on from Australian Capital Territory Cannabis Legalisation" (1 Feburary 2021), online: *Canex* <https://canex.co.uk/a-year-on-from-australian-capital-territory-cannabis-legalisation/>

Lee, Josh, "Mexico to Vote on Legalization" (9 December 2021), online: *The Paper* <https://abq.news/2021/12/mexico-to-vote-on-legalization/>

Lintzeris, Nicholas, Mills, Llewellyn, Suraev, Anastasia, Bravo, Maria, Arkell, Thomas, Arnold, Jonathon, Benson, Mellisa & McGregor, Iain, "Medical Cannabis Use in the Australian Community Following Introduction of Legal Access: The 2018–2019 Online Cross-Sectional Cannabis as Medicine Survey" (2020) 17:37 Harm Reduction Journal

Long, Andrew, "Vermont's Focus on Small Marijuana Growers Could Cause Supply Issues with Adult-Use Rollout" (17 December 2021), online: *MJBiz Daily* <https://mjbizdaily.com/small-marijuana-cultivators-could-cause-supply-issues-in-vermont-adult-use-market/>

Lopez, Oscar, "Mexico Set to Legalize Marijuana, Becoming World's Largest Market" (19 March 20210), online: *The New York Times* <www.nytimes.com/2021/03/10/world/americas/mexico-cannabis-bill.html>

Lyman, Andy, "Legislators Seek to Reform Drug Laws" (13 January 2021), online: *NM Political Report* <https://nmpoliticalreport.com/2021/01/13/legislators-seek-to-reform-drug-laws/>

Mano, Ana, "Cannabis Firms Catch a Whiff of Opportunity in Brazil" (20 August 2021), online: *Recuters* <www.reuters.com/business/cannabis-firms-catch-whiff-opportunity-brazil-2021-08-20/>

Mansur, Sarah, "Drug-Decriminalization Bill Among Those That Miss Deadline for Illinois Legislature's Session" (2 June 2021), online: *The News-Gazette* <www.news-gazette.com/news/local/politics/drug-decriminalization-bill-among-those-that-miss-deadline-for-illinois-legislatures-session/article_1ae0007d-c00a-5752-ac4b-d76fd1e92118.html>

Maposa, Siseko, "Opinion: Siseko Maposa: The Complexities of SA's Cannabis Policy-More Integration Needed" (22 December 2021), online: *News24* <www.news24.com/news24/columnists/guestcolumn/opinion-siseko-maposa-the-complexities-of-sas-cannabis-policy-more-integration-needed-20211222>

Marino Jr., David, "More Than 90% of Maine Towns Still Don't Allow Recreational Marijuana Sales" (20 September 2021), online: *Maine Public* <www.mainepublic.org/news/2021-09-20/more-than-90-of-maine-towns-still-dont-allow-recreational-marijuana-sales>

Marino Jr., David, "There's More Illegal Activity in Maine's Medical Marijuana Market, State's Top Pot Official Says" (10 November 2021), online: *Bangor Daily News* <https://bangordailynews.com/2021/11/10/news/theres-more-illegal-activity-in-maines-medical-marijuana-market-states-top-pot-official-says-joam40zk0w/>

Martin, Michael, "5 Years After California Legalized Weed, the Illicit Market Dominates" (7 November 2021), online: *NPR* <www.npr.org/2021/11/07/1053387426/5-years-after-california-legalized-weed-the-illicit-market-dominates>

McCopin, Robert, "Boom Time for Marijuana Sales in Illinois, as Industry Expands with New Products- but Minority Businesses Get Left Behind" (1 January 2022), online: *Chicago Tribune* <www.chicagotribune.com/marijuana/illinois/ct-illinois-marijuana-2021-review-20220101-6ltav5lghfba3awognltyrzs4m-story.html>

McLaren, Bryan, "How Cannabis Legalization in Arizona Offers a Forecast for Commercial Real Estate in Other Markets" (13 December 2021), online: *Forbes* <www.forbes.com/sites/forbesbusinesscouncil/2021/12/13/how-cannabis-legalization-in-arizona-offers-a-forecast-for-commercial-real-estate-in-other-markets/>

Metello, Inês & Ricardo, Mariana, "Portugal Discusses Draft=Laws to Legalize Cannabis for Personal Use" (9 June 2021), online: *Lexology* <www.lexology.com/library/detail.aspx?g=e24f0994-b132-4057-a80f-e96f2621e78a>

Mikulic, Matej, "Topic: Medical Cannabis in the UK" (27 October 2021), online: *Statista* <www.statista.com/topics/6200/medical-cannabis-in-the-uk/>

Miller, Patricia, "First Medical Cannabis Prescription Issued in South Africa" (14 September 2021), online: *Cannabis & Tech Today* <https://cannatechtoday.com/first-medical-cannabis-prescription-issued-in-south-africa

Minhee, Christine & Calandrillo, Steve, "The Cure for America's Opioid Crisis? End the War on Drugs" (2019) 42:2 Harvard Journal of Law and Public Policy 547

Monk, Ginny, "How CT Plans to Protect Medical Marijuana Program as Recreational Use Begins" (15 October 2021), online: *CT Insider* <www.ctinsider.com/news/article/How-CT-plans-to-protect-medical-marijuana-program-16536544.php>

Neis Araujo, Felipe, "In Brazil, Bolsonaro Continues to Pump Blood to the War on Drugs" (29 January 2021), online: *IDPC* <https://idpc.net/alerts/2021/01/in-brazil-bolsonaro-continues-to-pump-blood-to-the-war-on-drugs>

Netherlands, *Controlled Cannabis Supply Chain Experiment Act* 2019

New Zealand Ministry of Health, "Medicinal Cannabis Agency – Background Information" (11 April 2020), online: *Ministry of Health NZ* <www.health.govt.nz/our-work/regulation-health-and-disability-system/medicinal-cannabis-agency/medicinal-cannabis-agency-background-information>

New Zealand Police, "Illicit Drugs – Offences and Penalties" online: <www.police.govt.nz/advice/drugs-and-alcohol/illicit-drugs-offences-and-penalties>

Nott, Robert, "New Mexico Issues Recreational Cannabis Rules" (29 December 2021), online: *Santa Fe News* <www.santafenewmexican.com/news/local_news/new-mexico-issues-recreational-cannabis-rules/article_bbe5e504-6819-11ec-ad3e-97b9eb68c5a2.html>

Nunn, Kenneth B., "Race, Crime and the Pool of Surplus Criminality: Or Why the 'War on Drugs' Was a 'War on Blacks'" (2002) 6 The Journal of Gender, Race & Justice 381

148 *Drug Legalization in Other Democracies*

Nutt, David, Bazire, Steve, Phillips, Lawrence D. & Schlag, Anne K., "So Near Yet So Far: Why Won't the UK Prescribe Medical Cannabis?" (2020) 10:9 BMJ Open

Obradovic, Ivana, "From Prohibition to Regulation: A Comparative Analysis of the Emergence and Related Outcomes of New Legal Cannabis Policy Models (Colorado, Washington State and Uruguay)" (2021) 91 International Journal of Drug Policy

O'Brien, Conor, "Spanish Government to Examine Benefits of Legalizing Medical Cannabis" (13 May 2021), online: *Prohibition Partners* <https://prohibitionpartners.com/2021/05/13/spanish-government-to-examine-benefits-of-legalising-medical-cannabis/>

O'Dowd, Liam, "Is the UK Any Closer to Legalizing Cannabis?" (4 January 2022), online: *Leafie* <www.leafie.co.uk/articles/will-the-uk-legalise-cannabis/>

Parks, Ken, "Uruguay Wants to Open Pot Market to Tourists: Cannabis Weekly" (13 September 2021), online: *Bloomberg*<www.bloomberg.com/news/articles/2021-09-13/uruguay-wants-to-open-pot-market-to-tourists-cannabis-weekly>

Parnes, Jamie, Bravo, Adrian, Conner, Bradley & Pearson, Matthew, "A Burning Problem: Cannabis Lessons Learned from Colorado" (2018) 26:1 Addiction Research and Theory 3

Pascual, Alfredo, "Brazil's New Medical Cannabis Rules Reject Domestic Cultivation, Potentially Setting Up Large Import Market" (4 December 2019), online: *MJBizDaily* <https://mjbizdaily.com/brazil-new-medical-cannabis-rules-reject-domestic-cultivation-potentially-setting-up-large-import-market/>

Pascual, Alfredo, "Paraguay Issues First 12 Medical Cannabis Production Licenses" (25 February 2020), online: *MJBizDaily* <https://mjbizdaily.com/paraguay-issues-first-12-medical-cannabis-production-licenses/>

Pascual, Alfredo, "Paraguay to Open Application Process for Medical Cannabis Production Licenses in October" (16 September 2019), online: *MJBizDaily* <https://mjbizdaily.com/paraguay-to-open-application-process-for-medical-cannabis-production-licenses-in-october/>

Pascual, Alfredo, "Three Years in, Uruguay's Recreational Cannabis Market 'Tangible' Success" (17 December 2021), online: *MJBizDaily* <https://mjbizdaily.com/3-years-after-legalization-uruguays-recreational-cannabis-market-tangible-success/>

Pardo, Bryce, "The Uneven Repeal of Cannabis Prohibition in the United States" in Decorte, Tom, Lenton, Simon & Wilkins, Chris, eds, *Legalizing Cannabis: Experiences, Lessons and Scenarios* (London: Routledge, 2020) 11

Parry, Charles, Myers, Bronwyn & Caulkins, Jonathan, "Decriminalisation of Recreational Cannabis in South Africa" (2019) 392:10183 The Lancet 1804 at 1805

Patten, Daniel, "The Mass Incarceration of Nations and the Global War on Drugs: Comparing the United States' Domestic and Foreign Drug Policies" (2016) 43:1 Social Justice 85

Pearce, Madeleine, "Five years After Massachusetts Voters Approve Marijuana Legalization, Some Lawmakers Seek Increased Restrictions" (8 December 2021), online: *The Berkshire Eagle* <www.berkshireeagle.com/state/massachusetts-marijuana-proposals-in-statehouse-would-increase-restrictions/article_4171f442-56c2-11ec-931d-c71f1d5e0fa4.html>

Planteo, El, "Adult-Use Cannabis Legalization Needs to Be Discussed, Says Argentina's President Alberto Fernàndez" (2 August 2021), online: *yahoo!finance* <https://finance.yahoo.com/news/adult-cannabis-legalization-needs-discussed-194908198.html>

Drug Legalization in Other Democracies 149

Planto, El, "Chile's New President Gabriel Boric Says He Smoked Marijuana in University, Passes Drug Test Before Election" (21 December 2021), online: *Benzinga* <www.benzinga.com/markets/cannabis/21/12/24727381/chiles-new-president-gabriel-boric-says-he-smoked-marijuana-in-university-passes-drug-test-before>

Politi, Daniel, "Argentina to Allow Medicinal Marijuana to Be Grown at Home" (11 December 2020), online: *New York Times* <www.nytimes.com/2020/11/12/world/americas/argentina-cannabis-marijuana.html>

Pozzebon, Stefano, "With Export Restrictions Eased, Colombia's Medical Cannabis Business Is Poised for Liftoff" (25 October 2021), online: *CNN Business* <www.cnn.com/2021/10/24/business/legal-cannabis-colombia-export/index.html>

Queirolo, Rosario, "Uruguay: The First Country to Legalize Cannabis", in Decorte, Tom, Lenton, Simon & Wilkins, Chris, eds, *Legalizing Cannabis: Experiences, Lessons and Scenarios* (London: Routledge) 116

Quinton, Sophie, "Oregon's Drug Decriminalization May Spread, Despite Unclear Results" (3 November 2021), online: *PEW* <www.pewtrusts.org/en/research-and-analysis/blogs/stateline/2021/11/03/oregons-drug-decriminalization-may-spread-despite-unclear-results>

Radwin, Max, "Paraguay Shakes Up Drug Policy with First Medical Cannabis Licenses" (16 March 2020), online: *InSight Crime* <https://insightcrime.org/news/brief/paraguay-medical-cannabis/>

Rahal, Sarah, "How Michigan Marijuana Regulators Are Trying to Prevent a Monopoly of Dispensary Chains" (26 December 2021), online: *The Detroit News* <www.detroitnews.com/story/news/local/michigan/2021/12/27/michigan-cannabis-industry-social-equity-marijuana-entrepreneurs-dispensaries-chains/6336959001/?gnt-cfr=1>

Ramella, Alberto, Roda, Gabriella, Pavlovic, Radmila, Dei Case, Michele, Casagni, Eleonora, Mosconi, Giacomo, Cecati, Francisco, Minghetti, Paola & Grizzetti, Carlo, "Impact of Lipid Sources on Quality Traits of Medical Cannabis-Based Oil Preparations" (2020) 25 Molecules 2986 at 2987

Rehm, Jürgen, Elton-Marshall, Tara, Sornpaisarn, Bundit & Manthey, Jakob, "Medical Marijuana. What Can We Learn from the Experiences in Canada, Germany and Thailand?" (2019) 74 International Journal of Drug Policy

Roberts, Chris, "'It's Gonna Be a Bloodbath': Epic Marijuana Over Supply Is Flooding California, Jeopardizing Legalization" (31 August 2021), online: <www.forbes.com/sites/chrisroberts/2021/08/31/its-gonna-be-a-bloodbath-epic-marijuana-oversupply-is-flooding-california-jeopardizing-legalization/?sh=621534147ddb>

Roberts, Chris, "New York Is Already Doing Marijuana Legalization Wrong" (30 December 2021), online: *Forbes* <www.forbes.com/sites/chrisroberts/2021/12/30/new-york-is-already-doing-marijuana-legalization-wrong/>

Rocafort, Fred, "Chile's New Constitution: An Opportunity for Cannabis" (16 June 2021), online: *Cannalaw Blog* <https://harrisbricken.com/cannalawblog/chiles-new-constitution-an-opportunity-for-cannabis/>

Rocha, Ricardo, "Three Years of the Portuguese Medical Cannabis Law" (10 November 2021), online: *Mondaq* <www.mondaq.com/cannabis-hemp/1129956/three-years-of-the-portuguese-medical-cannabis-law>

Rodriguez, Cecilia, "Germany Moves to Legalize Cannabis, Second Country After Malta in Europe" (28 December 2021), online: *Forbes* <www.forbes.com/sites/ceciliarodriguez/2021/12/27/germany-moves-to-legalize-cannabis-second-country-after-malta-in-europe/?sh=57261>

150   *Drug Legalization in Other Democracies*

Rodriguez, Cecilia, "No More Cannabis Tourism in Barcelona? Court Overturns Regulations on 'Clubes Cannábicos'" (21 July 2021), online: *Forbes* <www.forbes.com/sites/ceciliarodriguez/2021/07/27/the-end-of-barcelonas-cannabis-tourism-court-overturns-regulations-on-clubes-cannbicos/?sh=2156832a272d>

Rodriguez-Ferrand, Graciela, "Decriminalization of Narcotics" (2016), online (pdf): *Law Library of the United States Congress* <https://tile.loc.gov/storage-services/service/ll/llglrd/2016479004/2016479004.pdf>

Rutledge, Garrett, "Revisiting New Jersey's Cannabis Legalization a Year Later" (28 December 2021), online: *New Jersey Digest* <https://thedigestonline.com/nj/new-jersey-cannabis-legalization/>

Rychert, Marta & Wilkins, Chris "Why did New Zealand's Referendum to Legalise Recreational Cannabis Fail?" (2021) 40:6 Drug and Alcohol Review

Rychert, Marta, Emanuel, Machel A. & Wilkins, Chris, "Foreign Investment in Emerging Legal Medicinal Cannabis Markets: The Jamaica Case Study" (2021) 17:38 Globalization and Health

Rychert, Marta, Emanuel, Machel A. & Wilkins, Chris, "Issues in the Establishment of a Therapeutic Cannabis Market Under Jamaica's Dangerous Drugs Amendment Act 2015" (2020) 86 International Journal of Drug Policy

Sabaghi, Dario, "These European Countries Could Legalize Cannabis in 2022" (29 December 2021), online: *Forbes* <www.forbes.com/sites/dariosabaghi/2021/12/29/these-european-countries-could-legalize-cannabis-in-2022/?sh=69687afe2514>

Sabet, Kevin, "Lessons Learned in Several States Eight Years After States Legalized Marijuana" (2021) 38 Current Opinion in Psychology

Safronova, Valeriya, "How Arizona Won the Weed Legalization Race" (1 April 2021), online: *The New York Times* <www.nytimes.com/2021/03/29/style/arizona-marijuana-legalization.html>

Salazar, Nikolás & Salvador, Cindy, "Market Development of the Cannabis in Peru" (20 February 2020), online: *ECOVIS* <www.ecovis.com/global/market-development-of-the-cannabis-in-peru/>

Samon Ros, Carla, "Peru's Chronically Ill Seeking Right to Grow Cannabis for Medicinal Use" (19 January 2021), online: *La Prensa Latin Media* <www.laprensalatina.com/perus-chronically-ill-seeking-right-to-grow-cannabis-for-medicinal-use/>

Schauer, Gillian, Dilley, Julia, Roehler, Douglas, Sheehy, Thomas, Filley, Jessica, Broschat, Sara, Holland, Kristin, Baldwin, Grant, Holmes-Chavez, Amy & Hoots, Brooke, "Cannabis Sales Increases During COVID-19: Findings from Alaska, Colorado, Oregon and Washington" (2021) 98 International Journal of Drug Policy

Schlag, Katrin A., "An Evaluation of Regulatory Regimes of Medical Cannabis: What Lessons can be Learned for the UK?" (2020) 3:1 Medical Cannabis and Cannabinoids

Schlag, Katrin A., Baldwin, David S., Barnes, Michael, Bazire, Steve, Coathup, Rachel, Curran, Valerie H., McShane, Rupert, Phillips, Lawrence D., Singh, Ilina & Nutt, David J., "Medical cannabis in the UK: From principle to practice" (2020) 34:9 Journal of Psychopharmacology 931

Scilippa, Phil, "Schedule 1 and 2 drugs have officially been defelonized in Colorado" (5 March 2020), online: *edm.com* <https://edm.com/news/schedule-1-2-narcotics-defelonized-colorado>

Drug Legalization in Other Democracies 151

Scottish Drugs Forum, "Westminster committee believes UK should consider decriminalization" (23 October 2020), online: *SDF Scottish Drugs Forum* <www.sdf.org.uk/tag/decriminalisation/>

Sebele, Sipho, "South Africa's Cannabis Bill Is Widely Unpopular – Here's Why" (2 September 2021), online: *Mugglehead Magazine* <https://mugglehead.com/south-africas-cannabis-bill-is-widely-unpopular-heres-why/>

Selsky, Andrew, "Oregon First U.S. State to Decriminalize Possession of Hard Drugs" (1 February 2021), online: *CTV News* <www.ctvnews.ca/world/oregon-first-u-s-state-to-decriminalize-possession-of-hard-drugs-1.5291021>

Shiner, Michael, Carre, Zoe, Delsol, Rebekah & Eastwood, Niamh, "The Colour of Injustice: 'Race', Drugs and Law Enforcement in England and Wales" (31 January 2019), online (pdf): *Release* <www.release.org.uk/publications/ColourOfInjustice>

Small, Jim, "Arizona Adults Spent $58 Million on Recreational Marijuana in October" (9 December 2021), online: *AZMirror* <www.azmirror.com/blog/arizona-adults-spent-58-million-on-recreational-marijuana-in-october/>

Smart, Charlie, "Penalties for Drugs" (3 June 2015), online: *PBS* <www.ctpublic.org/politics/2015-06-03/connecticut-senate-backs-cutting-penalties-for-drugs>

Smith, Rachel, "Legal Weed Shops May Not Hit in 2022, New York. Here's What We Need to Know" (21 December 2021), online: *The City* <www.thecity.nyc/2021/12/21/22848537/waiting-to-inhale-legal-weed-shops-may-not-hit-nyc-in-2022>

South Africa, *Minister of Justice and Constitutional Development and Others v Prince* [2018] ZACC 30

South African Health Products Regulatory Authority, "Cultivation of Cannabis and Manufacture of Cannabis-Related Pharmaceutical Products for Medicinal and Research Purposes" (November 2019), online (pdf): <https://sahpra.org.za/wp-content/uploads/2020/01/93b0b4262.44_Cannabiscultivation_v2_Nov2019.pdf>

Stover, Heino, Michels, Ingo I., Werse, Bernd & Pfeiffer-Gerschel, Tim, "Cannabis Regulation in Europe: Country Report Germany" (February 2019), online (pdf): *Transnational Institute* <www.tni.org/files/publication-downloads/cr_german_10062019.pdf>

Subritzky, Todd, Pettigrew, Simone & Lenton, Simon, "Issues in the Implementation and Evolution of the Commercial Recreational Cannabis Market in Colorado" (2016) 27 International Journal of Drug Policy

Sutton, Matt, "Drug Decriminalization in Oregon, One Year Later: Thousands of Lives Not Ruined by Possession Arrests, $300 Million+ in Funding for Services" (3 November 2021), online: *DrugPolice.org*<https://drugpolicy.org/press-release/2021/11/drug-decriminalization-oregon-one-year-later-thousands-lives-not-ruined>

Teehan, Sean, "New York Cannabis in 2021 in Review: Marijuana Industry Finally Gets Rolling" (29 December 2021), online: *Syracuse* <www.syracuse.com/marijuana/2021/12/new-york-cannabis-in-2021-in-review-marijuana-industry-finally-gets-rolling.html>

Tierney, Allison, "The Costa Rica model: Why Decriminalization of Drug Use Sometimes Isn't Enough" (5 April 2017), online: *VICE* <www.vice.com/en/article/kbjvax/the-costa-rica-model-why-decriminalization-of-drug-use-sometimes-isnt-enough>

152 *Drug Legalization in Other Democracies*

Tindale, Kathryn, "Peru Allows Medical Cannabis Cultivation by Patient Associations" (6 August 2021), online: *Mugglehead* <https://mugglehead.com/peru-allows-medical-cannabis-cultivation-by-patient-associations/>

Toner, Casey, Rutecki, Jared & Main, Frank, "Oregon's the First State to Ticket Narcotics Users, but Reform Has Yet to Live Up to What Was Promised" (3 December 2021), online: *Chicago Sun Times* <https://chicago.suntimes.com/2021/11/30/22644894/oregon-drug-reform-decriminalization-addictions-help>

Tonry, Michael, "Race and the War on Drugs" (1994) 1 University of Chicago Legal Forum 25

Travis, Alan, "Cannabis Laws Eased in Drug Policy Shakeup" (24 October 2001), online: *The Guardian* <www.theguardian.com/society/2001/oct/24/drugsandalcohol>

Tsavkko Garcia, Raphael, "The Struggle for Medical Marijuana Access in Brazil" (14 December 2020), online: *Filter* <https://filtermag.org/struggle-medical-marijuana-brazil/>

Tsirtsakis, Anastasia, "Changes to Medicinal Cannabis Prescribing Pathways" (23 November 2021), online: *NewsGP* <https://www1.racgp.org.au/newsgp/clinical/changes-to-medicinal-cannabis-prescribing-pathways>

United Kingdom, *Misuse of Drugs Act* 1971, c 38

United Kingdom, *The Misuse of Drugs Regulations* 2001, No 3998

United Nations International Narcotics Control Board, "Report of the International Narcotics Control Board for 2020" (February 2020), online (pdf): <www.incb.org/documents/Narcotic-Drugs/Technical Publications/2020/Narcotic_Drugs_Technical_publication_2020.pdf>

Unlu, Ali, Tammi, Tuukka & Hakkarainen, Pekka, "Drug Decriminalization Policy" (September 2020), online (pdf): *Finnish Institute for Health and Welfare* <http://fileserver.idpc.net/library/drug_decriminalisation_policy_2020_report.pdf>

Van de Bunt, Henk & Muller, Thaddeus, "The Bankruptcy of the Dutch Cannbis Policy: Time for a Restart" in Hans Nelen & Dina Siegel, eds, *Contemporary Organized Crime: Developments Challenges and Responses*. 2nd ed. (Switzerland: Springer, 2021)

Vaughn, Carol, "Lawyer and Activist Grows Marijuana on Terrace Overlooking Costa Rica Court House" (3 February 2022), online: *The Costa Rica Star* <https://news.co.cr/lawyer-and-activist-grows-marijuana-on-terrace-overlooking-costa-rica-court-house/82523/>

Virani, Hakique & Haines-Saah, Rebecca, "Drug Decriminalization: A Matter of Justice and Equity, Not Just Health" (2020) 58:1 American Journal of Preventive Medicine

Vitiello, Michael, "Marijuana Legalization, Racial Disparity, and the Hope for Reform" (2019) 23:3 Lewis and Clark Law Review

Vivian, Jesse, "Dispensing Cannabis" 41:2 US Pharmacist

Wang, Frances Kai-Hwa, "Detroit Just Decriminalized Psychedelics and 'Magic Mushrooms.' Here's What That Means" (3 November 2021), online: *PBS* <www.pbs.org/newshour/politics/detroit-just-decriminalized-psychedelics-and-magic-mushrooms-heres-what-that-means>

Weatherburn, Don, Alexeev, Sergey & Livingston, Michael, "Changes in and Correlates of Australian Public Attitudes Toward Illicit Drug Use" (2021) Drug and Alcohol Review, DOI: <https://doi.org/10.1111/dar.13426>

Yates, Dave & Speer, Jessica, "Over and Under-Regulation in the Colorado Cannabis Industry – A Data-Analytic Perspective" (2018) 59 International Journal of Drug Policy

YouGov, "Daily Question: 06/04/2021" (6 April 2021), online: *YouGov* <https://yougov.co.uk/topics/politics/survey-results/daily/2021/04/06/fcf4a/3>

Zaami, S., Di Luca, A., Di Luca, N. M. & Montanari, G., "Medical Use of Cannabis: Italian and European Legislation" (2018) 22 European Review for Medical and Pharmacological 1161

Zhang, Mona, "Maine's Mom and Pop Weed Scene Sweats Corporate 'Gentrification'" (20 June 2021), online: *Politico* <www.politico.com/news/2021/06/20/maines-fight-over-big-marijuana-493472>

Zobel, Frank, "Cannabis Regulation in Europe: Country Report Switzerland" (17 March 2019), online: *Transnational Institute* <www.tni.org/en/publication/cannabis-regulation-in-europe-country-report-switzerland>

5 Lessons Learned and Future Challenges

Previous chapters of this book have extensively analyzed: 1) Canada's long racist and classist drug policy history;[1] 2) issues with provincial implementation of cannabis legalization, including those pertaining to federalism and Indigenous exclusion;[2] and 3) comparative approaches to cannabis (and wider drug) policy liberalization in jurisdictions around the world.[3] These analyses have shed light on lessons that should be learned as the Cannabis Act[4] goes through its period of statutory review. As per Section 151.1(1) of the Cannabis Act, a statutory review of the legislation is required within a three-year period of the legislation coming into force, requiring review findings to be laid before each House of Parliament within 18 months of the day on which the review begins.[5] The section of the Cannabis Act that stipulates review notes "the impact of cannabis on Indigenous persons and communities" as being of "particular" focus.[6] Similarly, this chapter begins its discussion of lessons to be learned by focusing on the issue of Indigenous exclusion in the development, passage, and implementation of Canada's cannabis legalization legislation.[7] It then moves on to address the inadequate attention paid to redress for communities historically most disproportionately affected by cannabis criminalization, with a specific focus on what is an ineffective system of pardons for past cannabis convictions.[8] It is subsequently argued that there are policy areas where Canada can and should learn from other jurisdictions, namely: 1) the development of social equity provisions to encourage participation of historically marginalized groups in the cannabis industry;

---

1 Chapter 2
2 Chapter 3
3 Chapter 4
4 *Cannabis Act*, SC 2018, c 16
5 *Ibid*, s 151.1 (2): There are already reports that the Cannabis Act's review is running late. See Israel, Solomon, "Canada's Cannabis Legalization Review Running Late, as Industry Hopes for Reforms" (25 February 2022), *MJBiz Daily* <https://mjbizdaily.com/canadas-cannabis-legalization-review-running-late-as-industry-hopes-for-reforms/>
6 *Ibid*, s. 151.1 (1)
7 Chapter 5.1
8 Chapter 5.2

DOI: 10.4324/9781003200741-5

Lessons Learned and Future Challenges 155

2) the further liberalization of drug policy extending *beyond* cannabis to other illicit substances; and 3) moving away from a criminal justice approach to a harm reduction approach to drug use and addiction.[9] Finally, the chapter concludes by identifying issues that, whilst not readily apparent at the time of the passage of the Cannabis Act, are nonetheless future challenges that have manifested during its implementation and must be addressed.[10]

5.1 Lessons Learned: Indigenous Exclusion Must Be Addressed

It is a welcome development that the Cannabis Act specifically mentions the impacts of cannabis on Indigenous communities as an area of "particular" focus for its statutory review. That said, there is ample evidence throughout this text to make one sceptical about whether Indigenous communities will be sufficiently considered, consulted, and included in any review of, or amendments to, the Cannabis Act. The legislative process behind, and eventual passage of, the Cannabis Act has been characterized as a missed opportunity because of its complete failure to sufficiently consult and consider Indigenous communities.[11] This exclusion began from the earliest stage of the process, when "The campaign promise to legalize cannabis was void of any mention of engagement with Indigenous peoples or addressing the disproportionate negative impacts of decades of prohibition and criminalization".[12] Moreover, the public consultation process provided further evidence of Indigenous exclusion, as both the consultation document[13] and the summary of comments received during the public consultation made little to no mention of Indigenous perspectives and opinions on the legislation.[14] This (rightly) prompted the Standing Senate Committee on Aboriginal Peoples to recommend delaying the legislation for a year, citing "an alarming lack of consultation, particularly given this Government's stated intentions of developing a new relationship with Indigenous people".[15] The decision of the federal government to deny this request, and to move forward with the negotiation and signing

---

9 Chapter 5.3
10 Chapter 5.4
11 Chapters 2.6–2.7
12 Andrew Crosby, "Contesting Cannabis: Indigenous Jurisdiction and Legalization" (2019) 62:4 Canadian Public Administration 634 at 635
13 Health Canada, *Proposed Approach to the Regulation of Cannabis* (Ottawa: Health Canada, 2017)
14 Health Canada, *Proposed Approach to the Regulation of Cannabis: Summary of Comments Received During the Public Consultation* (Ottawa: Health Canada, 2018): In the former, the word "Indigenous" is found a grand total of two times in 75 pages. In the latter, it is found 3 times in 40 pages
15 Canada, Parliament, Senate, Standing Senate Committee on Aboriginal Peoples, *The Subject Matter of Bill C-45: An Act Respecting Cannabis and to Amend the Controlled Drugs and Substances Act, the Criminal Code and Other Acts* (May 2018) (Chair: Lillian Eva Dyck) at 8

156   *Lessons Learned and Future Challenges*

of the Coordinated Cannabis Taxation Agreements (which Indigenous people were excluded from),[16] has certainly not aged well.

As noted in Chapter 3,[17] absent the proper consideration of these issues prior to passing the Cannabis Act, the subsequent implementation of this legislation at the provincial level has led to a myriad of issues in Indigenous communities. These issues were loudly and forcefully proclaimed by both academics and Indigenous community leaders. Provinces went about the business of implementation largely by mirroring their alcohol distribution systems, thus replicating an unfortunate historical process whereby "First Nations governments play a subordinate role in these systems. This approach serves to replicate and perpetuate settler colonial systems of authority, to the exclusion of Indigenous self-determination".[18] The federal and provincial governments are now once again faced with an entirely foreseeable jurisdictional issue, as "illegal" dispensaries continue to operate on Indigenous lands with communities having "no mechanism to collect revenues from cannabis sales".[19] As noted by the Indigenous community leaders who participated in the research for this book, the current situation is not only unsustainable in the long term but is also leading to very real concerns in the short term, including the prevalence of the black market in Indigenous communities[20] and serious amounts of money being lost to organized crime rather than flowing through the mainstream system.[21] For their part, despite decades of disappointment, Indigenous community leaders have continuously expressed a willingness to work within the confines of Canada's legal cannabis regime.[22] It is time for the federal government to meet them halfway. Fostering Indigenous participation in the cannabis economy is not only the "right" thing to do in the name of reconciliation, but it is also the logical thing to do in the furtherance of a key government legalization objective: eliminating the black market.

16 Andrew Crosby, "Contesting Cannabis: Indigenous Jurisdiction and Legalization" (2019) 62:4 Canadian Public Administration 634 at 636
17 Chapter 3.2
18 Jared Wesley, "Beyond Prohibition: The Legalization of Cannabis in Canada" (2019) 62:4 Canadian Public Administration 533 at 541
19 Stephanie Ben-Ishai, "Bankruptcy for Cannabis Companies: Canada's Newest Export?" (2020) 27:2 University of Miami International and Comparative Law Review 226 at 244
20 Participant F, 26 May 2021: "It's the layering effect I call it. It's one ill-conceived issue after another and complete denials by the government that they're going to allow us to participate in any part of this economy. And what happens at that point: the economy just goes underground"
21 Participant J, 3 June 2021: "How much dormant capital has Canada lost? How much dormant capital have First Nations lost because the government says you can't bring that monetary value into the mainstream system. . . . Somebody needs to ask some serious economic questions here because I think this issue is much bigger and the impact is much bigger than Canadians really think"
22 *Ibid*: "Our efforts need to be about widening the path and having Indigenous participation in Canada's cannabis industry in a way that is at least making an attempt to look and mutual benefit and consideration"

Often overshadowed in the historical accounts of Liberal leader Justin Trudeau's 2015 election campaign promise to legalize cannabis is the fact that he also postured himself as a leader who would promote reconciliation with Indigenous people.[23] At least on the issue of cannabis, the analyses above and throughout this book suggest that he has not lived up to expectations. As one Indigenous community leader put it:

> But the problem with that Daniel is everything's been passed already and we're now left with a bad situation where we can't even get legislative amendments in for the next four or five years to recognize First Nations supply chain models. So yeah I'm going to give the Liberals a failing grade on that.[24]

The statutory review of the Cannabis Act, with its supposed focus on Indigenous communities, has an opportunity to change this failing grade and address the currently untenable jurisdictional issue of cannabis on Indigenous lands. Wesley has argued that "It is difficult to see how governments can continue to exclude Indigenous communities and municipalities from these high-level discussions".[25] It is indeed difficult, especially given the fact that Indigenous exclusion from the cannabis industry is not only an unjust recreation of the historical settler colonial policies surrounding alcohol and tobacco, but also because said exclusion allowing the black market to continue to thrive, thus directly contradicting a primary government objective behind cannabis legalization. That said, until something happens to change the narrative, Indigenous community leaders will likely hold on to beliefs such as these: "Are they actually gonna go back, there's no politician that's going to walk back onto the playing field to correct the score after they've won the game, it's never happened, and it won't happen".[26] The federal government may have been able to cite "tight timelines" when it first entirely excluded Indigenous communities from consultation and participation in the cannabis industry. This time around, a similar justification will not be acceptable.

5.2 Lessons Learned: Time to Write a New Chapter in Canada's Racist Drug History

Aside from the Indigenous issues discussed above, there was no greater failing of the Cannabis Act than its complete lack of social justice provisions. This was the second way in which the legislative process behind, and eventual passage of, the Cannabis Act was characterized as a *missed opportunity*.[27] The federal government

---

23 Amy Smart, "Reconciliation, Indigenous Engagement in Question Ahead of Election" (13 October 2019), online: *CBC News* <www.cbc.ca/news/politics/reconciliation-indigenous-engagement-in-question-ahead-of-election-1.5319899>
24 Participant J, *supra* note 21
25 Wesley, *supra* note 18, at 545
26 Participant F, *supra* note 20
27 Chapters 2.6–2.7

158 *Lessons Learned and Future Challenges*

had a unique opportunity to address the country's long racist and classist drug policy history alongside cannabis legalization legislation. Doing so would have intuitively and logically fit with the message that was being sent by legalization: societal views towards the prohibition of cannabis have changed, and so too must the law. Instead, from an early stage in the legislative process, addressing the historically disproportionate impact of cannabis criminalization on minority and marginalized groups did not appear on the agenda. Any mention of redress in the name of social justice for past wrongs is conspicuously absent from *The Final Report* of the Task Force on Cannabis Legalization and Regulation.[28] While the members of the Task Force undoubtedly possess a wealth of expertise and institutional knowledge, not one of them is representative of a community that has historically been disproportionately affected by cannabis criminalization.[29] It is thus unsurprising that the Cannabis Act has been criticized for being "entirely void of any complementary social justice measures . . . leaving intact laws that have disproportionately and prejudicially impacted Indigenous people and people of colour".[30] While the Task Force explicitly mentioned its analyses of several jurisdictions[31] as part of its study, redress for racialized and marginalized communities was clearly not an area of focus. The comparative analyses in Chapter 4 of this book have indeed shown that there is much that should be learned from other jurisdictions in this area. Several jurisdictions have implemented automatic record expungements alongside their cannabis legalization legislation, including, but not limited to: 1) California, which went further than just expungements and adjusted the length of prior convictions;[32] 2) Illinois, which provided automatic expungements of convictions up to the same maximum possession amount as Canada (30 grams);[33] 3) New York, which added further social equity provisions to be discussed in the next section; and 4) Vermont, which allowed for automatic expungement for past cannabis convictions up to a maximum of two ounces.[34]

These jurisdictions (as well as several others discussed below) also enacted social equity provisions that go beyond the simple issue of record expungement. Before discussing these, it is important to highlight just how insufficient Canada's

---

28 Canada, Task Force on Cannabis Legalization and Regulation, *A Framework for the Legalization and Regulation of Cannabis in Canada: The Final Report of the Task Force on Cannabis Legalization and Regulation* (Ottawa: Health Canada, 2016)

29 "Annex 1: Biographies of Task Force on Cannabis Legalization and Regulation Members" (30 November 2016), online: *Health Canada* <www.canada.ca/en/health-canada/services/drugs-medication/cannabis/laws-regulations/task-force-cannabis-legalization-regulation/framework-legalization-regulation-cannabis-in-canada.html#ann1>

30 Jenna Valleriani et al, "A Missed Opportunity? Cannabis Legalization and Reparations in Canada" (2018) 109 Canadian Journal of Public Health 745 at 745

31 Task Force, *supra* note 39, at 2: "The Task Force looked internationally (e.g., Colorado, Washington State, Uruguay) to learn from jurisdictions that have legalized cannabis for non-medical purposes"

32 Chapter 4.4.3

33 Chapter 4.4.6

34 Chapter 4.4.16

social justice response in the area of past cannabis-related conviction pardons has been. The Cannabis Act was quickly criticized for not providing "redress to racialized communities disproportionately affected by drug prohibition in the same way that American legalization does".[35] While the government subsequently passed legislation in 2019 to deal with the issue of pardons for simple cannabis possession,[36] the system implemented has proven ineffective: as of October 2021, only 484 pardons had been issued.[37] This was despite the fact that the government's own initial estimates suggested that nearly 10,000 Canadians would be eligible for the pardons.[38] Drug policy expert Patricia Erickson has argued that the low number of pardons issued is due to a costly and cumbersome process that re-marginalizes the people who most need pardons and are also the least able to access the process, suggesting that "A blanket pardon is the only thing that would have any real impact".[39] The jurisdictions cited above show that there is indeed precedent for this social justice measure found in several comparable U.S. jurisdictions. Moreover, automatic record suspensions or expungements (a purely federal, criminal law issue) should be viewed as both practical and strategic for the federal government, insofar as: 1) they would likely be politically popular, as they are a progressive step forward and have no real impact on the wide majority of the Canadian public; 2) they presumably shouldn't be expensive or difficult to implement, as it is the government who already holds the conviction records of those affected; and 3) they would be in line with liberal, progressive values (generally speaking) and, more specifically, in line with the values of cannabis legalization as a whole (i.e. the changing societal and government views towards the substance).

Just like the Cannabis Task Force, the provisions for review of the Cannabis Act found in Section 151.1 make absolutely no mention of minority or marginalized communities. It can only be hoped that the government goes beyond the scope and purview of review dictated by the legislation and looks at the issue of reform from a wider, social justice viewpoint. Put more forcefully, at an **absolute minimum,** the government needs to institute a system of automatic record expungement for past cannabis-related possession offences that are no longer illegal. If it fails to do at least this, it will leave itself open to the continued criticism that cannabis legalization in this country represents a missed opportunity to

---

35 Akwasi Owusu-Bempah & Alex Luscombe, "Race, Cannabis and the Canadian War on Drugs: An Examination of Cannabis Arrest Data by Race in Five Cities" (2020) 91 International Journal of Drug Policy 1 at 1

36 Bill C-93, *An Act to Provide No-Cost, Expedited Record Suspensions for Simple Possession of Cannabis,* 1st Sess, 42nd Parl, 2015 (as passed by the House of Commons 21 June 2019)

37 Peter Zimonjic, "Only 484 Marijuana Pardons Have Been Granted Since Program Started in 2019" (31 October 2021), online: *CBC News* <www.cbc.ca/news/politics/pot-pardons-still-low-484-1.6230666>

38 *Ibid*

39 *Ibid*

160 *Lessons Learned and Future Challenges*

address a long-standing racist and classist drug policy history. Moreover, without automatic record expungement, the government will continue to preclude participation from minority and marginalized communities, including the "legacy market", all of whom could otherwise usefully contribute to the government's stated objective of eliminating the illicit market. As noted by De Koning & McArdle, "Those individuals seeking to transition from the illegal to the legal market, a stated goal of policy and regulatory reform, faced difficulty in doing so, as a conviction for a drug-related offence would bar them from eligibility for a licence".[40] This is not just an academic or philosophical concern, but rather it is practically manifesting itself in gross amounts of disparity within the current legal cannabis market. As noted by the Centre on Drug Policy Evaluation, Black (1%) and Indigenous (2%) people are severely underrepresented in leadership positions in the Canadian cannabis industry.[41] Similarly, the "legacy market", i.e. members of the public who have run therapeutic and compassionate cannabis dispensaries for decades,[42] would also greatly benefit from record expungements and would potentially bring years of acquired knowledge and expertise into the legal cannabis market (rather than being forced to operate outside of it). Providing redress for these historically marginalized and over-criminalized groups is the bare minimum that the government must do to provide some basic measure of social justice. As is discussed below, several jurisdictions have already gone much further.

5.3 Lessons Learned from Abroad: Other Jurisdictions Have Done More to Promote Social Equity, Broader Drug Policy Liberalization, and Harm Reduction Approaches

The basic mechanism of automatic record expungement discussed above was referred to as an issue of *social justice*, which speaks to the core, irreducible minimum of what is required for basic fairness. Measures discussed here are referred to as *social equity* in that they extend beyond a basic measure of minimum fairness and rather are oriented towards providing for a more equitable

---

40 Alice De Koning & John McArdle, "Implementing Regulation in an Emerging Industry: A Multiple-Province Perspective" (2021) 55:2 Journal of Canadian Studies 362 at 370

41 Nazlee Maghsoudi et al, "How Diverse is Canada's Legal Cannabis Industry? Examining Race and Gender of Its Executives and Directors" (October 2020), online: *Centre on Drug Policy Evaluation* <>https://cdpc.org/publication/how-diverse-is-canadas-legal-cannabis-industry-examining-race-and-gender-of-its-executives-and-directors/> at 1

42 See Phillippe Lucas, "Regulating Compassion: An Overview of Canada's Federal Medical Cannabis Policy and Practice" (2008) 5 Harm Reduction Journal 5: Lucas argues that "legacy market" compassionate dispensaries were crucial in providing cannabis as medicine while the legal medical framework struggled to provide access

Lessons Learned and Future Challenges 161

landscape in the cannabis industry. It has been argued that the current Canadian cannabis

> regulatory environment actively discourages participants in the black and grey market from applying to legally participate in the cannabis business. There are also questions about whether adequate access to capital, sufficient licensing opportunities, and opportunities to participate in the market are available to ethnic and racial minorities, or to Canada's Indigenous population.[43]

Several jurisdictions surveyed in Chapter 4 of this book have moved beyond basic social justice provisions and have additionally added provisions for social equity into their legal cannabis regulatory schemes. As such, there is again much comparative experience for Canada to learn from. For example, California has removed a prohibition that previously prevented someone with a cannabis conviction from securing a license and has further moved to give priority for licenses to applicants who were in the cannabis business prior to legalization (i.e. "the legacy market").[44] In Illinois, a social equity program that prioritizes equity applications for licenses and provides access to financial resources for start-up costs was put in place alongside its cannabis legalization.[45] Massachusetts has made social equity access to the cannabis industry, particularly through grants for applicants, a priority heading into 2022 and beyond.[46] New Jersey prioritizes applications from minority and veteran applicants, relaxes application requirements for microbusinesses, and features application fees as low as $100.[47] The State of New York set a minimum goal of 50% of its licenses to go to social equity applicants.[48] Vermont's Cannabis Control Board oversees a robust prioritization of social equity and small-scale cultivator applicants.[49] Even the traditionally conservative and punitive state of Virginia has stated that it will prioritize social equity applicants in the first year of license applications and waive a percentage of the application fees.[50] Far from only making sense on logically intuitive grounds, the implementation of similar social equity programs across Canada would address two very real practical problems: 1) the severe lack of minority and marginalized participation in the cannabis industry noted above; and 2) the very real future

43 De Koning & McArdle, *supra* note 40, at 390
44 Chapter 4.4.3
45 Chapter 4.4.6: The State's Cannabis Regulation and Tax Act also earmarks nearly 25% of every cannabis tax dollar collected to go to community groups that fund programs in communities most harmed by violence, excessive incarceration, and economic disinvestment
46 Chapter 4.4.8
47 Chapter 4.4.12
48 Chapter 4.4.14
49 Chapter 4.4.16
50 Chapter 4.4.17

162 *Lessons Learned and Future Challenges*

challenge of market concentration to be discussed further below.[51] Social equity programs resembling those implemented in various U.S. states would likely fall under provincial jurisdiction (retail), but, as was noted in Chapter 3's discussion of federalism,[52] the federal government carries coercive force and could again dictate policy in this area by implementing social equity provisions pertaining to federally licensed producers, thus sending a clear message to the provinces to follow suit.

Similarly, the Canadian federal government should take note of a global trend towards broader drug policy liberalization, as any future changes in this area would certainly fall under its federal jurisdiction over criminal law. Several of the jurisdictions surveyed in Chapter 4 have liberalized their drug policy *beyond* cannabis, extending reforms to personal possession of other illicit or "hard" drugs. For example, several states within Australia have long been focused on alternatives to arrest and diversionary measures that remove criminal penalties for the use and possession of all illicit drugs.[53] In the United Kingdom, the Scottish National Party and the country's Health and Social Care Committee have supported the decriminalization of drug possession for personal use, becoming a civil matter rather than a criminal offence.[54] Drug use is not a criminal offence in the Czech Republic, where possession of small quantities of heroin, cocaine, hash and ecstasy are subject only to a monetary fine.[55] In Germany, no differentiation of penalties is made between different types of drugs, with personal possession of minor amounts of all drugs open to the possibility of prosecution diversion.[56] In Italy, the current law decriminalizes possession for personal use of all drugs, with the availability of milder alternative sanctions.[57] Malta subjects possession of small amounts of drugs for personal use to a minimum fine of 75–125 euros.[58] Portugal famously decriminalized all drugs more than two decades ago, and its public health-oriented model has since become a globally-recognized success story.[59] Spain deals with consumption and minor possession of drugs in public places as a non-criminal offence, opting instead to impose fines.[60] A whole number of Latin American countries have either decriminalized

---

51 Chapter 5.4.4
52 Chapter 3.1
53 Chapter 4.1.1
54 Chapter 4.1.5
55 Chapter 4.2.1
56 Chapter 4.2.2: Moreover, a coordinated and voluntary drug support service aimed at preventing drug dependence has operated for more than 15 years in the country, with around 120 project locations currently located across the country. For more information, see: Heino Stover et al, "Cannabis Regulation in Europe: Country Report Germany" (February 2019), online (pdf): *Transnational Institute* <>www.tni.org/files/publication-downloads/cr_german_10062019.pdf> at 2
57 Chapter 4.2.3
58 Chapter 4.2.4
59 Chapter 4.2.6
60 Chapter 4.2.7

Lessons Learned and Future Challenges   163

personal drug possession or dealt with it through non-criminal sanctions, including Argentina,[61] Chile,[62] Columbia,[63] Costa Rica,[64] Paraguay[65] and Peru.[66] Uruguay never criminalized the possession of drugs for personal consumption and further formalized its policy of decriminalization through legislative changes in 1974 and 1998.[67]

Opponentsof this global trend towards broader drug policy liberalization may suggest that these countries are all too far removed (geographically, culturally, and politically) from Canada. Even if this (debatable) point was to be taken, the same opponents would have a hard time explaining the similar trend that has been sweeping its way through the United States. As was noted in Chapter 2,[68] Canadian drug policy history is rife with examples of how the United States' punitive drug policy has had an impact on Canada. It may soon be time for this script to be flipped, with Canada instead deciding to ride the sweeping wave of drug policy liberalization that has been making its way throughout the United States. In a truly historic moment in June 2021, decriminalization of possession of all illicit drugs made its way into a congressional bill at the _federal_ level in the United States.[69] Regardless of its success or failure, it is indicative of a broader wave of drug policy reform sweeping throughout several U.S. states, including: 1) California, where drug possession was defelonized in 2014 and 2022 legislation seeks to decriminalize possession of several psychedelic drugs;[70] 2) Colorado, where possession of heroin, cocaine, ecstasy and most other illicit drugs was defelonized in 2020, removing the possibility of imprisonment for amounts under four grams;[71] 3) Connecticut, where drug possession has been defelonized to a misdemeanor since 2015, allowing for the avoidance of imprisonment in certain circumstances; 4) Illinois, where similar defelonization efforts were proposed in 2021 and will likely be returned to in 2022;[72] 5) Maine, where 2021 legislation that would have decriminalized possession of all illicit drugs passed through the state House before falling to a very slim minority in the Senate;[73] 6) Massachusetts, where a proposed bill to replace criminal penalties for the possession of any controlled substance with a civil fine of $50 is currently under consideration in the State legislature;[74] 7) New Jersey, where a 2021 bill

61 Chapter 4.3.1
62 Chapter 4.3.3
63 Chapter 4.3.4
64 Chapter 4.3.5
65 Chapter 4.3.7
66 Chapter 4.3.8
67 Chapter 4.3.9
68 Chapter 2.3
69 Chapter 4.4
70 Chapter 4.4.3
71 Chapter 4.4.4
72 Chapter 4.4.6
73 Chapter 4.4.7
74 Chapter 4.4.8

164 *Lessons Learned and Future Challenges*

reclassified possession of up to an ounce of psilocybin mushrooms as a disorderly persons offence;[75] 8) New Mexico, where the state Senate is currently also considering defelonizing possession of more serious drugs;[76] 9) New York, where the state Senate is currently also considering decriminalization of possession of certain controlled substances;[77] 10) Oregon, where possession of small amounts of heroin, methamphetamine, LSD, and other hard drugs have been decriminalized since 2020;[78] 11) Vermont, where early 2022 legislation seeking to decriminalize possession and distribution of low levels of currently illicit drugs has quickly gained support in the state House;[79] 12) Virginia, where state lawmakers in 2022 introduced legislation that would decriminalize possession of small amounts of peyote, ibogaine, or psilocybin;[80] and, finally 13) Washington State, where 2021 defelonization legislation made all drug possession for personal use a misdemeanor, requiring police to divert the person's first two offences to treatment before the case can even be made to a prosecutor.[81]

Unlike automatic record expungements, decriminalization of illicit substances other than cannabis in Canada would likely create some controversy and carry political risks for any federal government, regardless of the presence of a global trend towards drug policy liberalization. That said, these political risks would likely be tempered if any (or some combination) of the following (entirely foreseeable) circumstances were present in the future: 1) if the United States, at the federal level, decriminalized possession of drugs other than cannabis; 2) if the opioid crisis in both Canada and the United States continued to rage on, further shedding light on the failure of treating drug addiction as a criminal justice rather than public health issue;[82] 3) if the review of the Cannabis Act finds that previously feared impacts of cannabis legalization (increased use in general, increased youth use specifically, increased use of other drugs, increased impaired driving, etc.) have not materialized; 4) if societal views in Canada towards the criminalization of other illicit substances change in the same way that popular opinion towards cannabis has changed; and 5) if other comparable jurisdictions, specifically federalist constitutional democracies within the G20 group of countries, also make moves towards further drug policy liberalization. Make no mistake, as was the case with cannabis legalization, a number of these circumstances (particularly favourable Canadian societal attitudes) would need to be present for further drug policy liberalization

---

75 Chapter 4.4.12
76 Chapter 4.4.13
77 Chapter 4.4.14
78 Chapter 4.4.15
79 Chapter 4.4.16
80 Chapter 4.4.17
81 Chapter 4.4.18: The legislation also gives further discretion to the prosecutor in deciding whether to divert subsequent cases away from the formal criminal justice system. Moreover, in 2022, a pair of state lawmakers introduced legislation that would establish a legal, regulated psilocybin industry available to all adults of a legal age
82 For more on the opioid crisis as a failure of the war on drugs and the broader issue of a criminal justice approach to drug addiction, see: Christine Minhee & Steve Calandrillo, "The Cure for America's Opioid Crisis? End the War on Drugs" (2019) 42:2 Harvard Journal of Law and Public Policy 547

Lessons Learned and Future Challenges   165

to occur. Governments in Canada (or elsewhere) historically do not choose to act when doing so is vastly unpopular with their electorate. That said, if (and hopefully when) circumstances allow for potential wider drug policy reform, Canada would do well to consider comparative experience (and its own history) in an area that would necessarily need to accompany any form of further drug decriminalization: a move towards harm reduction approaches, to which focus now turns.

Decriminalizing personal possession of "harder" illicit substances is an easy policy change to implement in comparison to the once in a century policy endeavour that was cannabis legalization in Canada. The substances don't become legal or regulated by the government, possession over certain amounts, trafficking, cultivation, and other related activities remain illegal, and the federalism issues that required so much policy effort for cannabis legalization (provincial jurisdiction over sales, agreements on tax collection, setting up licensed production, etc.) simply don't exist. Governments can (as several of the jurisdictions above have done) simply choose between any number (or a combination) of policy options, including: 1) impose fines rather than criminal sanctions; 2) divert prosecution where appropriate; or 3) mandate treatment where appropriate. Whatever the policy choice, there is an immediate positive impact for the addict (remove/minimize criminal justice system contact, be directed towards treatment) and for the state (re-orient police resources to focus on supply and organized crime, clear prosecutorial and court backlogs to focus on complex criminal cases, and reduce costs related to incarceration). What is more difficult is implementing some form of decriminalization alongside the necessary harm reduction measures needed to truly re-orient a country towards treating drug addiction as a public health issue rather than criminal justice issue. Several of the jurisdictions surveyed in Chapter 4 simply decriminalized/defelonized personal use possession without any additional harm reduction measures. That said, a number of jurisdictions instead chose to combine decriminalization with harm reduction measures as part of a wider project towards re-orienting their country's approach to drug addiction, thus providing useful comparative experience for Canada to consider. The Czech Republic is far more advanced than Canada in this regard, with nationwide needle and syringe programs operating in all regions of the country, funded through grant systems established at both national and regional levels.[83] The same is true of Portugal, arguably the world's most successful example of a complete shift from treating drug addiction as a criminal justice issue to a public health issue.[84] Needle exchanges, methadone substitution programs, and heroin prescription

---

83 Chapter 4.2.1

84 Chapter 4.2.6: As noted in this chapter, Portugal invested heavily in harm reduction, treatment, and prevention alongside its decriminalization policy change. Various metrics have been pointed to as evidence of the country's success, including: 1) The consumption of drugs has actually decreased since its implementation; 2) The number of HIV cases in drug users also decreased, and the number of deaths by drug overdose stabilized (currently one of the lowest in all of the EU); 3) Drug consumption by young adults is remarkably low; 4) Fears that Portugal would become a drug tourism destination never materialized; and 5) The number of drug users seeking medical treatment increased. See Chapter 4.2.6, *supra* notes 30 and 31 for further reading on the success of Portugal's system

166 *Lessons Learned and Future Challenges*

centres have existed across Switzerland since the 1980s, and the country's citizens have formally recognized harm reduction (through a 2008 referendum) as an institutional pillar of the country's drug policy.[85] In the United States, harm reduction measures have proliferated alongside cannabis legalization over the last few years, including in: 1) California, where state Senator Scott Wiener has put forward a 2022 proposal for state-sanctioned safe consumption sites;[86] 2) Maine, where 2022 will see a debate on legislation that proposes to protect people who report drug overdoses from a small set of criminal offences;[87] 3) Massachusetts, where decriminalization has been accompanied by a provision allowing an individual to forego fines if they enrol in "needs screening" to identify any potential treatment. A proposed bill that would establish a 10-year pilot program to study the feasibility and effectiveness of safe drug consumption sites has also been tabled;[88] 4) New Mexico, where safe injection and consumption sites are also under consideration;[89] 5) New York, where Bill S1284, if enacted, would establish a drug decriminalization task force aimed at developing recommendations to treat substance use disorder as a disease rather than a criminal behavior;[90] 6) Oregon, where the state allocates more than $100 million dollars per year towards substance abuse treatment centres, with an estimated 70 organizations in 26 of the state's 36 counties having already received funding as of 2021, and with an additional $302 million dollars in funding earmarked for further funding of harm reduction and recovery services in the next two years;[91] and 7) Washington State, where (in addition to the diversionary measures mentioned above) it is estimated that for every $1 billion dollars in revenue collected from legal cannabis sales tax, nearly $600 million dollars is funneled into public health initiatives.[92]

To be clear, there is also an abundance of Canadian domestic historical experience with harm reduction that could be usefully drawn upon if the country were to ever seriously consider institutionalizing a broader public-health oriented approach to drug addiction. As noted in Chapter 2,[93] the work of the LeDain Commission created a new dialogue around drug use in Canada and effectively began the conversation around harm reduction in the country. As a result of this dialogue, publicly funded treatment services grew following the recommendations of the Commission.[94] By the mid-1980s, there was a growing societal

---

85 Chapter 4.2.8
86 Chapter 4.4.3
87 Chapter 4.4.7
88 Chapter 4.4.8
89 Chapter 4.4.13
90 Chapter 4.4.14
91 Chapter 4.4.15
92 Chapter 4.4.18
93 Chapter 2.3
94 Susan Boyd & Donald MacPherson, "Community Engagement – The Harms of Drug Prohibition: Ongoing Resistance in Vancouver's Eastside" (2018) 200 BC Studies 87 at 90

Lessons Learned and Future Challenges 167

acknowledgement of "the serious limitations of law enforcement and education in reducing the demand for drugs".[95] Nixon's War on Drugs effectively put an end to any serious consideration of harm reduction at the federal level in Canada, resulting in the passage and implementation of the punitive *Controlled Drugs and Substances Act*[96] in 1996. The resurgence of harm reduction in the early 2000s was similarly stifled once again during Prime Minister Stephen Harper's years in office, during which time the dialogue around harm reduction in the country suffered a serious regression.[97] There has nonetheless been a consistent segment of civil society and academia that has continued to argue for the institutionalization of harm reduction in Canada's federal drug policy, and there is plenty of evidence of regional efforts throughout the country to treat drug addiction as a public health issue rather than a criminal justice issue. Syringe programmes operated in Toronto as early as 1988 and spread to Montreal and Vancouver (as well as other urban and rural communities across Canada) in the following years.[98] Methadone programmes have existed across the country in some form since the early 1990s.[99] It has been argued that

> Those who witnessed the 1990s never thought another crisis could happen. Yet, due to the fact that drug prohibition continues and harm reduction services – including flexible drug substitution programs and overdose prevention sites – were never fully set up, by 2010 illicit drug overdoses again began to increase.[100]

Drug overdose deaths continue to climb throughout Canada (and the U.S.) at present. The Canadian Centre on Substance Use and Addiction has declared that Canada is in the midst of an opioid crisis.[101] To its credit, in February 2017, the federal government announced $65 million dollars in federal funding to support

---

95 Walter Cavalieri & Diane Riley, "Harm Reduction in Canada: The Many Faces of Regression" in Richard Pates & Diane Riley, eds, *Harm Reduction in Substance Use and High-Risk Behaviour: International Policy and Practice* (London: Wiley-Blackwell, 2012) 382, at 383: This article gives a detailed history of the prevelance (and regression) of harm reduction initiative across Canada, including a comprehensive description of harm reduction measures implemented in various provinces and territories

96 SC 1996, c 19

97 Benedikt Fischer, Cayley Russell & Neil Boyd, "A Century of Cannabis Control in Canada" in Tom Decorte, Simon Lenton & Chris Wilkins, eds, *Legalizing Cannabis: Experiences, Lessons and Scenarios* (England: Routledge, 2020) 89, at 89 at 92

98 Cavalieri & Riley, *supra* note 95, at 384

99 *Ibid*

100 Boyd & MacPherson, *supra* note 94, at 94

101 For more information, see: "Prescription Opioids (Canadian Drug Summary)" (June 2020), online (pdf): <www.ccsa.ca/sites/default/files/2020-07/CCSA-Canadian-Drug-Summary-Prescription-Opioids-2020-en.pdf>

168 *Lessons Learned and Future Challenges*

a new Drugs and Substances Strategy.[102] It also passed Bill C-37,[103] which, among other things, streamlines the application process for communities that want and need supervised consumption sites. As argued above, the government could further bolster these harm reduction efforts through the decriminalization of personal possession of illicit substances beyond cannabis. This would be a relatively easy (if not politically risky) policy change that could open the door for a wider future re-orientation of this country's approach to drug addiction. If (and hopefully when) the government decides to take this next step, it will have a wealth of comparative and domestic experience to draw upon.

5.4 Future Challenges: The Government Should Listen to the "Voices" of its Industry

The "lessons learned" above no doubt pertain to issues that will continue to pose significant challenges to the future success of cannabis legalization (and wider drug policy reform) in this country. It is fair to argue that these issues should have been foreseen and dealt with during the legislative process that led to the eventual passage of the Cannabis Act. That said, the government also faces several future challenges that were perhaps less foreseeable but have nonetheless manifested themselves as real issues in the early years of legalization's implementation. This section discusses these future challenges in greater depth than space in previous chapters allowed. In doing so, it once again relies on both academic viewpoints and the crucial "voices" of Indigenous community and cannabis industry leaders who face these challenges on the front lines as part of their day-to-day work within the industry. The opinions of these cannabis industry leaders, and those of the wider cannabis industry (where publicly available or through consultation), should be extensively considered and listened to as the federal government goes through its Cannabis Act review process and (hopefully) considers consequential legislative and regulatory reform.

5.4.1 Future Challenges: Changes to the Excise Tax and Related Issues

The current excise tax structure for cannabis in Canada was a persistent concern amongst participants who contributed interviews for this book. Indigenous community leaders noted that the current excise tax arrangements are driving up overall costs of cannabis and, as such, are leading to the proliferation of the

---

102 Canada, Parliament, *Government Response to the Report of the Standing Committee on Health Entitled Report and Recommendations on the Opioid Crisis in Canada* (Ottawa: House of Commons, 2017)

103 Bill C-37, *An Act to amend the Controlled Drugs and Substances Act and to make related amendments to other Acts,* 1st Sess, 42nd Parl, 2015 (as passed by the House of Commons 18 May 2017)

black market in their communities.[104] Moreover, it has been argued that "Cannabis excise stamps signify that the applicable cannabis duty has been paid on the packaged cannabis products and ensure that the product is legal. However, since each province has a different stamp, there is an increased chance of mislabeling and other errors".[105] A cannabis industry leader confirmed that it would instead be preferable to make the excise stamp uniform across the country.[106] A group of legal experts has agreed, arguing, "The current excise stamp process is inefficient and creates both an administrative and economic burden to producers, especially for those companies that sell their products across Canada. A national excise stamp would meaningfully reduce this burden".[107] Moreover, a cannabis industry leader described a related practical issue that also stems from the non-uniformity of excise: "If I'm sending something to Ontario and Ontario doesn't want it after three months, it creates what we call a Return to Vendor. I can't take that product and repurpose it and send it to another province because of the way the excise structures have been created".[108] If the government is serious about its objective of combatting the illegal market, it may very well need to contemplate modifying the current levels of cannabis taxation. As one cannabis industry leader noted,

> The Government is taking their cut off it on their stamp. . . . I think that's kind of really hurt the objective of tackling the black market because the margin which we're charging, they've got to take their cut first and we kinda take our cut it makes it difficult for us companies to make money at this and it makes the black market better positioned in terms of how they're selling their product.[109]

104 Participant F, *supra* note 20: "When you look at cannabis, it can be produced for about two dollars a gram. The federal and provincial government takes out about seven dollars per gram. Well if you got a first nation that's twenty minutes away guess where you're gonna go. You're gonna go to where you're gonna get it for five dollars a gram". Another participant added: "The Excise Tax would become the first major blowout because that Excise Tax portion could have actually assisted with the black market issue"

105 P. Bowal et al, "Regulating Cannabis: A Comparative Exploration of Canadian Legalization" (2020) 57:4 American Business Law Journal 677, at 708

106 Participant K, 22 July 2021: "With excise, like you need a separate excise stamp if you wanna send product to Manitoba or Saskatchewan or Ontario. . . . From the start the government should have just made the stamp uniform across the whole country"

107 Eric Foster et al, "Legal Cannabis Under Review: How Canada Can Fix the Cannabis Act, Drive Growth, and Ease Regulations" (8 December 2021), online: *Lexpert* <www.lexpert. ca/legal-insights/legal-cannabis-under-review-how-canada-can-fix-the-cannabis-act-drive-growth-and-ease-regulations/362344>

108 Participant K, *supra* note 106

109 Participant S, 30 June 2021: Questions were also raised about whether tax proceeds were being effectively redirected to social initiatives and combatting of the black market: "You've got a Crown corporation taking a good chunk of margin before we can get to the product. . . . You would hope anyways then that the proceeds from that are going into or being redistributed through programs and initiatives that are in line with you know wider societal change and ideals towards the system. And obviously tackling the illicit market which is you know not paying tax and causing more harm than good"

170 *Lessons Learned and Future Challenges*

A similar sentiment was echoed by another cannabis industry leader:

> We as an industry have gone there. We've created convenience and accessibility. The quality is there now and some of the pricing is even better than the illicit market. The challenge is, the way you've structured taxation and the channels that we need to go through to get the product to market. Like the producers aren't making the money it's all the government.[110]

The wider cannabis industry has also become more vocal about this concern. The "Stand for Craft" campaign, a coalition of craft licensed producers, processors, and micro cultivators, is calling on the government to reform what it calls "systemic financial dysfunction in the current excise regime".[111] Karine Cousineau, the co-chair of the national cannabis working group at the Canadian Chamber of Commerce, has publicly stated that the cannabis industry's sustainability and long-term success are at risk if the government doesn't modify the excise tax to better reflect legalization's economic goals alongside its health goals.[112] Both the British Columbia and Ontario chambers of commerce have joined their national counterpart in calling for excise tax reform.[113]

5.4.2 *Future Challenges: The Inadequacy of Health Canada Must Be Addressed*

Members of the cannabis industry operate within their provincial regulatory frameworks and have faced issues with their provincial regulators. Chapter 2's analyses gave various examples of these issues, shedding light, most specifically, on some of the inefficiencies surrounding the Ontario Cannabis Store and the Alcohol and Gaming Commission of Ontario.[114] That said, regardless of which area within the cannabis industry they work, industry leaders have been consistent and comprehensive in their criticism of the inadequacy of Health Canada as a federal regulator. One cannabis industry leader argues

---

110 Participant K, *supra* note 106
111 Solomon Israel, "Canadian Campaign Seeks Reduced Cannabis Excise Taxes" (17 December 2021), online: *MJBiz Daily* <>https://mjbizdaily.com/new-canadian-campaign-seeks-reduced-cannabis-excise-taxes/> The campaign is backed by more than 50 cannabis cultivators
112 Patrick Brethour, "Three Years After Legalizing Cannabis, Ottawa's Tax Structure Is Killing the Buzz for Small Producers" (1 October 2021), online: *The Globe and Mail* <www.theglobeandmail.com/business/article-small-scale-cannabis-producers-face-squeeze-from-tax-rules-falling/>
113 Matt Lamers, "Plunging Cannabis Prices Add Fuel to Efforts to Lower Tax Rate for Canadian Producers" (16 February 2022), online: *MJBiz Daily* <https://mjbizdaily.com/plunging-cannabis-prices-fuel-efforts-to-lower-tax-rate-for-canadian-producers/>
114 Chapter 3.4

Lessons Learned and Future Challenges 171

that Health Canada hasn't been effective as a regulator by detailing their own personal experience:

> I received a letter from Health Canada with respect to some marketing issues . . . and what happens is you just never hear back and they don't give you a response. So you just continue on until you hear otherwise. So I find that the execution of the Cannabis Act and Health Canada's purview has been kind of weird. It hasn't been effective.[115]

Another cannabis industry leader suggested that Health Canada needs to be better resourced in order to do its job effectively: "It's hard on the government to monitor these things and regulate them and enforce them and inspect them. Clearly Health Canada's been so underwater just trying to deal with everything that easing the burden on them would also seem to be a logical place to go".[116] Another industry leader has reported Health Canada response times exceeding more than two months.[117] The participant has further argued that the inefficiency of Health Canada has become something of a running joke in the industry, with industry members currently interpreting a lack of correspondence from the regulator as an implicit nod to their compliance.[118] This is obviously not a desirable way for regulation to function for either the industry (which is financially dependent on consistency in regulation and transparency in expectations for compliance) or for the government (which requires stringent and effective regulation to meet its stated objectives and policy goals). A group of legal experts has further made this point, arguing that,

> The listing process has become inefficient and considerably expensive for producers while they must wait sixty days to often receive no formal reply. Reducing the listing process to thirty days and including a requirement that

---

115 Participant S, *supra* note 109
116 Participant R, 30 June 2021
117 Participant K, *supra* note 106: "It's a ton of red tape. It's very difficult to ever get in front of Health Canada. So bureaucratic, so understaffed and under-resourced. Like pathetic response time. There's only one way to essentially reach them there's a number you leave a message. For LPs specifically, if they have questions about a new product innovation, being able to double back and check if its 'kosher'. . . . One of our partners put out a call based on some stuff they were working on and they got a call back like two and a half months later. How can you operate like that?"
118 *Ibid*: "When we launch a new product, we have to submit NNCPs, which is basically like a new product notice to Health Canada that stipulates "here's what we're launching, here's what it's going to look like, here's the potency range" and then they need to review and approve or disapprove. . . . And it's this joke in the industry: you literally send an NNCP and you have to count down sixty days because after sixty days if there's no response it's essentially been granted approval . . . and they had to adjust the law and the timeline because Health Canada was so overwhelmed with the influx of new innovation. . . . I don't think I've ever heard of any one LP ever receiving any correspondence within sixty days, so if I may be blunt, what the fuck is the point of it"

172 *Lessons Learned and Future Challenges*

Health Canada must advise producers of any comments or issues within that timeframe would have a material beneficial impact on producers.[119]

In a truly ironic and disappointing development, it appears as though the inadequacy of Health Canada may also already be contributing to a delay in the statutory review of the Cannabis Act.[120] Health Canada spokesperson Tammy Jarbeau recently indicated that "preparations are underway for the launch of the legislative review"[121] that, based on the three-year timeline noted above, should have begun in October 2021. The recent history of cannabis in Canada has shown that "tight timelines" are generally to the detriment of a thorough, thoughtful, and comprehensive consultation. It is thus of the utmost importance that a review of the Cannabis Act be started immediately. The government should take note of this development and of the criticisms of Health Canada discussed above. If it is truly committed to its goal of eliminating the black market, it needs to invest heavily in appropriately resourcing Health Canada so that it can perform its regulatory functions efficiently and adequately.

5.4.3 *Future Challenges: Marketing and Advertising Restrictions Need to Be Relaxed*

As was noted in Chapter 3, restrictions on cannabis marketing represent an area of regulation where the federal government has heavily dictated policy implementation in the provinces.[122] As noted by Bowal et al,

> The remarkably high level of regulatory detail makes compliance virtually impossible without legal advice or the ability of a person to otherwise parse thousands of words of legalese. . . . An unregulated market is not the answer, but imposing microregulations results in higher costs and other consequences. Brands enjoy little opportunity to build trust with customers at points of sale. Craft producers struggle to inform prospective customers about their product specialties[123]

This academic proposition was widely supported by the cannabis industry leaders who shared their opinions. One participant suggested that the stringent marketing restrictions around cannabis may be the result of an over-correction related

---

119 Eric Foster et al, *supra* note 107

120 Solomon Israel, "Canada's Cannabis Legalization Review Running Late, as Industry Hopes for Reforms" (25 February 2022), online: *MJBiz Daily* <https://mjbizdaily.com/canadas-cannabis-legalization-review-running-late-as-industry-hopes-for-reforms/>

121 *Ibid*: Health Canada declined to provide a timeline for when the review might begin

122 Chapter 3.3

123 Bowal et al, *supra* note 105, at 720

Lessons Learned and Future Challenges 173

to the historically less stringent regulations in the sphere of alcohol.[124] Similar to the academic point made above, another cannabis industry leader also expressed frustration about a specific example of a "microregulation":

> There's so many things that don't make any practical sense. So for example they say you can only have a logo that's no more than 9 cm, like just really really silly prescriptive requirements. So that's been tricky to navigate through and it's left a lot of questions in industry to try and resolve.[125]

The participant went on to further note the contradiction between cannabis and alcohol regulations in this area, expressing a hope for relaxed marketing rules that could one day lead to a similar normalization or de-stigmatization that exists with regard to alcohol.[126] Yet another cannabis industry leader, whilst expressing an understanding of the government's goal of preventing increased youth use, nonetheless argued that the restrictions are making it incredibly difficult to compete in the cannabis market.[127] Legal experts agree that the marketing and promotional restrictions of the Cannabis Act are overly restrictive and are in need of reform.[128] It thus appears that this is another area of cannabis legalization where we see the twin objectives of the government at odds with one another. From a public health perspective, it is essential that youth are not targeted by marketing

---

124 Participant R, *supra* note 116: "Just because you can do it in alcohol doesn't mean the governments happy about it. It's almost like they can't reverse that anymore and they're stuck with it and they don't wanna get the same problem again with cannabis"

125 Participant S, *supra* note 109

126 *Ibid*: "The number one thing I'd like to see improved upon would be . . . marketing regulations and some of the rules around the prescriptive regulations with respect to people seeing it in the store or not having minors be able to come into the store if they're accompanied with a parent. You know, try to be more progressive, just like liquor has evolved over the days, try to make it more socially acceptable and stop making the barriers there so the stigma can start to go away"

127 Participant K, *supra* note 106: "One other thing that prevents us from being able to do our job properly and that's on both the marketing and sales limitations that we have as an industry. Also, the ability to sample and pull product off the lines and again this is a federal issue. . . . I understand the need to keep it out of the hands of kids . . . but in order to be successful in the recreational channel you need to be able to speak and educate the consumer on how you're different than the competition. Right now, the only way to compete is on price and potency"

128 Eric Foster et al, *supra* note 107: "The marketing and promotional restrictions of the Act and the regulations relating to packaging of cannabis products are overly restrictive and prevent cannabis companies from developing a distinct brand and engaging with their consumers and patients. As a result, most products appear bland, indistinctive, and unappealing to consumers who ultimately decide to not engage with those products and turn to the illicit market. Amending and relaxing certain marketing, promotional and packaging restrictions will allow the regulated market to better engage with their consumers and build a distinct brand. Industry stakeholders believe it is essential that cannabis companies have reasonable freedom of choice with respect to how they want to promote and design their products, as is the case in almost every other consumer packaged goods industry"

174   *Lessons Learned and Future Challenges*

that may encourage increased consumption, which would defeat the purpose of one of the government's stated policy objectives. That said, as has been argued above, overly restrictive marketing restrictions are having an undue impact on the ability of companies to effectively compete in the legal market space. Without such competition, there is a chance that the black market benefits, thus defeating the other crucial policy objective of legalization. Relatedly, without this ability to compete and differentiate, smaller market players may find themselves going out of business or selling to larger market players, contributing to the rapidly increasing issue of market concentration that deserves its own separate analysis.

5.4.4 Future Challenges: The Issue of Market Concentration

Chapter 3 of this book concluded by (briefly) addressing the issue of market concentration,[129] but the issue requires far more analysis. As noted by Levesque, three of the biggest cannabis industry stakeholders (Aphria, Canopy Growth, and Aurora) now account for more than 60% of the market and "an oligopoly for the selling of a product like this one is not good news for any stakeholder in legalization, whether it is the other companies, regulatory agencies, public health experts or users".[130] As one cannabis industry leader noted:

> Look at the stats. Look at the amount of cannabis consumers vs. what Canopy is growing. Like just one LP has more supply now for two years than all of the others combined that can service the cannabis market. It's absolutely ridiculous. . . . What's going to end up happening is one of two things: they're [smaller producers] all going to go bankrupt, or they're all going to sell to the big guys and it's going to be a market that's controlled by the big players like it is in alcohol, you know Labatt and Molson.[131]

In fact, market concentration in the international beer market actually pales in comparison to the current market concentration exhibited in Canada's cannabis industry. For example, the three largest companies in the international beer market (Inbev, SAB Miller and Anheuser-Busch) share around 37% of the market,[132] far below the 60% cited above shared by Aphria, Canopy Growth, and Aurora. It has been suggested that "One of the factors explaining the trend towards rapid concentration of industry is the set of regulatory and financial constraints imposed on private actors".[133] In other words, market concentration may be more usefully viewed as a symptom of several of the regulatory issues noted above and

---

129 Chapter 3.11
130 Gabriel Levesque, "Cannabis Legalization in Canada. Case Studies: British Columbia, Ontario and Quebec" (2020), online (pdf): *French Monitoring Centre for Drugs and Drug Addiction* <https://en.ofdt.fr/BDD/publications/docs/ASTRACAN_Levesque-EN.pdf> at 70
131 Participant K, *supra* note 106
132 Levesque, *supra* note 130, at 38
133 *Ibid* at 40

Lessons Learned and Future Challenges 175

throughout this book. Larger companies are better able to assume the costs of regulation, thus leading to their greater concentration in the market. It is thus reasonable to argue that if the federal government eased some of this regulatory burden (particularly in relation to smaller market players), some of this market concentration would be alleviated. Market concentration could also be addressed at both the federal and provincial levels by allowing for greater prioritization and support of social equity business applicants. As noted in Chapter 5.3 above, there is much comparative experience from other jurisdictions that suggests a way forward towards a market with more equitable participation and less concentration.

5.4.5 Future Challenges: The Regulation of Consumption Lounges

One cannabis industry leader had this to say about the issue of consumption lounges:

> Their inabilities to license and regulate lounges is also a problem right now. People are going to need a place to consume. . . . Not even just catering to your locals but then to the tourists. . . . The inability for us to be able to cater to that is an issue . . . Some condo boards, rental properties, hotels still do not make accommodations for individuals who are looking to consume cannabis. Like how can you make a substance legal but then not create the appropriate spaces for an individual to consume it legally? In essence, you're kind of pushing this person into situations where they're doing illegal activity indirectly.[134]

This was an issue that the state of Nevada also found difficult, leading to 2021 legislation that allowed for cannabis consumption lounges in order to address the issue of consumption being limited to private residences and thus limiting its market's ability to cater to its famous tourism industry.[135] Another cannabis industry leader agreed that consumption lounges in Canada could usefully help drive tourism and the cannabis market economy.[136] Clearly, the issue is also on the mind of various provincial governments. While Ontario launched a public consultation in February 2020 to look at the viability of consumption lounges in the province, it had not provided any further guidance on the issue as of September 2021, prompting some businesses to open consumption spaces in the absence of any regulatory guidance and potentially illegally.[137] British Columbia also held a consultation with its cannabis industry stakeholders on the issue of consumption

---

134 Participant A, 21 July 2021
135 Chapter 4.4.11
136 Participant S, *supra* note 109
137 David George-Cosh, "Shops Open Consumption Spaces" (3 September 2021), online: *BNN Bloomberg* <www.bnnbloomberg.ca/cannabis-canada-weekly-shops-open-consumption-spaces-household-spending-nears-2b-1.1647828>

176 *Lessons Learned and Future Challenges*

lounges in August 2021, but there has not yet been further progress.[138] The cannabis industry has been vocal in its requests for consumption lounges to be introduced and regulated, arguing that they would provide necessary spaces for consumption and help drive tourism desperately needed in a broader entertainment industry that has suffered heavily during the COVID-19 pandemic.[139] While consumption lounges would fall within the purview of provincial jurisdiction, the federal government might consider providing the provinces with further guidance on an issue that appears to be one of future concern.

5.4.6 Future Challenges: The Need for More Transparent Data

As was noted in Chapter 3, the availability of data pertaining to various aspects of cannabis implementation in provinces across the country is sparse.[140] To its credit, at the federal level, Health Canada developed the Canadian Cannabis Survey (CCS) in 2017 and has been conducting the survey annually with an eye towards examining patterns of use, including: 1) quantities of cannabis consumed; 2) the use of cannabis for medical purposes; 3) the sources of cannabis and pricing; and 4) issues of public safety, such as impaired driving.[141] Nonetheless, this is but one set of data that is largely focused on consumption and relies upon self-reporting of cannabis-related activities. Most provincial governments have been very secretive about their pricing policies, making it difficult to discern average retail prices or make effective comparisons to the illicit market.[142] Provinces are indeed collecting and sharing this information with Health Canada, but researchers, industry stakeholders and other decision-makers are largely closed off from these crucial sources of data that could otherwise inform their analyses. It is worth noting that similar data is extensively collected and shared in U.S. states (particularly those that were first movers/leaders in the legalization movement sweeping across the country), allowing for sales to be broken down all the way to store level (Washington) or by county (Colorado).[143] As such, the literature pertaining to these U.S. states is far more robust, allowing for conclusions to be drawn about various cannabis-related

---

138 Kathryn Tindale, "BC Considering Cannabis Consumption Lounges" (26 August 2021), online: *Mugglehead* <https://mugglehead.com/bc-considering-cannabis-consumption-lounges/>

139 Tara Deschamps, "Canadian Cannabis Industry Laments Lack of Progress Toward Allowing Consumption Spaces" (27 September 2021), online: *The Globe and Mail* <www.theglobeandmail.com/business/article-canadian-cannabis-industry-laments-lack-of-progress-toward-allowing/>

140 Chapter 3.3

141 "Canadian Cannabis Survey 2020: Summary" (12 August 2021), online: *Health Canada* <www.canada.ca/en/health-canada/services/drugs-medication/cannabis/research-data/canadian-cannabis-survey-2020-summary.html>

142 Michael Armstrong, "Legal Cannabis Market Shares During Canada's First Year of Recreational Legalization" (2021) 88 International Journal of Drug Policy, DOI: <https://doi.org/10.1016/j.drugpo.2020.103028> at 8

143 *Ibid*

Lessons Learned and Future Challenges 177

health impacts. More available and transparent data also allows answers to be provided to broader questions about whether legalization is accomplishing its stated goals and objectives. Instead, "an almost generalized absence of provincial will to assess their cannabis legalization policies"[144] exists, leaving many of these questions largely unanswered. This is not a long-term sustainable approach to data collection and policy evaluation, especially in a remarkably complex, young, and constantly evolving regulatory sphere.

5.5 Conclusion: Where to Begin?

Several lessons learned and future challenges stemming from the early years of cannabis legalization have been discussed in this chapter and identified throughout this book. These include: 1) addressing the exclusion of Indigenous participation in the cannabis industry, which began at an early stage in the legislative process and continues today; 2) addressing the long racist and classist history of drug policy in this country, namely by providing for appropriate social justice mechanisms (automatic record expungement, in particular) that can afford redress to the communities historically most disproportionately affected by cannabis criminalization; 3) drawing from the experience of comparative jurisdictions to "catch up" in areas of social equity, broader drug policy liberalization and a movement towards a future re-orientation of drug policy that prioritizes harm reduction; 4) addressing the numerous concerns that Inidigenous community and cannabis industry stakeholders have identified, including problems with the excise tax, overly restrictive marketing regulations, market concentration, the ineffectiveness of Health Canada and the issue of consumption lounge regulation; and 5) addressing a very real data deficit that makes it incredibly difficult for academics, civil society members and private organizations to gauge the relative successes or failures of the first few years of cannabis legalization. This is a pretty long wish list of reforms for a government that is late to begin its statutory review of the Cannabis Act. Ultimately, many of these concerns may even fall outside of the relatively limited scope of focus that is within the legislative purview of said review. Regardless of what recommendations may be put forward by the statutory review, it is essential that the federal government adopt a much broader focus when it comes to cannabis (and wider drug) policy reform in the years to come. There is a wealth of domestic and comparative experience to draw upon, and Indigenous and cannabis industry leaders have clearly identified what they believe is needed for Canada's cannabis industry to move past its initial growing pains. If the government is truly committed to reconciliation, social justice, social equity, and the policy goal of eliminating the black market, it would do well to draw upon this experience, listen to the voices of those who have been most affected by cannabis (and wider drug) policy, and act fairly and comprehensively.

144 Gabriel Levesque, *supra* note 130, at 70

178 *Lessons Learned and Future Challenges*

Annexe 1: "Biographies of Task Force on Cannabis Legalization and Regulation Members" (30 November 2016), online: *Health Canada* <www.canada.ca/en/health-canada/services/drugs-medication/cannabis/laws-regulations/task-force-cannabis-legalization-regulation/framework-legalization-regulation-cannabis-in-canada.html#ann1>

Armstrong, Michael, "Legal Cannabis Market Shares During Canada's First Year of Recreational Legalization" (2021) 88 International Journal of Drug Policy, DOI: <https://doi.org/10.1016/j.drugpo.2020.103028> at 8

Ben-Ishai, Stephanie, "Bankruptcy for Cannabis Companies: Canada's Newest Export?" (2020) 27:2 University of Miami International and Comparative Law Review 226

Bill C-37, *An Act to Amend the Controlled Drugs and Substances Act and to Make Related Amendments to Other Acts*, 1st Sess, 42nd Parl, 2015 (as passed by the House of Commons 18 May 2017)

Bill C-93, *An Act to Provide No-Cost, Expedited Record Suspensions for Simple Possession of Cannabis*, 1st Sess, 42nd Parl, 2015 (as passed by the House of Commons 21 June 2019)

Bowal, Peter, Kisska-Schulze, Kathryn, Haigh, Richard & Ng, Adrienne, "Regulating Cannabis: A Comparative Exploration of Canadian Legalization" (2020) 57:4 American Business Law Journal 677

Boyd, Susan & MacPherson, Donald, "Community Engagement – The Harms of Drug Prohibition: Ongoing Resistance in Vancouver's Eastside" (2018) 200 BC Studies 87

Brethour, Patrick, "Three Years After Legalizing Cannabis, Ottawa's Tax Structure Is Killing the Buzz for Small Producers" (1 October 2021), online: *The Globe and Mail* <www.theglobeandmail.com/business/article-small-scale-cannabis-producers-face-squeeze-from-tax-rules-falling/>

Canada, Parliament, *Government Response to the Report of the Standing Committee on Health Entitled Report and Recommendations on the Opioid Crisis in Canada* (Ottawa: House of Commons, 2017)

Canada, Parliament, Senate, Standing Senate Committee on Aboriginal Peoples, *The Subject Matter of Bill C-45: An Act Respecting Cannabis and to Amend the Controlled Drugs and Substances Act, the Criminal Code and Other Acts* (Chair: Lillian Eva Dyck, May 2018)

Canada, Task Force on Cannabis Legalization and Regulation, *A Framework for the Legalization and Regulation of Cannabis in Canada: The Final Report of the Task Force on Cannabis Legalization and Regulation* (Ottawa: Health Canada, 2016)

"Canadian Cannabis Survey 2020: Summary" (12 August 2021), online: *Health Canada* <www.canada.ca/en/health-canada/services/drugs-medication/cannabis/research-data/canadian-cannabis-survey-2020-summary.html>

Cannabis Act, SC 2018, c 16

Cavalieri, Walter & Riley, Diane, "Harm Reduction in Canada: The Many Faces of Regression" in *Harm Reduction in Substance Use and High-Risk Behaviour: International Policy and Practice* (London: Wiley-Blackwell, 2012) 382

Controlled Drugs and Substances Act, SC 1996, c 19

Crosby, Andrew, "Contesting Cannabis: Indigenous Jurisdiction and Legalization" (2019) 62:4 Canadian Public Administration 634

De Koning, Alice & McArdle, John, "Implementing Regulation in an Emerging Industry: A Multiple-Province Perspective" (2021) 55:2 Journal of Canadian Studies 362

Deschamps, Tara, "Canadian Cannabis Industry Laments Lack of Progress Toward Allowing Consumption Spaces" (27 September 2021), online: *The Globe and Mail* <www.theglobeandmail.com/business/article-canadian-cannabis-industry-laments-lack-of-progress-toward-allowing/>

Fischer, Benedikt, Russell, Cayley & Boyd, Neil, "A Century of Cannabis Control in Canada" in Decorte, Tom, Lenton, Simon & Wilkins, Chris, eds, *Legalizing Cannabis: Experiences, Lessons and Scenarios* (England: Routledge, 2020) 89

Foster, Eric, Ruggolo, Stuart, Moulton, Emeleigh & Burns, Kimberley, "Legal Cannabis Under Review: How Canada Can Fix the Cannabis Act, Drive Growth, and Ease Regulations" (8 December 2021), online: *Lexpert* <www.lexpert.ca/legal-insights/legal-cannabis-under-review-how-canada-can-fix-the-cannabis-act-drive-growth-and-ease-regulations/362344>

George-Cosh, David, "Shops Open Consumption Spaces" (3 September 2021), online: *BNN Bloomberg* <www.bnnbloomberg.ca/cannabis-canada-weekly-shops-open-consumption-spaces-household-spending-nears-2b-1.1647828>

Health Canada, *Proposed Approach to the Regulation of Cannabis* (Ottawa: Health Canada, 2017)

Health Canada, *Proposed Approach to the Regulation of Cannabis: Summary of Comments Received During the Public Consultation* (Ottawa: Health Canada, 2018)

Israel, Solomon, "Canada's Cannabis Legalization Review Running Late, as Industry Hopes for Reforms" (25 February 2022), online: *MJBiz Daily* <https://mjbizdaily.com/canadas-cannabis-legalization-review-running-late-as-industry-hopes-for-reforms/>

Israel, Solomon, "Canadian Campaign Seeks Reduced Cannabis Excise Taxes" (17 December 2021), online: *MJBiz Daily* <https://mjbizdaily.com/new-canadian-campaign-seeks-reduced-cannabis-excise-taxes/>

Lamers, Matt, "Plunging Cannabis Prices Add Fuel to Efforts to Lower Tax Rate for Canadian Producers" (16 February 2022), online: *MJBiz Daily* <https://mjbizdaily.com/plunging-cannabis-prices-fuel-efforts-to-lower-tax-rate-for-canadian-producers/>

Levesque, Gabriel, "Cannabis Legalization in Canada. Case Studies: British Columbia, Ontario and Quebec" (2020), online (pdf): *French Monitoring Centre for Drugs and Drug Addiction* <https://en.ofdt.fr/BDD/publications/docs/ASTRACAN_Levesque-EN.pdf> at 70

Lucas, Phillippe, "Regulating Compassion: An Overview of Canada's Federal Medical Cannabis Policy and Practice" (2008) 5 Harm Reduction Journal 5

Maghsoudi, Nazlee, Rammohan, Indhu, Bowra, Andrea, Sniderman, Ruby, Tanguay, Justine, Bouck, Zachary, Scheim, Ayden, Werb, Dan & Owusu-Bempah, Akwasi, "How Diverse Is Canada's Legal Cannabis Industry? Examining Race and Gender of its Executives and Directors" (October 2020), online: *Centre on Drug Policy Evaluation* <https://cdpe.org/publication/how-diverse-is-canadas-legal-cannabis-industry-examining-race-and-gender-of-its-executives-and-directors/>

Minhee, Christine & Calandrillo, Steve, "The Cure for America's Opioid Crisis? End the War on Drugs" (2019) 42:2 Harvard Journal of Law and Public Policy 547

Owusu-Bempah, Akwasi & Luscombe, Alex, "Race, Cannabis and the Canadian War on Drugs: An Examination of Cannabis Arrest Data by Race in Five Cities" (2020) 91 International Journal of Drug Policy 1

180   *Lessons Learned and Future Challenges*

"Prescription Opioids (Canadian Drug Summary)" (June 2020), online (pdf): <www.ccsa.ca/sites/default/files/2020-07/CCSA-Canadian-Drug-Summary-Prescription-Opioids-2020-en.pdf>

Stover, Heino, Michels, Ingo I., Werse, Bernd & Pfeiffer-Gerschel, Tim, "Cannabis Regulation in Europe: Country Report Germany" (February 2019), online (pdf): *Transnational Institute* <www.tni.org/files/publication-downloads/cr_german_10062019.pdf>

Tindale, Kathryn, "BC Considering Cannabis Consumption Lounges" (26 August 2021), online: *Mugglehead* <https://mugglehead.com/bc-considering-cannabis-consumption-lounges/>

Valleriani, Jenna, Lavalley, Jennifer & McNeil, Ryan, "A Missed Opportunity? Cannabis Legalization and Reparations in Canada" (2018) 109 Canadian Journal of Public Health 745

Wesley, Jared, "Beyond Prohibition: The Legalization of Cannabis in Canada" (2019) 62:4 Canadian Public Administration 533

Zimonjic, Peter, "Only 484 Marijuana Pardons Have Been Granted Since Program Started in 2019" (31 October 2021), online: *CBC News* <www.cbc.ca/news/politics/pot-pardons-still-low-484-1.6230666>

6 Conclusion

Before reiterating recommendations for future change based on the analyses throughout this book, it is worth revisiting the objectives laid out in Chapter 1.[1] The first objective of this book was to provide a comprehensive analysis of the historical evolution of Canada's federal drug policy in order to better understand more recent developments, including the legalization of cannabis. The analyses in Chapter 2[2] made it abundantly clear that the historical evolution of Canada's federal drug policy has been largely driven by racist, classist, and colonial motivations. Understanding this aspect of Canada's drug policy history has usefully allowed the Cannabis Act[3] to be placed in historical context. This was particularly important for the purposes of the book's second objective. Analyses of the legislative process behind, and eventual passage of, the federal Cannabis Act, illustrated significant exclusion and lack of consideration of the communities historically most affected by drug prohibition, namely Canada's Indigenous, minority, and marginalized populations. It was thus possible to conclude that Canada's long racist and classist drug policy history was not sufficiently addressed by the Cannabis Act, leading it to be characterized as a missed opportunity.[4] The third objective of this book was to comprehensively survey provincial implementation of the federal legislation, with an eye towards identifying any notable similarities and differences amongst provinces and analyzing the complex interplay of jurisdictional issues that existed during this implementation. Chapter 3 detailed several ways in which provincial implementation of legal cannabis was similar across the country[5] whilst also noting distinct differences in the approaches of specific provinces (for example, the completely different policy choices made by Quebec and Alberta, which were representative of two very opposite policy implementation objectives).[6] The complex interplay of jurisdictional issues that existed during implementation was analyzed both in relation to further exclusion

---

1 Chapter 1.1
2 Chapter 2.1–2.6
3 *Cannabis Act*, SC 2018, c 16
4 Chapter 2.6
5 Chapter 3.3
6 Chapter 3.4–3.10

DOI: 10.4324/9781003200741-6

182 *Conclusion*

of Indigenous participation[7] as well as part of analyses of cooperation versus unilateralism when policy is implemented in federalist constitutional democracies.[8] The latter analyses helped to accomplish objective four, providing for an argument to be made that cooperative federalism was not a driving factor in the provincial implementation of legal cannabis. Instead, it was argued that the federal government largely acted unilaterally and coercively, greatly limiting the policy choices of the provinces.

The fifth and sixth objectives of this book were accomplished during a comprehensive survey of drug policy liberalization in jurisdictions around the world, with an eye towards placing Canada's past, present, and future wider drug policy in comparative context. In doing so, it was argued that lessons could be learned when the early years of Canada's cannabis legalization were placed alongside efforts to liberalize cannabis (and wider drug) policy in other federalist constitutional democracies. The comparative analyses in Chapter 4 were indeed a useful exercise. They helped to place Canada's cannabis legalization within a broader, sweeping movement towards cannabis legalization that is currently making its way through jurisdictions all around the world. Crucially, the comparative analyses also helped to highlight several ways in which other jurisdictions have done more than Canada to promote social justice and social equity in legal cannabis regimes, engaging in broader drug policy liberalization and implementing harm reduction approaches with an eye towards re-orienting their broader drug policy from a criminal justice issue to a public health issue. These "lessons learned" from abroad were highlighted as useful comparative experiences from which Canada can draw inspiration if (and hopefully when) it decides to engage in further drug policy reform in the future.[9] Lastly, this book had a stated aim of making a crucial contribution to a field of literature that is topical, ever-growing, and focused on a policy environment that is fast-moving. In order to accomplish this, it has argued that there are several lessons learned[10] and future challenges[11] that must be addressed as Canada moves into its next phase of cannabis (and wider drug) policy reform. Cannabis legalization is in its infancy and will soon be subjected to a (hopefully substantive) statutory review. As such, it is worth reiterating recommendations for future change that should be considered in the years to come.

6.1 Recommendations for Future Change to Cannabis (and Wider Drug) Policy in Canada

This section succinctly and concisely reiterates recommendations for future change to cannabis (and wider drug) policy in Canada. In doing so, it formats

7 Chapter 3.2
8 Chapter 3.1
9 Chapter 5.3
10 Chapters 5.1–5.2
11 Chapter 5.4

Conclusion 183

these recommendations in a manner similar to the commission of inquiry and parliamentary committee reports, with an eye towards appealing to a policy-focused audience. In some cases, these recommendations will be placed alongside select qualitative material from the Indigenous community and cannabis industry leaders who participated in the research for this book. In others, they are placed alongside select documentary material. In either case, the material is selected because it is illustrative of the larger, overall issue that is being targeted by the recommendation. In this sense, it provides a succinct and powerful snapshot of the broader arguments that were made throughout the book to support the recommendation. The recommendations are placed below, largely in the order of their consideration throughout the book.

Recommendation One: The federal government should immediately prioritize consultation and cooperation with Indigenous communities in order to address the significant exclusion of these communities in the development, passage, and implementation of the Cannabis Act. Importantly, this consultation and cooperation should be specifically focused on developing harmonization measures, through which Indigenous communities can benefit from the excise tax and begin to participate in the legal cannabis market across Canada.

As was argued by one Indigenous community leader: "Let's harmonize with the existing laws and let's create interface and let's work with leveling out the playing field on an economic level to address this".[12] This point was more forcefully and succinctly reinforced by another Indigenous community leader: "The Federal government needs to amend their legislation at a minimum to say they can enter into agreements with the First Nations governments to recognize our jurisdiction".[13] The statements of Indigenous community leaders throughout the book have consistently illustrated that they are open to conversations with the federal government about how they can participate in the mainstream framework of legal cannabis in Canada. To date, not only has the federal government failed to meet them halfway, but they have also consistently and consciously excluded Indigenous communities from consultation, participation and the benefits of tax sharing agreements. As a result, there is understandable scepticism of any future consultation or reform:

> Well isn't it a little bit damned late to do that after you've already amended all of that legislation, are they actually gonna go back, there's no politician that's going to walk back onto the playing field to correct the score after they've won the game, it's never happened, and it won't happen.[14]

12 Participant J, 3 June 2021
13 Participant T, 26 May 2021
14 Participant F, 26 May 2021

184   *Conclusion*

Until the federal government acts on the recommendation stated above, such scepticism will continue to be warranted.

Recommendation Two: The federal government should immediately develop and implement a fair, accessible, and effective system of automatic record expungement to provide redress to the minority and marginalized communities historically most disproportionately affected by cannabis criminalization. The Cannabis Act's glaring lack of social justice and social equity mechanisms needs to be addressed as a matter of urgent priority. The current system for pardons is ineffective and inaccessible and needs to be repealed and replaced. Furthermore, the federal government should implement social equity provisions (including prioritization of social equity license applicants, provision of financial assistance and grants to social equity applicants, and dedicated reinvestment of cannabis tax revenues to communities historically most affected by cannabis criminalization) similar to those that have been enacted alongside legalization in several U.S. states.

As noted by one cannabis industry leader, the federal government

> made it seem as though supporting individuals who have been wrongly affected by this, and those within marginalized communities, would have definitely been front and centre, but it was quickly pushed to the wayside ... The legislation could have been tweaked to allow for a more equitable landscape for people to participate.[15]

In order for legal cannabis in this country to be viewed as anything but a missed opportunity, the federal government needs to act to address the systemic reasons why a very real and severe lack of diversity exists in the cannabis industry.[16] Several comparative analyses throughout this book have provided examples of jurisdictions that have better provided for social justice and social equity alongside cannabis legalization.[17] The federal government should take the lead in implementing these provisions for its federally licensed producer applications, sending a strong message to the provinces to also implement similar provisions in their retail license applications. Following the lead of Saskatchewan and British Columbia, other provinces should take note of successful attempts to encourage cannabis industry participation amongst Indigenous (and other marginalized) communities.

Recommendation Three: The federal government should establish a Commission of Inquiry to thoroughly study the potential for broader drug policy reform in Canada. More specifically, the possibility of decriminalizing

---

15 Participant A, 21 July 2021

16 Nazlee Maghsoudi et al, "How Diverse Is Canada's Legal Cannabis Industry? Examining Race and Gender of Its Executives and Directors" (October 2020), online: *Centre on Drug Policy Evaluation* <https://cdpe.org/publication/how-diverse-is-canadas-legal-cannabis-industry-examining-race-and-gender-of-its-executives-and-directors/>

17 Chapter 5.3

personal possession of substances beyond cannabis should be considered alongside a broader analysis of the country's federal drug strategy. The further institutionalization of harm reduction measures, with an eye towards fundamentally re-orienting Canada's approach to drug addiction from a criminal justice issue to a public health issue, should be considered in great depth, in line with the broader global trend towards wider drug policy liberalization.

As noted extensively in the comparative analyses of this book, wider drug policy liberalization is sweeping through jurisdictions around the world, including in the historically punitive United States. If various states within that country can re-write their drug policy history, Canada can at least give it serious consideration. It has been more than 50 years since the LeDain Commission created a new dialogue around drug use in Canada and effectively began the conversation around harm reduction in this country. The various periods of regression of harm reduction as a viable alternative to dealing with drug addiction in this country are unfortunately manifesting themselves in a new and dangerous drug crisis. As has been previously noted,

> Those who witnessed the 1990s never thought another crisis could happen. Yet, due to the fact that drug prohibition continues and harm reduction services – including flexible drug substitution programs and overdose prevention sites – were never fully set up, by 2010 illicit drug overdoses again began to increase.[18]

This disturbing increase is continuing, despite commendable attempts from the federal government to support a new Drugs and Substances Strategy. Canada finds itself in the middle of an opioid crisis. The time to consider a fully institutionalized alternative approach to drug addiction, based on decriminalization and harm reduction, is now.

Recommendation Four: The federal government should immediately amend its cannabis excise tax formula to address industry concerns that the current excise tax is making it virtually impossible for smaller market players to succeed. Relatedly, following common practice in several comparable jurisdictions, the government should be transparent about how the taxes collected from cannabis sales are being used.

As one cannabis industry leader noted,

> The Government is taking their cut off it on their stamp. . . . I think that's kind of really hurt the objective of tackling the black market because the margin which we're charging, they've got to take their cut first and we kinda take our cut it makes it difficult for us companies to make money at

---

18 Susan Boyd & Donald MacPherson, "Community Engagement – The Harms of Drug Prohibition: Ongoing Resistance in Vancouver's Eastside" (2018) 200 BC Studies 87 at 94

186   *Conclusion*

this and it makes the black market better positioned in terms of how they're selling their product. . . . You've got a Crown corporation taking a good chunk of margin before we can get to the product. . . . You would hope anyways then that the proceeds from that are going into or being redistributed through programs and initiatives that are in line with you know wider societal change and ideals towards the system. And obviously tackling the illicit market which is you know not paying tax and causing more harm than good.[19]

It has been made abundantly clear that the current excise tax formula is largely responsible for the difficulties faced by many companies in the cannabis industry. Modifying the excise tax balance would allow more companies to compete within the industry, leading to better prices and more options outside of the black market, thus furthering a key policy objective of cannabis legalization. The federal government needs to listen to the wider voices of its cannabis industry, including the Canadian Chamber of Commerce, the British Columbia Chamber of Commerce, and the Ontario Chamber of Commerce, all of whom have called for excise tax reform.[20] Moreover, the federal government should be more transparent about how taxes collected from cannabis sales are being used, with an eye towards scrutiny and appropriate allocation to causes directly related to the public health objectives of legalization.

Recommendation Five: The federal government must immediately allocate additional resources to the various branches of Health Canada involved in regulating the cannabis industry. The current inadequacy of Health Canada as a federal regulator must be addressed.

Cannabis industry leaders have been consistent and comprehensive in their criticism of the inadequacy of Health Canada as a federal regulator. One cannabis industry leader argues that Health Canada hasn't been effective as a regulator by detailing their own personal experience:

I received a letter from Health Canada with respect to some marketing issues . . . and what happens is you just never hear back and they don't give you a response. So you just continue on until you hear otherwise. So I find that the execution of the Cannabis Act and Health Canada's purview has been kind of weird. It hasn't been effective.[21]

Another cannabis industry leader suggested that Health Canada needs to be better resourced in order to do its job effectively:

It's hard on the government to monitor these things and regulate them and enforce them and inspect them. Clearly Health Canada's been so underwater

---

19 Participant S, 30 June 2021
20 Chapter 5.4.1
21 Participant S, *supra* note 19

Conclusion   187

just trying to deal with everything that easing the burden on them would also seem to be a logical place to go.[22]

Another industry leader has reported Health Canada response times exceeding more than two months.[23] As the Canadian cannabis industry is still in its infancy, efficient and effective regulation within this complex and ever-evolving policy sphere is necessary for both the industry (who requires it to thrive) and the government (whose policy objectives are at risk if its regulator is not effectively monitoring compliance). A group of legal experts has further made this point, arguing that,

> The listing process has become inefficient and considerably expensive for producers while they must wait sixty days to often receive no formal reply. Reducing the listing process to thirty days and including a requirement that Health Canada must advise producers of any comments or issues within that timeframe would have a material beneficial impact on producers.[24]

Implementing this regulatory reform, and properly resourcing Health Canada so that it can carry it out, should be made a priority.

Recommendation Six: The federal government needs to acknowledge that it miscalculated its original marketing and advertising restrictions. The government should act immediately to relax these marketing and advertising restrictions, so a better balance can be struck between the government's twin objectives of discouraging increased use while also seeking to eliminate the black market.

Legal experts agree that the current marketing and promotional restrictions of the Cannabis Act are overly restrictive and in need of reform.[25] Cannabis industry

---

22 Participant R, 30 June 2021

23 Participant K, 22 July 2021: "It's a ton of red tape. It's very difficult to ever get in front of Health Canada. So bureaucratic, so understaffed and under-resourced. Like pathetic response time. There's only one way to essentially reach them there's a number you leave a message. For LPs specifically, if they have questions about a new product innovation, being able to double back and check if its 'kosher'. . . . One of our partners put out a call based on some stuff they were working on and they got a call back like two and a half months later. How can you operate like that?"

24 Eric Foster et al, "Legal Cannabis Under Review: How Canada Can Fix the Cannabis Act, Drive Growth, and Ease Regulations" (8 December 2021), online: *Lexpert* <www.lexpert. ca/legal-insights/legal-cannabis-under-review-how-canada-can-fix-the-cannabis-act-drive-growth-and-ease-regulations/362344>

25 *Ibid*: "The marketing and promotional restrictions of the Act and the regulations relating to packaging of cannabis products are overly restrictive and prevent cannabis companies from developing a distinct brand and engaging with their consumers and patients. As a result, most products appear bland, indistinctive, and unappealing to consumers who ultimately decide to not engage with those products and turn to the illicit market. Amending and relaxing certain marketing, promotional and packaging restrictions will allow the regulated market to better engage with their consumers and build a distinct brand. Industry stakeholders believe it is essential that cannabis companies have reasonable freedom of choice with respect to how they want to promote and design their products, as is the case in almost every other consumer packaged goods industry"

188   *Conclusion*

leaders have strongly echoed this concern and their desire for these restrictions to be relaxed. As one participant stated,

> The number one thing I'd like to see improved upon would be . . . marketing regulations and some of the rules around the prescriptive regulations with respect to people seeing it in the store or not having minors be able to come into the store if they're accompanied with a parent. You know, try to be more progressive, just like liquor has evolved over the days, try to make it more socially acceptable and stop making the barriers there so the stigma can start to go away.[26]

More than one cannabis industry leader made the comparison to the alcohol industry, and it was suggested that the stringent marketing restrictions around cannabis may be the result of an over-correction related to the historically less stringent regulations in the sphere of alcohol.[27] At the time the Cannabis Act was passed, the government's motivation to prevent the excessive marketing and promotion that exists in the alcohol industry from reoccurring in the cannabis industry was reasonable. Nearly four years later, it now clearly stands out as an over-correction that needs to be rectified. Almost everyone understands the objective of protecting youth from excessive promotion but, as is often the case, it appears that the right balance has not been struck, and the industry (and wider policy objectives like black market elimination) are suffering because of it. This issue should be firmly within the purview of the Cannabis Act's review, and, as such, the government should already have this issue on its agenda for future reform.

Recommendation Seven: The federal government should address the rapidly growing problem of market concentration through caps on licenses for large industry players, mirroring a trend practiced in other jurisdictions. The federal government should also exercise their coercive policy force to guide provinces towards the prioritization of licenses for smaller market players, including members of the legacy market.

As noted by Levesque, three of the biggest cannabis industry stakeholders (Aphria, Canopy Growth and Aurora) now account for more than 60% of the market and "an oligopoly for the selling of a product like this one is not good news for any stakeholder in legalization, whether it is the other companies,

---

26 Participant S, *supra* note 19
27 Participant R, *supra* note 22: "Just because you can do it in alcohol doesn't mean the governments happy about it. It's almost like they can't reverse that anymore and they're stuck with it and they don't wanna get the same problem again with cannabis"

regulatory agencies, public health experts, or users".[28] As one cannabis industry leader noted:

> Look at the stats. Look at the amount of cannabis consumers vs. what Canopy is growing. Like just one LP has more supply now for two years than all of the others combined that can service the cannabis market. It's absolutely ridiculous. . . . What's going to end up happening is one of two things: they're [smaller producers] all going to go bankrupt, or they're all going to sell to the big guys and it's going to be a market that's controlled by the big players like it is in alcohol, you know Labatt and Molson.[29]

Market concentration has previously been argued to be a symptom of excessive regulation.[30] It is hoped that market concentration will be alleviated as the federal government implements some of the above recommendations, thus giving smaller industry players a greater chance to succeed and hopefully fostering greater amounts of diversity within the cannabis industry. Nonetheless, this in and of itself will not be enough to stem the tide of a market that is already more concentrated than the international beer market. Caps on federally licensed producers would be a significant step and would signal to the provinces that they, too, need to implement regulatory reform to address the issue.

Recommendation Eight: Provinces should continue (or begin) efforts to regulate consumption lounges within their jurisdiction. The federal government should provide guidance for the regulation of these consumption lounges.

One cannabis industry leader had this to say about the issue of consumption lounges:

> Their inabilities to license and regulate lounges is also a problem right now. People are going to need a place to consume. . . . Not even just catering to your locals but then to the tourists. . . . The inability for us to be able to cater to that is an issue. . . . Some condo boards, rental properties, hotels still do not make accommodations for individuals who are looking to consume cannabis. Like how can you make a substance legal but then not create the appropriate spaces for an individual to consume it legally? In essence, you're kind of pushing this person into situations where they're doing illegal activity indirectly.[31]

---

28 Gabriel Levesque, "Cannabis Legalization in Canada. Case studies: British Columbia, Ontario and Quebec" (2020), online (pdf): *French Monitoring Centre for Drugs and Drug Addiction* <https://en.ofdt.fr/BDD/publications/docs/ASTRACAN_Levesque-EN.pdf> at 70

29 Participant K, *supra* note 23

30 Chapter 5.4.4

31 Participant A, *supra* note 15

190   *Conclusion*

If the federal government has seen fit to legalize cannabis, it should logically follow that people should have safe and legal access to places to consume the substance. Provincial attempts to consult industry stakeholders on the issue of consumption lounges should continue, with guidance from the federal government provided. The comparative experience of Nevada may be usefully looked upon as a model for fostering tourism and economic activity.[32]

Recommendation Nine: Provinces should be more transparent in their cannabis industry data collection and sharing. The example of several U.S. jurisdictions that have successfully used open and transparent data to guide and shape their regulatory reform should be followed.

Provinces are already collecting and sharing information about the operation of their cannabis industries with Health Canada, but researchers, industry stakeholders and other decision-makers are largely closed off from these crucial sources of data that could otherwise inform their analyses. It is worth noting that similar data is extensively collected and shared in U.S. states (particularly those that were first movers/leaders in the legalization movement sweeping across the country), allowing for sales to be broken down all the way to store level (Washington) or by county (Colorado).[33] The provincial secrecy surrounding cannabis industry data discussed elsewhere in this book[34] is a detriment to effective policy evaluation and regulatory reform. Considering the relative infancy of the provinces' cannabis markets and the fast-moving nature of the regulatory space, this data deficiency needs to be addressed sooner rather than later.

Recommendation Ten: The federal government should IMMEDIATELY begin its statutory review of the Cannabis Act, which is already behind schedule.[35] Moreover, given this delay and the limited purview of the review, future reviews should be mandated alongside any new legislative reform.

While various aspects of the federal Cannabis Act were criticized throughout this book, the fact that the legislation included a provision for automatic statutory review[36] within three years of the legislation's operation was a welcome development. Ongoing and automatic statutory review should be a consistent feature of any subsequent legislative reform made to Canada's cannabis policy going forward. It is hard to overemphasize the scale of the undertaking that was cannabis legalization in this country. This book has already elucidated several areas of necessary reform, and more will present themselves as the country moves

---

32 Chapter 4.4.11
33 Michael Armstrong, "Legal cannabis market shares during Canada's first year of recreational legalization" (2021) 88 International Journal of Drug Policy, DOI: <>https://doi.org/10.1016/j.drugpo.2020.103028> at 8
34 Chapter 5.4.6
35 Solomon Israel, "Canada's Cannabis Legalization Review Running Late, as Industry Hopes for Reforms" (25 February 2022), *MJBiz Daily* <https://mjbizdaily.com/canadas-cannabis-legalization-review-running-late-as-industry-hopes-for-reforms/>
36 Cannabis Act, *supra* note 3, s 151.1

past its initial growing pains. Consistent attention and focus will be necessary to monitor this ever-evolving and fast-moving regulatory space, with an eye towards providing the most fair, equitable, and profitable operation of the system as is possible.

6.2 Looking Towards the Future: Directions for Future Research

Future versions of this text and/or future related research projects will undoubtedly focus on monitoring the implementation of the recommendations made above. Similarly, future research will continue to engage with both Indigenous community and cannabis industry leaders. As was noted earlier in the book, "In a quickly moving policy area like cannabis reform, scholars must be in close contact with practitioners in the public, private, and non-profit sectors in order to stay abreast of new developments and advancements in the field".[37] This statement is as true now as it ever was, and, as such, further engagement with stakeholders beyond those surveyed in this book will be a goal of future research. Qualitative interviews for this project were limited by time and resource constraints, but future research could certainly involve broader engagement with the wide array of public, private and non-profit actors that are involved in the legal cannabis industry.

Furthermore, future versions of this text will undoubtedly focus on what will likely be a continued trend towards cannabis (and wider drug) policy liberalization throughout the world, including, hopefully, right here at home in Canada. By the time this book is published, there may very well already be a handful of new jurisdictions that have moved towards drug policy liberalization. This is what some in academia may refer to as a "good problem", as the field of analysis seems likely to grow in the years to come. In the hopeful event that some of the recommendations noted above are acted upon within the coming years, there will be new policies to discuss and analyze. One can only hope that these policies are developed in a way that considers lessons learned from Canada's long racist and classist drug policy history. Similarly, speaking from the perspective of someone who heard the frustrations and scepticism of Indigenous community leaders first-hand, it is genuinely hoped that the federal government finally decides to do more than pay lip service to the project of reconciliation with Indigenous communities. The future of cannabis policy reform represents a significant opportunity to finally engage and consult with Indigenous communities sufficiently. It is hoped that the federal government seizes this opportunity.

It is also hoped that in the future, researchers will be afforded the opportunity to rely on relevant and accessible data when working in this field. It is still remarkably difficult to draw concrete conclusions about whether cannabis

---

37 Jared Wesley, "Beyond Prohibition: The Legalization of Cannabis in Canada" (2019) 62:4 Canadian Public Administration 533 at 546

192   *Conclusion*

legalization in this country is effectively meeting its stated goals and objectives. There are still many questions left unanswered about whether cannabis legalization has increased consumption and use, and these questions will need to be answered for future broader drug policy debates to be properly informed. Moreover, future research will also necessarily have to be focused on accurate analyses of whether legalization has effectively combatted the elicit market. To a large extent, the pathway towards black market elimination has already been laid out: foster greater amounts of participation of Indigenous and other marginalized members in the industry, relax various regulations that are making it impossible for smaller industry players to compete, and tweak excise tax rules that are having a disproportionate impact on market concentration and allowing the black market to continue thriving.

To conclude, it is important to once again remember the words of the Task Force on Cannabis Legalization and Regulation:

> The current paradigm of cannabis prohibition has been with us for almost 100 years. We cannot, and should not, expect to turn this around overnight. While moving away from cannabis prohibition is long overdue, we may not anticipate every nuance of future policy.[38]

Nearly six years after these words were written, there are still nuances of future cannabis (and wider drug) policy in Canada that are hard to anticipate. This comes part and parcel with such a fundamental, once in a lifetime policy change. The need for future research in this field will thus likely never cease. Along the way, it can only be hoped that the volumes of research that are produced will be considered thoughtfully and comprehensively by governments, with an eye towards accomplishing the future goal of attaining a cannabis (and wider drug) policy that is fair, equitable, profitable, and accessible to all Canadians.

Armstrong, Michael, "Legal Cannabis Market Shares During Canada's First Year of Recreational Legalization" (2021) 88 International Journal of Drug Policy, DOI: <https://doi.org/10.1016/j.drugpo.2020.103028>

Boyd, Susan & MacPherson, Donald, "Community Engagement – The Harms of Drug Prohibition: Ongoing Resistance in Vancouver's Eastside" (2018) 200 BC Studies 87

Canada, Task Force on Cannabis Legalization and Regulation, *A Framework for the Legalization and Regulation of Cannabis in Canada: The Final Report of the Task Force on Cannabis Legalization and Regulation* (Ottawa: Health Canada, 2016)

Cannabis Act, SC 2018, c 16

Foster, Eric, Ruggolo, Stuart, Moulton, Emeleigh & Burns, Kimberley, "Legal Cannabis Under Review: How Canada Can Fix the Cannabis Act, Drive Growth, and

---

38 Canada, Task Force on Cannabis Legalization and Regulation, *A Framework for the Legalization and Regulation of Cannabis in Canada: The Final Report of the Task Force on Cannabis Legalization and Regulation* (Ottawa: Health Canada, 2016) at 1

Ease Regulations" (8 December 2021), online: *Lexpert* <www.lexpert.ca/legal-insights/legal-cannabis-under-review-how-canada-can-fix-the-cannabis-act-drive-growth-and-ease-regulations/362344>

Israel, Solomon, "Canada's Cannabis Legalization Review Running Late, as Industry Hopes for Reforms" (25 February 2022), *MJBiz Daily* <https://mjbizdaily.com/canadas-cannabis-legalization-review-running-late-as-industry-hopes-for-reforms/>

Levesque, Gabriel, "Cannabis Legalization in Canada. Case Studies: British Columbia, Ontario and Quebec" (2020), online (pdf): *French Monitoring Centre for Drugs and Drug Addiction* <https://en.ofdt.fr/BDD/publications/docs/ASTRACAN_Levesque-EN.pdf>

Maghsoudi, Nazlee, Rammohan, Indhu, Bowra, Andrea, Sniderman, Ruby, Tanguay, Justine, Bouck, Zachary, Scheim, Ayden, Werb, Dan & Owusu-Bempah, Akwasi, "How Diverse Is Canada's Legal Cannabis Industry? Examining Race and Gender of its Executives and Directors" (October 2020), online: *Centre on Drug Policy Evaluation*<https://cdpe.org/publication/how-diverse-is-canadas-legal-cannabis-industry-examining-race-and-gender-of-its-executives-and-directors/>

Wesley, Jared, "Beyond Prohibition: The Legalization of Cannabis in Canada" (2019) 62:4 Canadian Public Administration 533

Index

1988 Law 1.340 106
1989 Law 23737, Argentina 98–99
2018 Cannabis Act 1; Bill C-45 31–32; Bill C-46 33; 2015 Liberal government election promise 29; missed opportunity 34; recommendations, Task Force 30

academic concern, Cannabis Act: federal government 36, 39; jurisdictional issue 38; lack of consultation, indigenous communities 40; legacy market 37; licensing 37; social justice component, lack of 36; underrepresentation, black and indigenous people 36
Act to Tax and Regulate the Production, Sale and Use of Marijuana 113
adult-use cannabis legalization 95, 100
adult-use licenses 127
AGCO *see* Alcohol and Gaming Commission (AGCO)
AGLC *see* Alberta Gaming, Liquor and Cannabis (AGLC)
Alaska 113–114
Alberta Gaming, Liquor and Cannabis (AGLC) 64
Alberta provincial implementation, cannabis legalization 64–65
Alcohol and Gaming Commission (AGCO) 61, 170
American financial institutions 109
Aphria 174
Arden, Jacinda 82
Argentina 98–100, 163
Arizona 114–115
Arizona's medical system 114
Armstrong, Michael 4, 54
Arriola 99

Assessment of Drug Addiction, Consumption and Traffic 93
Aurora 174
Australia 77–79
automatic record expungement to provide redress 184

B.C. Indigenous cannabis project 68
BC Liquor Distribution Branch (LDB) 67
Ben-Ishai, Stephanie 50
Bill C-7 21–22
Bill C-38 25
Bill C-45 31–32
Bill C-46 33
Bill C-85 21
Bill S-19 19
Black Candle, The (Murphy, Emily) 15
black market 39–40, 52, 54–55, 61, 66–67, 71–73, 95, 122, 156–157; benefits 174; economy 84; elimination 73, 188, 192; in Indigenous communities 156, 169
Boric, Gabriel 102
Bowal, Peter 46, 55, 172
Boyd, Neil 14, 28
Brazil 100–101
British Columbia (BC) provincial implementation, cannabis legalization: B.C. Indigenous cannabis project 68; LDB 67; licenses 67–68; sales and per capita sales numbers 67

California 115–117, 161, 166
Canada *see* federal drug policy, Canada
Canada's Constitution Act, 1867 46
Canada's Drug Strategy 20–21
Canada's legal cannabis regime 156
Canada's racist drug history 157–160

Index 195

Canadian Cannabis Survey (CCS) 176–177
Canadian Centre on Substance Use and Addiction 167
Canadian Chamber of Commerce 170
cannabis 77; adult-use recreational sales 122, 124–125, 127–129; business 161; coffeeshops, selling in 91–92; conviction 161; criminalization 158, 177; cultivation and possession in Malta 90–91; cultivation in New Zealand 81; delivery companies 123; excise tax formula 185–186; exemptions to all cannabis laws 80; Indigenous community 168; legal age for possession 80; legalization, Alaska 113; legalization, Arizona 114; legalization, Canada 165; legalization, Peru 107–108; legalization, South Africa 83; legalization of production 92, 157–158, 182; legalization of recreational possession and cultivation of, Maine 121; legal market 160, 177; market economy 175; medical 82; possession 84, 88, 122; recreational legalization 82; sale of 88; taxation 169; *see also* drug prohibition and legalization
Cannabis Act 109, 154–159, 164, 168, 173, 181, 183
cannabis (and wider drug) policy in Canada, recommendations 182–191; cannabis excise tax formula 185–186; cannabis industry data collection and sharing 190–191; Commission of Inquiry 184–185; consultation and cooperation with Indigenous communities 183–184; market concentration through caps on licenses 188–189; regulate consumption lounges 189–190; resources to various branches of Health Canada 186–187; system of automatic record expungement to provide redress 184
Cannabis as Medicine Act 88
cannabis-based medicine 95
Cannabis-Based Products for Medicinal Use (CBPMs) 85
Cannabis Control Authority 134
Cannabis Control Board 129–130, 132
Cannabis Control Commission 123
Cannabis Control Division 128

Cannabis Expiation Notice 78
Cannabis for Private Purposes Bill 83
cannabis industry data collection and sharing 190–191
cannabis legalization 154; legislative process 1; *see also* federalism; provincial implementation
Cannabis Licensing Authority 80
Cannabis policy in the United States 111
Cannabis Regulation and Tax Act 120
cannabis regulation in Alaska 113
Cannabis Regulatory Commission (CRC) 127
cannabis social clubs (CSCs) 96
Canopy Growth 174
CAQ government *see* Coalition Avenir Quebec (CAQ) government
Carstairs, Catherine 15
Cavalieri, Walter 19, 26
CCS *see* Canadian Cannabis Survey (CCS)
CDSA *see* Controlled Drugs and Substances Act (CDSA)
Centre on Drug Policy Evaluation 160
Chile 101–102, 163
Christie, Chris 127
civil penalty schemes 78
classism 2–3, 7, 9, 13, 15, 17, 21, 34, 42, 81, 84, 120, 121, 154, 158, 160, 164, 177, 181, 191
Coalition Avenir Quebec (CAQ) government 66
cocaine 106–107
Cole memorandum 112
colonialism 7–8, 42, 51, 156–157, 181
Colorado 117–119
Colorado Department of Revenue Marijuana Enforcement Division 117
Columbia 102–103, 163
commercialization 103
commercial market 82
commonwealth jurisdictions 9
Commonwealth jurisdictions, drug prohibition and legalization in: Australia 77–79; Jamaica 80–81; New Zealand 81–82; South Africa 82–83; United Kingdom 84–86
community resolutions 84
Compassionate Use Act in 1996 115
concessionaire model, New Brunswick 71
Connecticut 119–120, 163
consumption lounges 189–190

196   *Index*

consumption lounges, regulation of 10
Control, Regulation, and Taxation
   of Marijuana and Industrial Hemp
   Act 131
Controlled Cannabis Supply Chain
   Experiment Act, 2019 92
Controlled Drugs and Substances Act
   (CDSA) 7, 21, 167
Controlled Substances Act 112
cooperative federalism 8, 46, 48, 182
Coordinated Cannabis Taxation
   Agreements 156
Costa Rica 103–104, 163
Cousineau, Karine 170
COVID-19 pandemic 5, 59, 81, 96,
   105, 114, 123, 132, 176
Criminal Code Article 299, Peru 107
Crosby, Andrew 30
Cultivation of Cannabis and
   Manufacture of Cannabis-Related
   Pharmaceutical Products for Medical
   and Research Purposes regulations 82
Cuomo, Andrew 130
Czech Republic 86–87

Dangerous Drug Amendment Act 80
decriminalize/decriminalization 9–10,
   19, 22, 25, 94, 112, 128, 164;
   cannabis possession 22, 24, 35, 98;
   drug 85, 89, 94, 103, 125, 128;
   drug use 103; model 80; personal
   possession 162–165, 168; possession
   of all illicit drugs 25, 122, 133, 163;
   policy of 104; recreational cannabis
   use 28; task force 130, 166
defelonization 9, 116, 121, 125, 128,
   137, 163–164; bills 128; drug
   possession 120; legislation 136, 164
De Koning 58, 62, 67
demon drug mythology 20
Dias, Giselle 17
diversionary programs 78
dope fiend mythology 17
drugs: decriminalization 125;
   decriminalization task force 130, 166;
   occasional vs. habitual use 94; policy
   liberalization 91, 117, 163–164, 177,
   182, 191; policy reform 24–26, 113;
   tourism destination 94
drug prohibition and legalization 77;
   Commonwealth jurisdictions 77–86;
   European countries 86–98; Latin
   America 98–111; United States
   111–137

Drugs and Drug Trafficking Act 83
Duque, Ivan 103

Eastern Provinces provincial
   implementation, cannabis legalization
   71–72
economic disinvestment 121
Edmonton juvenile court 15
Erickson, Patricia 159
Erickson, Patricia E. 18–20, 23–24
European countries, drug prohibition
   and legalization in: Czech Republic
   86–87; Germany 87–89; Italy 89–90;
   Malta 90–91; Netherlands 91–93;
   Portugal 93–96; Spain 96–97;
   Switzerland 97–98
European Union's drug laws 88
excessive incarceration 121
excise tax 10, 52, 177, 192; collection
   32; and related issues 168–170
expungements 164

federal drug policy, Canada: academic
   concerns 34–41; 2018 Cannabis Act
   7, 29–34; Controlled Drugs and
   Substances Act 19–23; indigenous
   community and cannabis industry
   leaders 34–41; LeDain Commission
   Inquiry 7, 17–19; legal challenges,
   medical cannabis regulation 26–29;
   Opium Act 6, 14–17; reform 24–26;
   War on Drugs 7, 19–23
federalism 162; absent of action,
   federal government 54; cooperative
   48; excise tax 52; federal and
   provincial regulators 50; Federal
   Government 51–52; imposed
   decision, federal government 48;
   indigenous communities, exclusion
   from legal system 51, 53; logistical
   issue 49; Section 88, Indian Act 51;
   unilateralism 48
Fernandez, Alberto 99
Fischer, Benedikt 28

German Cannabis Agency 88
German Narcotic Drugs Act 88
Germany 87–89
Green Party 79

Half Circle, The 71
harm reduction 19–21, 23, 26, 86–87,
   94, 97, 101, 160–168
Harper, Stephen 25

Index 197

Hathaway, Andrew 17
Health and Social Care Committee 162
Health Canada 57, 171–172, 176;
  inadequacy of 170–172; resources to
  various branches of 186–187
health-driven policies 95
heroin 106
House of Commons Special Committee,
  the 24–25
Hyshka, Elaine 24

I-502 135
Illinois 120–121, 163
inadequacy, Health Canada 10
inadequacy of Health Canada 170
indigenous: exclusion 3, 8–9, 46;
  federal government 51–52; federalism
  50–51; impacts of cannabis 155–157;
  tax sharing discussions 51
inflexible unilateralism 48
International Narcotics Control
  Board 85
Italy 89–90

Jamaica 80–81
Jarbeau, Tammy 172
Johnson, Boris 85

Khan, Sadiq 85
Kulfas, Matias 99

labour demonstration, 1907 14
Lamont, Edward 119
Latin America, drug prohibition and
  legalization in: Argentina 98–100;
  Brazil 100–101; Chile 101–102;
  Columbia 102–103; Costa Rica
  103–104; Mexico 104–106; Paraguay
  106–107; Peru 107–108; Uruguay
  108–111
Lavoie, Jessie 70
Law on the Protection of Citizens'
  Security, 2015 96
LeDain Commission 166; amendments,
  Criminal Code 19; Bill S-19 19;
  Final Report 17; *Interim Report* 18;
  possession convictions, cannabis 19
legacy market 8, 37, 58, 67–68,
  161, 188
legal cannabis system 91
LePage, Paul 122
LGCA *see* Liquor, Gaming and Cannabis
  Authority (LGCA)
liberalization of drug policy 155

Liberal Party of Canada 1
Liquor, Gaming and Cannabis Authority
  (LGCA) 70

Mackenzie, William Lyon 14
Maine 121–122, 163, 166
Maine State Legislature 121
Malta 90–91
Malta's 2014 Drug Dependence
  (Treatment not Imprisonment)
  Act 90
Manitoba, legal cannabis
  implementation 70–71
marginalized communities 2, 7, 13, 26,
  37, 42, 158, 160, 181, 184, 192
Marihuana for Medical Purposes
  Regulations (MMPR) 28–29
marijuana 107
marijuana, legalization of 105
Marijuana Medical Access Regulations
  (MMAR) 27–28
Marijuana Policy Project, S.B. 1201 119
Marijuana Regulation and Taxation Act
  (MRTA) 129
market concentration 10, 46, 73, 162,
  174–175, 177, 189, 192
market concentration through caps on
  licenses 188–189
marketing and advertising restrictions
  10, 172–174
Marley, Bob 80
Massachusetts 122–124, 163, 166
Massachusetts' drug policy reform 122
McArdle, John 58, 62, 67
medical cannabis 79; Australia 79;
  Chile 102; Columbia 103; Czech
  Republic 87; Jamaica 80; legal access
  26–28; Maine 121–122; Malta 91;
  Mexico 105; Michigan 124; MMAR
  27; MMPR 28; New Zealand 82;
  non-medical market 29; Peru 107;
  regulation 26–28; scheme, 2020
  82; South Africa 82; Switzerland 98;
  system 87; Vermont 132; Virginia
  133; *Wakeford* case 26
medical preservation plan 119
Medicines and Related Substances
  Control Act 83
Mexico 104–106
Michigan 124–125
microregulation 173
Mills, Janet 122
Misuse of Drugs Act, 1971 84
Misuse of Drugs Act, 1975 81

198 *Index*

Misuse of Drugs (Medicinal Cannabis) Amendment Act, 2018 82
Misuse of Drugs Regulations, 2001 85
MMAR *see* Marijuana Medical Access Regulations (MMAR)
MMPR *see* Marihuana for Medical Purposes Regulations (MMPR)
Montana 125–126
Montana Department of Revenue 125
Mulroney, Brian 20
Murphy, Emily 15
Murphy, Phil 127

Narcotic Control Act, 1961 16
Narcotic Drug Act 14
Narcotic Drugs Amendment Act 79
National Anti-Drug Secretariat 106
National Drug Policy Council 101
National Health Service (NHS) 86
National Institute for Health and Care Excellence (NICE) 86
National Narcotics Council 103
National Narcotics Statute 102
needle and syringe programs 87
Netherlands 91–93
Nevada 126–127
Nevada Cannabis Compliance Board 127
New Jersey 127–128, 163
New Mexico 128–129, 164, 166
New York 129–130, 164, 166
New Zealand 81–82
Nixon's War on Drugs 167

OCS *see* Ontario Cannabis Store (OCS)
Office of Cannabis Management 129
Office of Medicinal Cannabis (OMC) 93
Ogden Memorandum 111
Ontario Cannabis Store (OCS) 62–63, 170
Ontario provincial implementation, cannabis legalization: licenses 60; lottery system, license 60–61; OCS 62–63; political regime changes 60; private market approach 62; retail rollout 61; stores 63
Ontario Supreme Court 27
Opium Act 6; Chinese drug users 15; dope fiend mythology 17; legislative provisions 15–16; marijuana prohibition 15–16; Opium and Narcotic Drug Act, 1911 14; opium trade, British Columbia 14; white drug addicts 15

Opium and Narcotic Drug Act, 1929 16
Oregon 130–132, 164, 166
Oregon Liquor Control Commission (OLCC) 131
organized criminals 111–112

Paraguay 106–107, 163
Peru 107–108, 163
policy liberalization, jurisdictions 9
Polis, Jared 118
Portugal 93–96
Portuguese Institute for Drugs and Addiction 94
Production of Cannabis for Medical and Research Purposes Act 91
prohibition *see* drug prohibition and legalization
pro-legalization activism 89
provincial implementation, cannabis legalization 7; adequate supply, issue of 54; Alberta 64–65; British Columbia 67–68; cooperative federalism 8, 48; Eastern Provinces 71–72; federalism 50–54; indigenous exclusion 46, 50–54; legacy market 8, 58; Manitoba 70–71; national supply shortages 55; online retail sales 59; Ontario 60–64; Quebec 65–67; Saskatchewan 68–69; social justice and social equity provisions, lack of 58; strict marketing and advertising rules 55; trends and issues 8, 54–60; wholesale distribution 59
public consultation process 155

Quebec Court of Appeal 67
Quebec provincial implementation, cannabis legalization: black market 66; home cultivation ban 66–67; medical cannabis 66; product choice 66; restrictive approach 65–66; SAQ 65; stakeholder endorsement 65

racism 2, 3, 7, 9, 13, 15, 17, 21, 42, 155, 157, 158, 160, 177, 181, 191
Ravin v. State 113
Reagan, Ronald 20
recreational cannabis 90–91, 133; laws 87; legalization 82; market 93
recreational legalization 117
regulation consumption lounges 175–176
Rehm, Jürgen 27–28

Index 199

research methodology: documentary analyses 4; provincial cannabis agencies 4; qualitative interviews, cannabis industry leaders 4; qualitative interviews, indigenous community leaders 5; snowball sampling 5
Return to Vendor 169
Riley, Diane 16, 18–19, 22, 26
Royal College of Physicians 86
Russell, Cayley 28

Salazar, Mario 104
SAQ *see* Société des alcools du Québec (SAQ)
Saskatchewan provincial implementation, cannabis legalization: indigenous owners and partners 69; licenses 69; open market system 69; SLGA 68
Sativex 95
Scottish National Party 79
Searching for Hope 107–108
Secure and Fair (SAFE) Banking Act 112–113
Senate Special Committee on Illegal Drugs, the 24
small-scale initiatives 78
Snow, Dave 48
social educational sentences 100
social equity 8–10, 42, 58, 118–120, 123, 131–132, 137, 155, 158, 160–162, 177, 182, 184; licensees 118; provisions 8, 10, 42, 58, 154
Social Equity Council 119
Social Equity Program (SEP) 123, 161–162
social justice 2, 7–9, 33–36, 116, 118, 158, 160–161, 171
Social Security and Health Commission of the Council of States 96
Société des alcools du Québec (SAQ) 65
South Africa 82–83
Spain 96–97
Stand for Craft campaign 170
Standing Senate Committee on Aboriginal Peoples 155
state-licensed medical cannabis system 130
substance abuse treatment 131
Supreme Court of Canada 48

Switzerland 97–98
systemic financial dysfunction 170

Task Force on Cannabis Legalization and Regulation 158
Therapeutic Goods Administration, Australia 79
tourism industry 175
traffickers 112
Train, Andrew 48
Trudeau, Justin 29, 156

United Kingdom 84–86
United States, drug prohibition and legalization in 111–113; Alaska 113–114; Arizona 114–115; California 115–117; Colorado 117–119; Connecticut 119–120; Illinois 120–121; Maine 121–122; Massachusetts 122–124; Michigan 124–125; Montana 125–126; Nevada 126–127; New Jersey 127–128; New Mexico 128–129; New York 129–130; Oregon 130–132; Vermont 132–133; Virginia 133–134; Washington State 134–137
Uruguay 108–111

Vancouver drug panic 15
Vermont 132–133, 164
Vermont's Cannabis Control Board 161
violence 121
Virginia 133–134, 164

Wakeford case 26
War on Drugs 20; Bill C-7 21–22; Bill C-85 21; Canada's Drug Strategy 20–21; CDSA 21–22; 1986 declaration, United States President 20; demise, drug strategy 21; 'demon drug' mythology 20; Federal Drug Secretariat 20; harm reduction, policy of 19; political indifference, drug law reform 20
Washington State 134–137, 164, 166
Wesley, Jared 4, 51, 53
Wiener, Scott 166
Wright, Tremaine 130

Youngkin, Glenn 134

Printed in the United States
by Baker & Taylor Publisher Services